BOVINE ECONOMY OF INDIA
CONCEPTUAL ANALYSIS AND EMPIRICAL EVIDENCE

BOVINE ECONOMY OF INDIA

CONCEPTUAL ANALYSIS AND EMPIRICAL EVIDENCE

R. Albert Christopher Dhas

SERIALS PUBLICATIONS
NEW DELHI (INDIA)

First Published - 2010

ISBN: 978-81-8387-279-9

Published by

SERIALS PUBLICATIONS
4830/24, Prahlad Street, Ansari Road
Darya Ganj, New Delhi-110002 (India)
Phone: 23245225 Fax : 91-11-23272135
E-mail: serials@satyam.net.in

DEDICATED TO

MY FATHER AND MOTHER

CONTENTS

FOREWORD

Livestock sector has gained considerable importance in India's rural economy in recent decades. This is evident from the increasing share of livestock output to the output originating from agriculture and allied sectors. There have been also considerable changes taking place in the species, age, sex and size distribution of livestock population across different regions in the country.

Though this sector has assumed importance in shaping the income, employment and nutrition of India's population, there are not many studies conducted by researchers to unravel the various facets of this sector and influence the process of decision making at different levels. Several eminent economists like Prof. K.N. Raj, Prof. V.M. Dandeker, Prof. A. Vaidyanathan, Prof. C.H. Hunumantha Rao have done pioneering work on this subject in Sixties and Seventies. Of late, there are only very few comprehensive study on this subject. The present study by R. Albert Christopher Dhas carried out for the state of Tamil Nadu is an important contribution that unravels the livestock sector in a regional perspective.

In this book, the role of bovines in Tamil Nadu economy and its changes over time during the first half of the 20th century are analysed to obtain a historical perspective. The analysis about the role of bovines as a source of motive power indicated that while the agro-climatic and irrigation factors played a major role in shaping the work animal density prior to the mid-1970s, the technological, economic and institutional factors are important in recent years. The observed trends in work and milch animal population and the trends in milk production, demand and consumption clearly indicated that dairying has been gaining importance in the bovine economy of Tamil Nadu. The changes in size, composition and distribution of bovines are found to be broadly in response to the development of dairying in Tamil Nadu. The findings of the study have indicated the prospects for increasing the production and productivity of the bovine sector of Tamil Nadu. Though the arguments are primarily based on Tamil Nadu data, the questions raised have relevance for other regions and for other regions of the country.

I congratulate Dr. Dhas for conducting this study and making it available for larger audience. The book will be of great interest to academic researchers, policy makers in particular and those who are interested in India's livestock sector in general.

Prof. K. Narayanan Nair
Director
Centre for Development Studies
Thiruvananthapuram, Kerala

PREFACE

This book analyses the transition in the bovine economy with the historical perspective. The conceptual analysis is basically with reference to India and the empirical evidences are provided with a special focus on Tamil Nadu. The present volume is drawn from my doctoral thesis carried out at the Centre for Development Studies (CDS), Trivandrum and submitted to the Jawaharlal Nehru University (JNU), New Delhi.

It is with profound sense of gratitude that I thank Prof. K. N. Nair and Prof. P. S. George, my research supervisors, for all their guidance and support towards my research work. The guiding force that mooted the idea of this book is Prof.K.N.Nair, Director, CDS, He provided me all support to execute this task within a short span of time and wrote the foreward for this book. Special thanks are due to Dr P. R. Gopinathan Nair for shaping the quality of my academic presentation. I also thank Dr. G. N. Rao, Dr. Chandan Mukerjee and Dr. K. Navaneetham for their help and critical comments.

During the initial stages of my work, I was fortunate to have several interactions with Dr. K. N. Raj, Dr. V. M. Dandekar, Dr. T. N. Krishnan, Dr. P. G. K. Panicker, Dr. A.Vaidyanathan, Prof. N. Krishnaji, Dr. Martin Doornbos, Dr. Sakthi Padhi and Dr. Rammanohar Reddy. I record my thanks to them.

My Colleagues at The American College, Madurai were always a source of encouragement. My special gratitude goes to The Principal, Bursar, Deans, Heads of the Department, and all the faculty members of the Economics Department. I record my gratefulness to Dr. T. Arul Pragasam (Head, P.G. Economics), Dr R.Mohan (Head, U.G. Economics), Prof. M. Isaac Samraj (Rtd. Head, P. G. Economics), Major S. Stanley Jeyasingh (Rtd. Vice-Principal), Dr. C. Gopinath (Rtd. Director, Centre for Management Development, Trivandrum), Prof. K. Balraj (PSG College of Arts and Science, Coimbatore) and Dr. V. C. Retnam (Rtd. Professor of Economics, Scott Christian College, Nagercoil) for their constant encouragement.

In connection with my research work, I had visited several Institutes, Universities, Libraries, Departments and Offices. Particular mention may be made of Madras Institute of Development Studies, Institute of Social and Economic Change, Centre for Economics and Social Studies, Tamil Nadu Agricultural University, Tamil Nadu Veterinary and Animal Science University, National Dairy Development Board, Institute of Rural Management Anand, Tamil Nadu Animal Husbandry Department, Directorate of Economics and Statistics, Department of Evaluation and Applied Research and Tamil Nadu Cooperative Milk Producer's Federation Ltd.,. I thank the officials, faculty members, librarians and library staff, and the administrative staff of all these institutions for their unstinted cooperation and help.

I have received help and encouragements from several friends, relatives and CDS community. To name a few, Albin, Anand, Anandaraj, Ancy, Anilkumar, Anitha, Baby, Beena, Christopher, Dennis, Gunamalai, Gopikuttan, Harilal, Kabir, Ramesh, Roy, Sanjith, Sanu, Soman, Udayakumar, Vijay, Uma and so on. I bow to them all in gratitude. I specially thank the CDS community, particularly the staff of the library, computer and administration wings for all their sincere help.

I acknowledge Indian Council of Social Science Research (ICSSR), Kerala Research Programme on Local Level Development (KRPLLD) and Centre for Development Studies (CDS) for the financial support for conducting the research and converting the same as a book.

My father and mother had high expectations about my academic achievements. But, they are no more to see this book. The support of my brothers-Daniel, Paulraj, Jeya Chandran and Justin–and their families, mother-in-law, Uncles & Aunts are worth recording. The encouragement and understanding of my wife Helen, son Jason and daughter Jenie helped me bring this effort into fruition. My heartfelt thanks go to them.

I also thank Serials Publications for their interest in bringing out this volume and for the good presentation and timely release of the book.

Above all, I praise the Lord, The Almighty for giving me courage, guidance and resolve for accomplishing this challenging job.

R. ALBERT CHRISTOPHER DHAS

ABBREVIATIONS

AI	Artificial Insemination
AMC/NSA	Adult Male Cattle per Net Sown Area
BC/NSA	Breeding Cows per Net Sown Area
CDS	Centre for Development Studies
CR	Calving Rate
CSO	Central Statistical Organisation
CULT	Cultivators
DAP	Draught Animal Power
DCP	Digestible Crude Protein
EEC	European Economic Community
FC	Female Calves
FCB	Female Calves Born
FP	Farm Power
FP/NSA	Farm Power per Net Sown Area
GCA	Gross Cropped Area
GDP	Gross Domestic Product
GIA	Gross Irrigated Area
GOI	Government of India
GOTN	Government of Tamil Nadu
IARS	Institute of Agricultural Research Statistics
IASRI	Indian Agricultural Statistics Research Institute
ICAR	Indian Council of Agricultural Research
ICDP	Intensive Cattle Development Programme
ICMR	Indian Council of Medical Research
IDC	Indian Dairy Corporation

IRDP	Integrated Rural Development Programme
ISS	Integrated Sample Survey
KDMPU	Kaira District Cooperative Milk Producers' Union
KVS	Key Village Scheme
MIDS	Madras Institute of Development Studies
MMPO	Milk and Milk Products Order
MP	Mechanical Power
MT	Metric Tonnes
NCAER	National Council of Applied Economic Research
NDDB	National Dairy Development Board
NIA	Net Irrigated Area
NIA/NSA	Net Irrigated Area per Net Sown Area
NNER	Normal North East Rainfall
NP	Number of Pumpsets
NSA	Net Sown Area
NSA/CULT	Net Sown Area per Cultivators
NSA/CULT2	Square of Net Sown Area per Cultivators
NSS	National Sample Survey
NSSO	National Sample Survey Organisation
NSWR	Normal South West Rainfall
NT	Number of Tractors
NTR	Normal Total Rainfall
OF	Operation Flood
PMP	Percentage of Mechanical Power
PNNER	Percentage of Normal North East Rainfall
PNSWR	Percentage of Normal South West Rainfall
PPP	Percentage of Pumpsets Power
PTP	Percentage of Tractor Power
RRm	Replacement Rate of Males
SFDA	Small Farmers Development Agency
SMP	Skimmed Milk Powder
SRm	Survival Rate of Males

TCMPF	Tamil Nadu Cooperative Milk Producers' Federation Ltd.
TDN	Total Digestible Nutrient
TIVJ	The Indian Veterinary Journal
TIVJ	The Indian Veterinary Journal
TPP	Tons Per Annum
URAA	Uruguay Round Agreement on Agriculture
WAC	World Agricultural Census
WAP	Work Animal Population
WAP/ NSA	Work Animal Population per Net Sown Area
WIA	Well Irrigated Area
WTO	World Trade Organisation
YSMC/ AMC	Young Stock Male Cattle per Adult Male Cattle

1

INTRODUCTION

India had 283 million bovines in 2003 of which cattle accounted for 65 per cent and buffaloes the rest (GOI 2002), which constituted about one-sixth of the cattle and about one-half of the buffalo population of the world. The All-India Debt and Investment Survey (1991-92) had revealed that two-thirds of the rural households in the country owned livestock and that the average value of livestock per reporting household came to Rs 3,618 as on the 30th of June1991 (NSS, 48th round, GOI 1998a). According to this survey, bovines, cattle and buffaloes together, accounted for 90 per cent of the livestock wealth in India. The contribution of the livestock sector to total national gross domestic product (GDP) formed about 5 per cent in 2006-07 (Economic Survey:2006-07, GOI 2003a).

Though the contribution of agriculture and allied sectors to the GDP has been declining over time, the contribution of livestock to the gross output in the agricultural sector has been steadily on the increase accounting for about 27 per cent at present. Out of the total output originating from the livestock sector, the share of milk constitutes nearly two-thirds, as against only one-half during the early 1950's. India has now become the largest producer of milk in the world (Gupta 1997). The total milk production in India is estimated at about 100 million tonnes in 2006-07 and its per capita availability is 245 grams per day (Economic Survey: 2006-07).

It is estimated that the total annual employment in the livestock sector is about 20 million persons, approximately 11 million according to principal status and 9 million according to subsidiary status (Tenth Five Year Plan: 2000-2007). Women constitute about 70 per cent of the labor force in livestock farming. As the ownership of livestock is almost evenly distributed among landless labourers and marginal and small farmers, the progress of the livestock sector implies an equitable pattern of development of the rural economy. The export earnings from the livestock and the related sectors are progressively rising. Finished leather accounted for as high as 54 per cent (Rs.2,568 crore) and meat and meat products for 36 per cent (Rs.1,694 crore) of the total export earnings from the livestock sector during 2003-04 (Economic Survey: 2004-05). In sum, the importance of livestock in the Indian economy has been progressively increasing in recent decades.

The size, composition and productivity of India's livestock population have been undergoing significant changes. Right from ancient times, cattle formed an important part of the Indian agricultural system; they were kept primarily for draught purposes and as a sure source of manure. However, in recent years, consequent on the diffusion of agro-mechanical technologies in agriculture, the importance of work animals as draught power has gradually diminished. Farmers are being provided with assistance for owning agricultural machinery including tractors, and with training on their operation, maintenance and management. (Nair 1981a, 1981b, Economic Survey: 2004-05). During the past ten years (1991-92 to 2000-01), about 2.05 million tractors and 1,17,000 power tillers were sold in the country. The contribution of Draught Animal Power (DAP) to total power availability in Indian Agriculture has been declining over the years. The contribution, which was about 60 per cent in 1971-72, is estimated at 16 per cent in 2003-04. During this period, the total power availability increased from 0.3 kw/hectare to 1.4 kw/hectare. It is estimated that, at present, 22.78 per cent of the cultivated area is covered by tractors for tillage operations and 21.30 per cent for sowing operations. There has been considerable progress towards mechanisation in irrigation, harvesting and threshing operations too (Economic Survey: 2004-05). However, such rapid increase in mechanisation has made agriculture more sensitive to changes in international oil prices, since for running the machines imported oil was required. The wisdom of this type of integration of Indian agriculture with the international market through substitution of renewable resources (like animal draught power) with non-renewable sources of energy has been called into question by champions of sustainable agriculture. Recently, the National Commission on Cattle (GOI 2002) has also questioned the policy of indiscriminate promotion of mechanisation of agriculture and emphasised the need to preserve India's draught animal stock by banning slaughter of cattle.

Concerted efforts to increase milk production[1] in India began during the pre-independence period. During the Second World War, attempts had been made to meet the growing urban demand for milk and to ensure its regular supply for troops. Following Independence, the need for developing the livestock sector and increasing milk production received formal and official recognition. During the Five Year Plan periods, steps were taken to increase the supply of essential inputs for cattle development, to set up creameries and milk product factories and to strengthen dairy training and research programmes. Animal husbandry and dairy development programmes were also designed and implemented as part of the poverty alleviation strategies implemented in the country. The measures initiated to develop the livestock sector are reflected in the increase in the plan outlay on animal husbandry and dairying in the successive Five Year Plans. The total plan outlay for this sector which had been a mere Rs. 22 crore in the First Five Year Plan has increased to Rs. 2500 crore in the Tenth Plan (see Appendix Table 1. 1). As part of the poverty alleviation strategy, the Government of India gave priority to dairy development projects such as Small Farmers Development Agency (SFDA) and the Integrated Rural Development Programme (IRDP) as instruments for providing income and employment for the rural population.

Among the several policies and programmes implemented for improving the productivity and efficiency of India's livestock sector, the Key Village Scheme (KVS), Intensive Cattle Development Programme (ICDP) and Operation Flood (OF) projects have the pride of place. The aims, scope and coverage of these programmes have undergone significant changes over time. The Key Village Scheme introduced during the First Five Year Plan had aimed at increasing the quality of bovines by controlled breeding and by taking measures for proper feeding and disease control. Initially, its focus was on increasing the supply of breeding facilities, effective disease control measures, scientific management practices and organised marketing facilities. Towards the end of the Second Plan, there were 600 Key Village Centres in the country, covering an estimated 6 million cows and she-buffaloes. Since this scheme was not able to enhance milk supply to meet the growing urban demand and its contribution to the improvement in genetic quality and the productivity of the stock remained insignificant, a new project called the Intensive Cattle Development Project (ICDP), was started in the Third Plan. Its objectives were to provide facilities for cross-breeding of milch cattle, to supply other inputs to enhance production of milk and to link up the milk-shed areas with the urban milk market by improving marketing and processing facilities. In 1960, there were 62 ICDP units in the country. In some areas in which KVS existed, it was merged with ICDP; in all other areas KVS continued in the original form. However, since ICDP did not make any significant impact on the augmentation of milk production in the country, the Government of India formulated a new project called Operation Flood (OF) by the end of the Fourth Five Year Plan. This project was based on the experience of the Kaira District Cooperative Milk Producers' Union (KDMPU), Anand. Thus, during the late 1960s, the Government of India initiated major policy changes in the dairy sector to achieve self-sufficiency in milk production[2].

In the Fifth Plan, the Government of India implemented the OF project through the National Dairy Development Board (NDDB) and Indian Dairy Corporation (IDC) in selected milk sheds. The basic objective of this project was to increase milk production by (a) providing an assured market for milk to rural producers by linking rural milk sheds with urban milk markets (b) simultaneously providing facilities for cross-breeding and upgrading of milch animals and (c) ensuring supply of cattle feed and facilities for veterinary care for enhancing the productivity of milch animals. The first phase of this project (OF-I) began in 1970 and ended in March 1981. The total investment of this phase (about Rs.1165 million) was generated from the sale of milk products (1,27,517 MT Skim Milk Powder and 39,696 MT of Butter Oil) donated by the European Economic Community (EEC) through the World Food Programme. About 64 per cent of the total investment of Rs 742.2 million was used for production enhancement programmes and about 10 per cent for creating supporting infrastructure facilities like storage, long distance transport and project planning. OF-I aimed at setting up dairy co-operatives in 27 milk-sheds covering 10 states of India so as to link them with the 4 metro cities of Bombay, Calcutta, Delhi and Madras. This phase of this project resulted in the formation of 12000 village dairy co-operatives with a membership of 1.5 million farmers having 2.5 million milch animals spread over 27 milk shed areas (NDDB 1978). The second phase of the Operation Flood project (OF II) launched in 1979 covered 21 states and 4 Union Territories with a total financial outlay Rs 4855 million. A major part (49 per cent) of this investment was to be financed by dairy aid provided by the EEC and the rest by a World Bank Loan (36 per cent) and by proceeds of repayment of OFI loans (15 per cent). During this second phase, about 34500 dairy co-operative societies were organised in 136 milk sheds (NDDB:2003). The third phase (OF III) was intended to rectify the imbalances remaining after OF I and OF II and to extend the programme coverage to another 15000 villages and nearly 200 medium-sized urban centres. This phase involved a financial outlay of Rs 6806 million. An indicator of the success of Operation Flood is the amount of milk procured[3] and supplied to consumers. The average milk procurement increased from 2.56 million kg per day during Phase I to 11 million kg per day during Phase III. At present, over 60000 dairy co-operative societies function in 173 milk-sheds involving over 6 million farmer members and marketing 7.3 million kg of milk a day in over 535 cities and towns of the country. The total milk-processing capacity has reached 14 million kg. a day and powder production capacity 654 tonne a day.

As is evident from the preceding discussion, the aims and the strategy of bovine development programmes have undergone significant changes during the past four decades. The main features of these changes in strategy indicate the following: from multi-purpose bovines to single-purpose animals, from low-yielding to high-yielding milch animals, from home-based to commercialised milk production and from an indigenous model to a western model of dairy development (Nair and Jackson 1981). Such a shift in the development strategy has had significant impact on the bovine economy of the country. These policies and programmes were implemented in an overall policy environment in which the central government follows a policy of import-substitution by restricting imports and promoting domestic production. The policy was also considered a means to create livelihood for the small and marginal farming households and the landless wage earners, with milk production taking place in millions of rural households scattered across the country. Milk-processing and product manufacturing were restricted mainly to small firms and cooperatives. High import duties, non-tariff barriers, restrictions on imports and exports, and stringent licensing provisions provided incentives to Indian-owned small enterprises and cooperatives to expand production[4] in a protected market. Competition within the organized sector was regulated through licensing provisions, which prohibited new entrants into the milk-processing sector. Milk powder and butter oil were available in the international market at lower prices, a fact which made reconstitution of milk from these products cheaper than collection and sale of fresh milk. It was therefore necessary to restrict cheap imports with a view to promoting indigenous production.

During the early 1990s, the Government of India introduced major trade policy reforms that favoured privatization and liberalization of the economy. The dairy industry was delicensed in 1991 with a view to encouraging private sector participation and investment. However, in response to sociopolitical pressure, the government introduced the Milk and Milk Products Order (MMPO) in 1992 under the Essential Commodities Act of 1955, to regulate milk and dairy product production[5]

The government has amended the MMPO from time to time; the major amendment was made in March 2002, by which restrictions on setting up of milk-processing and milk product manufacturing plants were removed and the concept of milk-shed abolished. This amendment is expected to facilitate the entry of large companies, as a result of which competition in the domestic markets would definitely increase. A major development in the Indian dairy sector policy came when India signed the Uruguay Round Agreement on Agriculture (URAA) in 1994 and became a member of the World Trade Organization (WTO), an action which made India open up its dairy sector to world markets (Gulati et al. 1996, Sundaresan 2001). The import and export of dairy products was delicensed and decanalized, and free trade in dairy products was allowed with only certain inspection requirements in position. The first major step was taken in 1994-95, when the import of skimmed milk powder (SMP) and butter oil was decanalized; restrictions on the remaining products were removed in April 2002. Moreover, the import tariffs on dairy products were drastically reduced after trade liberalization. Further, India had bound its import tariffs for dairy products at low levels in the Uruguay Round schedules.

There exist conflicting arguments regarding the pros and cons of the liberalization process on the dairy sector. It is argued that milk prices in India are much higher than international prices (Sharma 2000, 2002, 2004, Sharma and Sharma 2002, 2002a, Sharma and Gulati 2003, Kumar 2004, Aswathi 2004, Jha 2004); with liberalization imports are likely to increase in India. At the same time, it is noted that the low prices in the major dairy exporting countries (mostly EU, USA and Canada) are due to high export subsidies and that, if the WTO negotiations could result in the withdrawal of these subsidies, these countries would not enjoy comparative advantage over India. The country would be able therefore to compete with them in the international market (Banerjee 1996, Jha and Debroy 2000, Saxena 2000, Sirohi 2002, Sharma 2001, 2004, Kumar 2004). Whatever be the merits of such arguments, it is clear that in the emerging environment of trade liberalization, the country may not be able to compete with other countries in the international market unless there happens considerable reduction in the domestic cost of production. This requires increase in productivity and efficiency of the sector.

Viewing from the vantage point of the present state of India's livestock sector, the integration of the Indian economy to the international market through increased use of imported oil and oil based products (chemical fertilizers) as substitutes to draught animal power and dung as manure in agriculture respectively, would definitely make agriculture more vulnerable to fluctuations in international oil prices. The rapid spread in mechanization would also result in the reverse tendency that has become widespread in agriculture, thereby pushing out the rural poor from agricultural production as a source of livelihood. Of course, it could be argued that the reduction in the number of work animals would release more feed for milch animals, thereby promoting dairying. However, the question that needs to be asked is the possibility for the poor resource-starved farmers to reduce their cost of production of milk and other livestock products and reap the advantages offered by the liberalization of trade. In order to provide insights into these questions, it is necessary to look at the changes taking place in the livestock sector and the underlying factors and processes. The present study is carried out against this background. Given the large variations in the different characteristics of the livestock sector such an analysis is best be done at the regional level.

Objectives and Scope

Analysis of the recent trends in India's livestock sector has highlighted the fact that here exists substantial differentiation in the characteristics of the livestock sector across states/ regions in the country. Some of these interesting and striking differentials may be summarized as follows.

(a) The density of work animals per hectare of net sown area has shown a mildly falling trend for the country as a whole; but in several states, especially in the states of Andhra Pradesh, Gujarat, Haryana, Kerala, Rajasthan and Tamil Nadu it has shown a secular decline. On the other hand, in some other states, it has shown a mixed pattern of mildly rising trend till the 1980s, and a mild fall thereafter. A few eastern states, namely West Bengal, Bihar and Orissa, have shown an invariably upward trend in work animal density.

(b) The cattle and buffalo sex ratios (number of males per 100 females) have been shifting in favour of females at varying rates in all the states except the states in eastern India, where they have showed an upward trend till the 1980s and remained more or less stable since then.

(c) The ratio of cows to she-buffaloes has shown an increasing trend in all the regions except the eastern region. This could be a reflection of the increased demand for milch cows. She-buffaloes are more suitable for more milk production in some parts of the northern and the southern regions.

(d) The diffusion of cross-breeding technology has been uneven across the major states. The classification of states, according to the share of crossbred cattle in the total cattle population in 1997 shows that the share remained above 60 per cent in Kerala and Punjab, it varied between 30 to 40 per cent in Tamil Nadu, Haryana and Jammu and Kashmir, it oscillated between 10 to 25 per cent in Karnataka, Maharashtra, and Uttat Pradesh and remained at less than 10 per cent in Gujarat , Madhya Pradesh, Andhra Pradesh, Rajasthan and West Bengal.

(e) Though the production of milk has shown an increasing trend in recent decades there exist considerable regional variations in the pattern of growth. The pattern of milk consumption has also shown considerable regional variations.

The trends in the pattern of bovine holdings summarised above are a reflection of the choices that farmers have made in allocating their resources in livestock-rearing to meet the changing demand conditions for milk products and services. It has been shown in some of the earlier studies that such choices are also shaped by demographic, economic, technological and institutional factors (Raj 1969 & 1972, Vaidyanathan 1978, Vaidyanathan, Nair and Harris 1982). Since, the magnitudes and interactions among such variables differ across regions, it is important to carry out disaggregated state-wise/regional analysis of the changes in the pattern of bovine holdings and the underlying factors and processes. The objective of the present study is to undertake such an analysis for the state of Tamil Nadu. Some of the reasons that motivated us to select Tamil Nadu for the study are: (i) it is one among the four states which experienced a secular decline in the stock of work animals (Nair and Dhas 1990, Sharma 2004); (ii) the production of milk has shown a steady increase over the past four decades (Dhas 1986 & 2001, Gurumurthy 1999) and (iii) the agricultural sector has been undergoing significant changes in terms of cropping pattern, degree of intensity of mechanization, etc (Madras Institute of Development Studies 1988, Rajalakshmi 2001 Naganathan 2002, GOTN 2003, GOI 2005c).

The overall objective of this study is to analyse the evolution of the bovine sector in relation to the changes taking place in the agricultural sector in particular and in the rest of the economy in general. In specific terms, the objectives of the study are outlined as follows:

(a) To examine the determinants of the size and composition of the cattle and buffalo population. An attempt will be made in this part of the analysis to bring out the influence of agro-climatic, technological and institutional factors in shaping the bovine complex;

(b) To bring out the changes in the distribution of bovine holdings and their utilization across size groups of land holdings;

(c) To analyze the factors shaping the supply of and demand for milk; and

(d) In the light of the above analysis, to highlight the prospects of development of the livestock sector.

In the past, a few state level studies attempted to unravel changes in the size and composition of the bovine population and the underlying factors (Nair 1981a, George and Nair 1990 and Yeshwanth 1990 for Kerala; Dhas 1986 for Tamil Nadu; Harold 1987 for Karnataka; Mohan 1989, Lakshmann et al. 1994 and Subramaniam, et al. 1995 for Andhra Pradesh; Shah 1997 for Maharashtra; Kurup 2003 for Orissa; Franco and Chand 1991and Saxena 1995 for Gujarat; Fahimuddin 1963 for Bihar; Sharma, R.K. 1981 and 2001for Haryana; Jain 1986 for Rajasthan; Kumar et al. 2004 for Himachal Pradesh; and Sastry *et al.* 1993 for Pondicherry). Since most of them were confined either to one or two specific aspects of the bovine sector, they do not make a comprehensive treatment of the different factors or processes at work which shape the bovine utilization patterns. An exception is the study for Kerala (Nair 1981a) that attempted to provide a comprehensive approach to the analysis of bovine holdings. One of the major limitations of the majority of these studies is that they lacked a historical approach. Research by economic historians (see for instance Thompson 1983) of Western Europe has pointed out in clear terms, how shifts from bullocks to horses as motive power in European agriculture had taken place consequent on the shift in the pattern of farming from one-crop rotation to two-crop rotation and changes in the types of ploughs and other implements used for ploughing and other agricultural operations; the link between movement of people from rural to urban areas consequent on the Industrial Revolution and the subsequent shortage of labour, which promoted labour-saving technologies in crop production and the manner in which horses emerged as a major source of farm draught power in European agriculture in the 18th and the 19th centuries. According to Thompson, it is this predominance of horses in European agriculture, and the fact that they were also very important in fighting wars, that contributed to the development of the taboo against the slaughter of horses and the eating of horsemeat in several countries in Western Europe. Though economic historians in India analyzed the influence of cattle wealth in shaping agriculture, the question how the cattle wealth in turn was shaped by changes in agriculture and in the rest of the economy has not attracted research attention. Historical insights are useful in understanding the contemporary resource utilization patterns in the livestock sector. In our approach to the study, we shall attempt to examine changes in the bovine holdings of Tamil Nadu in the light of the historical changes as have been analyzed as a background for the period 1900-1951.

Much of the quantitative analysis of the determinants of the size, composition and productivity of the bovine holdings in our study covers the period 1956-2000. For the analytical framework of the study, we have drawn from the works of Raj (1969) and Vaidyanathan (1988). One of the distinguishing features of their analysis is the enquiry into the different roles of bovine: as a mother machine since cows reproduce calves, as a source of intermediate goods (draught power and manure to agriculture and hides and skins for leather industry), as a producer of consumer goods since cows and she-buffaloes produce milk and also serve as a consumption good, since they are slaughtered for beef. We have attempted to look at these different roles of bovines, subject to the availability of data.

Sources of Data

Much of the historical analysis has been carried out using the data available from Indian Agricultural Statistics, Livestock Censuses, Statistical Abstracts of British India, Statistical Atlas of Madras Presidency, Season and Crop Reports of Madras Presidency and historical studies on agriculture in the Madras Presidency. The analysis for more recent periods was done by using data from Livestock Censuses, Season and Crop Reports for Tamil Nadu, Agricultural Censuses and Input Surveys, Reports of Consumption Expenditure and Landholdings Surveys published by the National Sample Survey Organisation, Integrated Sample Surveys (ISS) conducted by the Tamil Nadu Animal Husbandry Department, etc., and Farm Management Studies. A note on the sources and limitations of data on the livestock sector is given in Annexure. Because of the long delays in the publication of official data, the study could not extend the analysis to the most recent years.

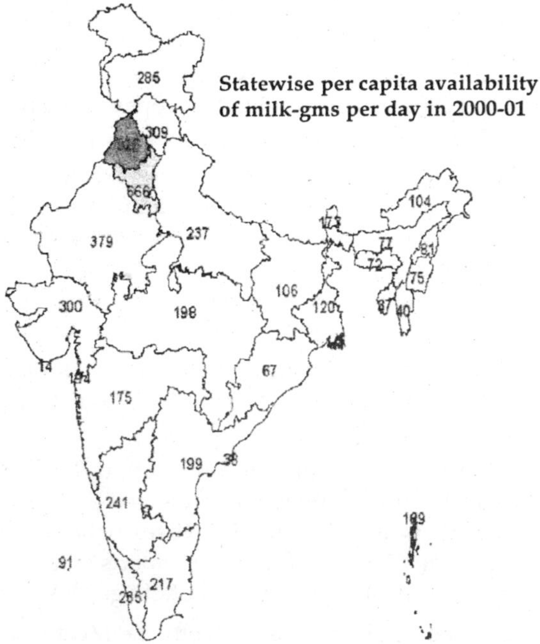

Data Source: "Basic Animal husbandry Statistics-2000", DAHD, GOI

Figure 1 : **Map showing the per capita availability of milk in India by state: 2000-01.**

Source: NDDB, Annual Report.

Chapter Outline

Following this introduction, chapter 2 will review the major studies that analysed the patterns and variations in bovine sex ratios in India. This will be followed by an analysis of the trends in the bovine economy of Tamil Nadu till 1951. With the help of analytical models, we shall examine the determinants of bovine sex ratios in chapter 4. Chapter 5 looks at the distributional changes in bovine holdings. The trends in milk production and the factors shaping them are examined in chapter 6. The final chapter summarizes the main findings and highlights their implications.

Notes

1. Milk production in India increased from 17 million tons in 1950-51 to 84.6 million tons in 2001-02. The trends in milk production and per capita availability of milk in India and across states between 1991-92 and 2001-02 are presented in Appendix Tables 1.2 and 1.3. The per capita details are also portrayed in a map (Figure 1).
2. Production of milk in rural areas, procuring of milk through producer cooperatives and moving processed milk to urban demand centres was the crucial elements of strategy of the government's dairy development policy. This policy initiative gave a boost to dairy development and initiated the process of establishing linkages between rural producers and urban consumers.
3. The growth of village milk producers' cooperative and procurement under Operation Flood (1970 to 1990) is depicted in Appendix Table 1. 4.
4. In order to promote domestic production, India followed an import-substitution strategy and protected the dairy sector from external markets through quantitative restrictions on imports and exports and canalization (restricting imports and exports through government or government-designated agencies).
5. The order required permission from state/central registration authorities to set up units handling more than 10,000 litres of milk per day or milk solids up to 500 tons per annum, depending on the capacity of the plant. The order included sanitary and hygienic regulations to ensure product quality. The status of registrations granted under the MMPO as of March 31, 2002, is shown in Appendix Table 1. 5.

APPENDIX

Appendix Table 1.1
Plan-wise Outlay and Expenditure (Rs. in crores) of Central and Centrally Sponsored Schemes under Animal Husbandry in India: 1950-55 to 2002-07

Plan/Year	*Animal Husbandry*		*Dairying*		*Total*	
	Outlay	*Exp.*	*Outlay*	*Exp.*	*Outlay*	*Exp.*
First Plan (1950-55)	14.19	8.22	7.81	7.78	22.00	16.00
Second Plan (1955-60)	38.50	21.42	17.44	12.05	55.94	33.47
Third Plan (1960-65)	54.44	43.40	36.08	33.60	90.52	77.00
Annual Plan (1966-67)	41.33	34.00	26.14	25.70	67.47	59.70
Fourth Plan (1967-72)	94.10	75.51	139.00	78.75	233.10	154.26
Fifth Plan	-	178.43	-	-	437.54	232.46
Sixth Plan (1980-85)	60.46	39.08	336.10	298.34	396.56	337.42
Seventh Plan (1985-90)	165.19	102.35	302.75	374.43	467.94	476.78
Annual Plan (1990-91)	43.71	36.18	79.67	41.43	123.38	77.61
Annual Plan (1991-92)	57.97	43.28	97.49	77.99	155.46	121.27
Eighth Plan	400.00	305.43	900.00	818.05	1300.00	1123.48
Ninth Plan (1997-2002)	1076.12	-	469.52	-	1545.64	-
Tenth Plan (2002-2007)	2145.00		355.00		2500.00	-

Note: *: Provisional.

Source: Basic Animal Husbandry Statistics 2002, Department of Animal Husbandry and Dairying, Ministry of Agriculture, GOI.
Tenth Five Year Plan (2002-2007). Planning Commission, GOI.

Appendix Table 1.2

Trends in Milk Production in Different States & Union Territories of India: 1991-92 to 2000-01

(thousands of metric tons)

State	*1991-92*	*1992-93*	*1993-94*	*1994-95*	*1995-96*	*1996-97*	*1997-98*	*1998-99*	*1999-00*	*2000-01*	*2001-02*
Andhra Pradesh	2943	3103	3766	4221	4261	4471	4473	4842	4730	4904	5145
Arunachal Pradesh	7	21	21	22	42	44	43	45	45	45.5	55
Assam	639	658	676	698	699	714	719	725	822	852	894
Bihar	3210	3195	3215	3250	3321	3410	3420	3440	3740	3878	4068
Chandigarh	34	37	38	39	41	42	43	43	42	44	46
Dadra & Nagar Haveli	3	10	7	8	5	4	4	8	10	10	1
Daman and Diu		1	1	1	0	1	1	1	1	1	11
Delhi	227	235	252	257	261	264	267	290	295	306	321
Goa	28	30	33	36	37	37	38	41	43	45	47
Gujarat	3591	3795	3935	4459	4608	4831	4913	5059	5124	5313	5573
Haryana	3565	3715	3850	4062	4055	4204	4373	4527	4673	4845	4976
Himachal Pradesh	597	610	654	663	676	698	714	724	745	772	810
Jammu and Kashmir	515	937	780	641	869	992	979	990	1000	1037	1088
Karnataka	2475	2590	2736	3003	3190	3460	3970	4231	4925	5106	5357
Kerala	1785	1889	2001	2118	2192	2258	2343	2420	2673	2771	2907
Lakshadweep	1	1	1	1	1	1	1	1	1	1	1
Madhya Pradesh	4806	4879	4975	5047	5125	5224	5377	5442	5600	5806	6091
Maharashtra	3955	4102	4250	4812	4991	5127	5193	5609	5810	5850	6024

Contd...

(thousands of metric tons)

State	1991-92	1992-93	1993-94	1994-95	1995-96	1996-97	1997-98	1998-99	1999-00	2000-01	2001-02
Manipur	83	83	84	64	57	61	62	65	67	69	73
Meghalaya	50	52	53	54	57	58	59	61	65	67	71
Mizoram	8	9	9	9	9	9	17	20	10	10	11
Nagaland	43	44	45	43	44	46	46	47.5	49.5	51	54
Orissa	505	542	565	584	648	687	672	733	795	824	865
Pondichery	27	27	32	33	33	38	36	36	35	36	38
Punjab	5382	5583	5970	6215	6424	6755	7165	7394	7700	7984	8375
Rajasthan	4474	4586	4958	5103	5449	5874	6487	6923	5820	6034	6330
Sikkim	29	30	30	32	33	34	35	34.5	43	44	46
Tamilnadu	3357	3468	3524	3695	3791	3976	4061	4273	4256	4413	4629
Tripura	32	34	35	38	39	44	57	76	49	51	53
Uttar Pradesh	10206	10649	10991	11321	11878	12387	12934	13618	15176	15735	16506
West Bengal	3019	3023	3095	3250	3341	3376	3415	3441	3750	3888	4079
India	55620	57962	60607	63804	66198	69147	71940	75182	78117	80817	84570

Source: NDDB, 2003.

Appendix Table 1.3

Trends in Per Capita Availability of Milk (gram/day) in Major States and Union Territories in India: 1991-92 to 2000-01

State	*1991-92*	*1992-93*	*1993-94*	*1994-95*	*1995-96*	*1996-97*	*1997-98*	*1998-99*	*1999-00*	*2000-01*
Andhra Pradesh	121	126	151	167	167	173	170	182	186	189
Arunachal Pradesh	22	65	64	65	121	124	119	121	118	117
Assam	78	79	80	81	80	80	79	79	88	89
Bihar	102	99	97	96	96	96	94	92	98	99
Chandigarh	145	153	152	150	153	151	150	145	137	138
Dadra & Nagar Haveli	59	189	126	138	82	63	60	114	136	130
Daman & Diu	0	26	25	24	0	22	21	20	19	18
Delhi	66	66	68	67	65	63	62	65	63	63
Goa	66	69	75	81	82	81	82	87	90	93
Gujarat	238	247	251	278	282	290	289	291	289	294
Haryana	593	603	610	628	611	618	627	634	638	645
Himachal Pradesh	316	318	335	335	336	341	343	343	347	354
Jammu & Kashmir	183	324	263	210	277	308	296	292	287	290
Karnataka	151	155	161	174	182	195	220	231	264	270
Kerala	168	176	185	194	199	203	209	214	234	241
Lakshadweep	53	52	51	51	50	49	48	47	47	46
Madhya Pradesh	199	198	198	197	196	195	197	195	197	200
Maharashtra	137	140	142	157	160	161	160	169	171	169
Manipur	124	121	119	88	77	80	79	81	81	81

Contd...

State	*1991-92*	*1992-93*	*1993-94*	*1994-95*	*1995-96*	*1996-97*	*1997-98*	*1998-99*	*1999-00*	*2000-01*
Meghalaya	77	78	78	77	79	79	78	78	81	82
Mizoram	32	35	34	33	32	31	58	66	32	32
Nagaland	97	95	92	84	82	81	77	76	75	74
Orissa	44	46	47	48	53	55	53	57	61	62
Pondichery	92	90	105	106	104	117	109	107	102	103
Punjab	727	741	778	795	807	834	869	880	900	917
Rajasthan	279	278	294	295	307	323	348	362	297	300
Sikkim	195	197	191	198	198	199	199	190	225	229
Tamilnadu	165	168	169	176	178	185	187	195	192	197
Tripura	32	33	34	36	37	41	52	68	43	44
Uttar Pradesh	201	205	207	208	214	218	222	229	249	253
West Bengal	121	120	121	125	126	125	125	123	132	135
India	180	184	189	195	198	203	207	213	217	220

Source: NDDB, 2003.

Appendix Table 1.4
Growth of Milk Producers' Cooperatives and Procurement under Operation Flood (1970-1990)

Project Phase	*Year*	*Number of Milk Cooperatives*	*Milk Producers ('000)*	*Annual Milk Procurement (million Tonnes)*
OF I	1970-71	1588	278	0.1898
	1971-72	1811	327	0.2372
	1972-73	2200	361	0.2774
	1973-74	2598	394	0.2226
	1974-75	2966	445	0.3175
	1975-76	4533	562	0.4197
	1976-77	7681	723	0.5657
	1977-78	9306	943	0.6205
	1978-79	10099	1213	0.7336
	1979-80	11436	1475	0.8614
	1980-81	13270	1747	0.9844
OF II	1981-82	18422	2124	1.0147
	1982-83	23496	2620	1.6133
	1983-84	28614	3116	1.9016
	1984-85	34523	3632	2.1097
OF III	1985-86	42692	4484	2.8762
	1986-87	49077	5097	2.8652
	1987-88	54525	5666	2.8105
	1988-89	58883	6250	2.9090
	1989-90	60825	7003	3.5821

Source: V. Venkatasubramanian *et. al.* (2003).

Appendix Table 1.5
Number of Dairy Plants Registered under Milk and Milk Products Order (MMPO) in India by States as on March, 2002.

States/Union	*Cooperative*		*Private*		*Others*		*Total*	
territories	*No.*	*Capacity*	*No.*	*Capacity*	*No.*	*Capacity*	*No.*	*Capacity*
By Central Authority								
Andhra Pradesh	13	2905	6	855	1	200	20	3960
Bihar	6	485	1	120	0	0	7	605
Delhi	0	0	0	0	8	6500	8	6500
Goa	1	30	0	0	0	0	1	30
Gujarat	14	6170	2	300	6	640	22	7110
Haryana	5	400	14	3390	0	0	19	3790
Himachal Pradesh	3	44	2	345	0	0	5	389
Karnataka	12	1833	5	495	1	400	18	2728
Kerala	4	400	3	125	0	0	7	525
Madhya Pradesh	7	1200	4	1100	0	0	11	2300

Contd...

States/Union territories	*Cooperative* No.	*Cooperative* Capacity	*Private* No.	*Private* Capacity	*Others* No.	*Others* Capacity	*Total* No.	*Total* Capacity
Maharashtra	17	3570	18	3900	15	2700	50	10170
Orissa	7	182	0	0	0	0	7	182
Pondicherry	1	50	0	0	0	0	1	50
Punjab	12	1570	12	3050	0	0	24	4620
Rajasthan	12	1290	9	1050	0	0	21	2340
Sikkim	1	15	0	0	0	0	1	15
Tamilnadu	13	3880	4	526	0	0	17	4406
Tripura	1	10	0	0	0	0	1	10
Uttar Pradesh	7	1540	33	6664	0	0	40	8204
West Bengal	2	216	0	0	2	820	4	1036
Total	138	25790	113	21920	33	11260	284	58970
By State Registering Authorities								
Andhra Pradesh	0	0	9	588	0	0	9	588
Bihar	0	0	0	0	0	0	0	0
Delhi	0	0	0	0	0	0	0	0
Goa	0	0	0	0	0	0	0	0
Gujarat	3	110	1	390	1	30	5	530
Haryana	0	0	23	1200	2	130	25	1330
Himachal Pradesh	0	0	0	0	0	0	0	0
Karnataka	2	75	14	615	0	0	16	690
Kerala	7	365	4	113	2	35	13	513
Madhya Pradesh	3	50	0	0	2	20	5	70
Maharashtra	18	636	50	1675	23	695	91	3006
Orissa	1	30	0	0	0	0	1	30
Pondicherry	0	0	0	0	0	0	0	0
Punjab	1	60	19	755	0	0	20	815
Rajasthan	2	47	8	547	0	0	10	594
Sikkim	0	0	0	0	0	0	0	0
Tamilnadu	12	485	12	345	0	0	24	830
Tripura	0	0	0	0	0	0	0	0
Uttar Pradesh	25	746	147	4177	0	0	172	4923
West Bengal	0	0	3	90	0	0	3	90
Total	74	2604	290	10495	30	910	394	14009
Total (Central + State registration)	212	28394	403	32415	63	12170	678	72979

Note: Capacity in thousands of liters/day
Source: GOI, 2002.

2

BOVINE SEX RATIOS IN INDIA: THEORIES AND EMPIRICAL FINDINGS

Introduction

Analysis of the variations in the sex ratios of human and animal populations across regions has been a subject of interesting debate among social scientists in India (Miller 1981, Bardhan 1974, Wadley and Derr 1987, Harris 1965, Crotty 1980, Vaidyanathan, Harris and Nair 1982). Demographers who worked on human sex ratios by age groups have shown a North-South divide in the preference for the male child, as reflected in the sex ratio of child mortality and the index of son preference (The index of son-preference is defined as 100 x E/c , were 'E' is the excess number of sons over daughters considered ideal and 'c' is the ideal family size. The index varies from -100 to 100). It is revealed from the analysis of Population Censuses and other sources of data on child mortality by sex, that the sex ratio (defined as male/female) of children below one year tends to be significantly higher in the North Indian states of Punjab, Haryana, Uttar Pradesh, Rajasthan, and Madhya Pradesh than in the South Indian States of Andhra Pradesh, Karnataka, Tamil Nadu and Kerala. (see for details Basu 1995). The index of son preference reveals that it is significantly higher in the North than in the South. A variety of explanations are offered for such variations in the preference for the male over the female, in terms of economic and cultural factors. According to Miller (1981) it is the higher demand for female labour in South Indian agriculture than in the North and the higher widespread practice of dowry in the North than in the South, that have contributed to the observed variations in son- preference. Recent research shows variations in the preference for male children over female children across districts in Tamil Nadu. The 'unwanted' female children are gotten rid of by deliberate starvation and infanticide (Rajan *et al.* 1991, Chunkath *et al.*1997, Sudha and Rajan 1999).

Somewhat in parallel to the above discussion, research by economists and social anthropologists has pointed out the prevalence of significant variations in the cattle and the buffalo sex ratios across states in India. It was Harris (1966) who showed first that the sex ratio of adult cattle was higher in the South, followed by the East and that the lowest was in the North Indian states. He attributed such variations to the relatively higher demand for draught animals in the rice-growing regions of the South and the East than in the North. He also noted the significantly higher preference for she-buffaloes over he-buffaloes in the North than in the East and the South and attributed it to variations in requirement of milk in the human diet: people in the North who are exposed to cold climate require a higher source of fat and protein from milk than those living in the other regions. Harris's cultural materialistic explanations were subjected to scrutiny by a number of researchers in India and abroad (see Dandeker 1967, 1969, Shah 1967, Heston 1971). In the midst of such debates, there took place attempts to quantify the existence of 'surplus cows'. The advocates of the 'surplus cows' hypothesis argued that given the reproductive efficiency of cows, it would be possible to meet the requirement of male cattle for traction in agriculture, by maintaining a smaller stock of cows that are better fed than the existing stock, that the existence of surplus is due to the Hindu religion's sentiments against consumption of beef and slaughter of cattle (see Dandekar: 1969 &1970, Mishra 1978) and that a deliberate policy of cattle slaughter would increase the economic welfare of the people.

Raj (1969) took the discussion on surplus cattle into new heights through his highly influential paper on the "Investment in Livestock in Agrarian Economy". With the help of an analytical model that captured the growth in demand for milk, draught power and other goods and services obtained from cattle on the one hand, and the factors operating from the supply side like the size distribution of land, ecological factors like irrigation, the use of land for crops and for the cultivation of fodder, on the other, he predicted that the size and composition of cattle maintained in the country is the stock that is needed to meet the demand. To illustrate his arguments, he also compared the Indian situation with that of the United States and found that his model correctly predicted the stock size that prevailed in that country. In the empirical part of his paper he looked at the systematic variations in the sex and species composition of bovine stock and accounted for the variations in terms of demographic, economic, ecological, technological and institutional factors. The line of analysis advocated by Raj was extended by Vaidyanathan (1978, 1988) through systematic empirical research. Since in-depth reviews of earlier studies are already available (Nair 1981a, Dhas 1986, Vaidyanathan 1989 and George 1996) we refrain from undertaking a repeated exercise on this aspect.

However, in order to sharpen the focus of the present exercise, we will attempt a limited survey of studies on India's bovine economy. The review is organized in the following sequence. In the light of the arguments that the primary function of cows is to produce male calves to be raised as draught animals and that the requirement of draught power in agriculture has been undergoing significant changes overtime, we shall first present a review of studies on the work-animal stock. This is followed by a review of studies on the milch animal stock, including trends in milk production, its sources of growth, changes in consumption and demand for milk. At the end of the review, we will present our main findings with a view to highlighting the focus of the present study.

Work Animal Population

The Royal Commission on Agriculture (1928) had observed that the number of bullocks per unit of cultivated area in a region is related to the number of cultivators, the average size of landholdings, the soil character, availability of irrigation, cropping pattern, time available for ploughing before sowing and the species composition of the work-animal population. Fahimuddin (1963) who examined the question with reference to Bihar found that work-animal density was intimately related to cropping pattern, size of holdings and quality of the soil.

Sharma (1981) in his analysis of the inter-district variations in the density of draught animals in Haryana explained the observed variations in terms of area cultivated, farm size and the degree of agricultural mechanisation, especially tractorisation. His analysis revealed that tractorisation has only a weak effect on the draught-animal stock.

Vaidyanathan (1978) and Vaidyanathan, Nair and Harris (1982) examined the changes in work-animal density across states in India by formulating the following hypothesis that explained not only the density of work animals, but also the way the sex ratio of bovines is decided.

> "As human population density rises, land is cultivated more intensively, and, since private property prevails, there is a progressive decline in the average size of holdings. Because of the seasonality of rainfall, plow animals function as a "energy gate". Hence, the decline in size of holding does not lead to a proportional decline in the number of plow animals per holding. Land has to be prepared for sowing in a short time during which it is too risky to depend on hiring someone else's animals. It is only by owning his own plow animals that the farmer can ensure timeliness of initial operations. As a result, the total number of plow animals may rise faster than the requirements of draft power. This leads to a lower rate of utilization and/or selection for smaller breeds. Beyond a certain point, however, increases in the cost of maintaining

> animals relative to the needs of human subsistence force farmers to give up the ownership of draft animals. The extent to which this occurs depends on the effectiveness of exchange and/or lease arrangements and the feasibility of substituting human for animal labour in cultivation" (Vaidyanathan 1982, p. 366).

The above hypothesis has two sets of relationships which may be written as follows: (i) with rise in human density, work animal density would tend to increase more rapidly than draught requirements upto a point, beyond which it would decline, and (ii) with increase in human density the proportion of adults in the bovine population would tend to increase upto a point, beyond which it would diminish. The above hypothesis did not take in to account the influence of other factors, especially the role of technological, economic and ecological factors in shaping the variations in density and sex ratios. Vaidyanathan (1989) further tested this inference by means of a regression model with work-animal densities as the dependent variable and rainfall, percentage of area under irrigation, average size of landholding and the average horse power from mechanical power on the other as independent variables. His model found all the variables to have significant influence on the density of work-animals. He further extended his analysis by bringing in factors like feed supply and those influencing the demand for milk to test the relationship between work-animal density and bovine sex ratios. His analysis revealed that demand for milk and the availability of feed supply exert a negative effect on the sex ratio of bovines.

There were also attempts to test this hypothesis by other researchers. Nair (1981a) analysed the density-dependent hypothesis using historical data (1920s to 1970s) for Kerala and all-India. He observed that while the country as a whole was still in the ascending phase of the relation between human density and bovine density, Kerala had already entered the declining phase. In Kerala, the density of adult male cattle had been declining and that of adult female cattle increasing. Among the young stock in the state, the density of the female stock was increasing. The decline in adult male density and increase in young female cattle density indicated that in the State, farmers had begun substituting milch animals for draught animals. Dolberg (1982) and Jabar and Green (1984) tested the density-dependent hypothesis with the data collected from Bangladesh and found that very small farms preferred to have small animals and that, while the size of the holding declined, the sex ratio changed in favour of milch animals. Dhas (1986) who examined the decline in the work-animal density in Tamil Nadu during 1951 to 1982, found patterns of change closely similar to those of Kerala.

Apart from population pressure on land and consequent reduction in the size of holding, mechanisation of agriculture has also been found to influence draught-animal holding. In the case of Punjab, Hanumantha Rao (1975) observed that mechanisation triggered by steeply rising wage rate of field labourers and increasing bullock prices, had led to reduction of the use of animal power in agriculture. Grewal and Kahlon (1973) had observed that tractorization also led to a significant change in the sex composition of cattle: a drastic decline in total animal population associated with rise in the proportion of milch animals.

Introduction of mechanical power does not necessarily lead to decline in draught animal population if it is associated with intensification of cultivation. For example, Sharma (1981) found that in Haryana there existed a positive relation between growth in mechanical power and work-animal density. He attributed this to (i) the introduction of pumpsets which led to more intensive land preparation which in turn involved a net increase in the requirement of animal power and (ii) the confinement of tractorization to only portions of the farms. Jarvis (1982) argued that an increase in the demand for milk and beef was also a factor that is likely to reduce the supply of draught power services in India, particularly in the context of mechanisation of agriculture.

Odend'hal (1988a) observed that the demand for bullocks in the Daltaic West Bengal during the period between 1977 and 1987 declined consequent on the increasing use of hand-operated tractors for ploughing even though the male cattle population had increased significantly in the upland regions of the state (Odend'hal: 1988b).

Nair and Dhas (1989, 1990) analysed, using data from the National Sample Survey (26th and 37th rounds), the factors shaping the density of draught animals per cultivated holding and their utilisation pattern across size groups of land holdings. Their study showed that in most parts of India, agricultural mechanisation had not resulted in any reduction in draught animal stock. Dhas (1989) observed that the draught animal population in Tamil Nadu had been declining from the mid-sixties and that the rate of decline had become higher from the mid-'seventies. These changes were analysed in relation to factors such as availability of mechanical power, size of land holdings, cropping pattern, feed supply and increasing requirements of milch animals. The study revealed that while the intensity of agricultural mechanisation had not contributed to a decline in the draught animal population, all the other factors had.

Sharma (1989) observed reduction in the draught animals in a village in west Uttar Pradesh during the period 1964 to 1984 and consequent very low rate of replacement of animals by tractors. But he argued that the introduction of tractors had resulted in a considerable shift in the ownership of draught power among different size groups of farms, which enabled farmers either to discard, or to maintain fewer, animals. Mishra and Sharma (1990) examined the changes in size, composition and regional variations in the draught animal population in India during 1951 to 1982. The study revealed that there had taken place a virtual stagnation in the draught animal population between 1961 and 1977 and that it was followed by a marginal reduction during 1977-1982. The steep reduction in draught animal population in Kerala and Tamil Nadu is attributed also to decline in the area under rice cultivation and large shifts of area to tree crops, particularly plantation crops. The shift was marginal till the end of the 1970s. Prabaharan (1991) examined the size, composition and utilisation of draught animals in Tamil Nadu across agro-climatic zones, based on a survey conducted during 1989-90. He observed the practice of hiring out draught animals for crop production activities as a method of their intensive utilisation.

Saxena (1995) observed that though a gradual decline in the draught animal population in Gujarat had begun as early as in 1966, inter-regional and inter-district disparities in the density of draught animals were pronounced, due primarily to differences in the level of tractorisation, size of operational holdings and availability of irrigation facilities. It was found that the rental markets for both animal and tractor power were becoming increasingly popular. Shah (1997) found that the structure of draught power in Maharashtra was undergoing a significant change during the period between 1956 and 1987. Mechanisation of irrigation and tractorisation was taking place at a much higher rate than increase in draught animal population. Similar trends were observed in Karnataka also (Brithal and Ravishankar: 1999).

The foregoing survey has brought out the factors that influenced the density of draught animals across regions in the country. It indicates the influence of agro-climatic factors, crop pattern, size of holding and degrees of mechanisation in determining work-animal density. It also establishes the linkage between the requirement of draught power in agriculture and the holding of milch animals. The review presented in the section that follows will further highlight these linkages.

Milch Animal Population

Traditionally, adult female cattle were maintained for the purpose of producing male calves to be raised as bullocks, the production of milk being considered a by- product. However, with the decline in the requirement of draught power in agriculture and the growth in the demand for milk, the stock of cows as milch animals has been increasing over time. Also, she-buffaloes, which are rated superior to cows for milk production, have gained more importance over time. There exist a large number of studies that attempted to examine the changing role of milch animals across regions and size of landholdings in the country. These studies have highlighted two important aspects of the bovine stock: (a) the size of the cow population in the economy is largely a function of the bullock population required; and (b) reduction of the required bullock population is difficult without significant changes in the techno-economic and institutional set up in agriculture. Such studies highlight a growing trend in milch animal population and a shift in the bovine sex ratio in favour of milch animals.

Sharma *et al.* (1987) estimated that the annual growth rates of breedable cattle and buffalo population in India were 1.01 and 1.49 per cent respectively during 1945-1972. The growth rates in milch animal population were found to have been different across states. Birthal and Ravishankar (1999) observed a declining growth rate of milch stock in Karnataka since 1976. (also see Singh and Sharma 1979, Sharma et.al. 1987, Arya and Rawat 1989, Singh *et al.* 1990, Dhas 2001, Sharma,R.K 2001). Species composition and breed composition of milch animal stock have also been topics of research since the early 1960s. Significant variations in the relative importance of she-buffaloes and cows for milk production are observed across regions in the country. The relative importance of she-buffaloes tends to increase in regions in which demand for milk is high and the supply of feed abundant. The productivity of she-buffalo is higher than that of cow. (Telang and Chavan 1965, Ram and Singh 1974, Reddy *et al.* 1980, Raut and Amble 1969, Acharya *et al.* 1973; Srivastava and Singh 1975, Sardiwal and Kalla 1975, Sharma *et al.* 1975, Lavania *et al.*1975, Phukan and Gohain 1975, Pichholiya 1975, Sivakumar 1978 a, Patel *et al.* 1982, Tripathi *et al.* 1986, Ramesh Chand 1995 Shiyani 1996 and Saxena 2000).

Studies have shown that the cost of production of buffalo milk is lower than that of cow milk. (Reddy *et al.* 1980, Raut and Amble 1969, Acharya *et al.* 1973, Srivastava and Singh 1975, Gangwar and Bhatia 1980, Acharya and Pawar 1980, Kalyankar 1980, Sharma and Singh 1994c Saxena 2000 and Pandey *et al.* 2002). The lactation period of she-buffalo is longer too than that of cows (Telang and Chavan 1965, and GOI 1984). An important advantage of she-buffalo over cow is the efficiency of buffaloes to convert feed into milk with higher fat content. The estimated fat content of buffalo milk is about 7.5 per cent and that of cow milk is roughly about 3.7 per cent (Aggarwala and Sharma 1961, Vaidyanathan 1982, Singh and Rai 1998). She-buffaloes have certain disadvantages over she-cattle. Their maintenance cost is higher (Srivatsava and Singh 1975, Reddy *et al.* 1980, Chopra and Katyal 1980, Tripathi *et al.* 1986, Singh and Gangwar 1989, Pandey *et al.* 2002), the inter-calving period is longer (Srivatsava and Singh 1975, Acharya and Pawar 1980), and, they are more costly and more expensive and only better-off farmers can afford to have them (Srivastava and Singh 1975, Reddy et.al.1980, Gangwar and Bhatia 1980 and Chopra and Katyal 1980). Since she-buffalo is a more profitable milch animal than she-cattle, with the growth in demand for milk and the increased commercialization of milk production, the species composition of milch animal holdings has been shifting in favour of the former. (Ram and Singh 1974, Ranganath 1977, Singh and Sharma 1979, Vaidyanathan 1982, Dhas 1986, Arya and Rawat, 1989, Singh and Gangwar 1989, Singh, *et al.* 1990, Ramesh Chand, 1995, Pandey 1995, Birthal and Ravishankar 1999, Singh and Rai 1998 Saxena 2000 and Sharma R.K, 2001). Vaidyanathan (1989) argued that the practice of substitution of buffaloes for cows is not universal and that it varies depending partly on the trends in feed supply and partly on ecology. It was also found that more buffaloes in-milk existed in the high rainfall areas.

The relative advantage of she-buffalo over she-cattle has been undergoing some changes due to the upgradation of cattle breeds through cross-breeding. Cross-breeding of cattle and upgrading of buffaloes are the main thrusts of the breeding technology used for increasing milk production in India. The underlying rationale for this strategy is the higher productivity and lower unit cost of milk production of crosbred animals (Acharya *et al.* 1973, Reddy and Mathur 1980, Yedev and Singh 1982, Ganpule and Desai 1983, Kalamani 1984, Patel *et al.* 1984, Pandey and Mishra 1985, Saxena 2000). Several scholars who have advocated a selective approach in this matter have called the claim of the superiority of crossbreds over the indigenous breeds of cattle into question. According to Surender Singh (1979), the increase in the number of cross-bred cows will result in increase in the severity of the shortage of feeds and fodder in India. Vaidyanathan (1989) argued that the diffusion of cross-bred cows is greater in areas where the bullock population has stabilised or is declining and where buffaloes do not have a clear advantage over cows in terms of milk-yields and feed productivity. He attributed the success of the cross-breeding programme in Kerala to the decline in bullock population and the dominant role of cows as the source of milk. In general, the studies on the breed composition of milch animals indicate that there has taken place a change in the composition in favour of cross-bred and upgraded milch animals, though their intensity varies across regions. Nair (1982) highlighted the steady increase in the cross-bred population in the 'seventies and the early 'eighties in Kerala. According to him, it is the sharp decline in the requirement of draught animals in agriculture and increase in the demand for milk that contributed to the rapid diffusion of cross-breeding in Kerala. Studies conducted in other regions of the country indicate that the requirement of draught animals in agriculture as an important factor contributing to the diffusion of cross breeding technology.

Studies on the distribution of milch animal population across size groups of landholding have provided certain interesting insights. Ram and Singh (1974) noted that the larger holdings had maintained larger number of milch animals and vice versa, but that the proportion of cows tended to increase with increase in the size of holding only upto a point. Beyond the 5-10 acres size group it was the proportion of buffaloes that increased with increase in the holding size. Sivakumar (1978a, 1978b) who examined the distribution of cows and buffaloes across big, medium, small and landless households in two villages of Tamil Nadu found a positive relation with size of landholding. According to Desai and Verma (1978) the pattern in certain parts of Gujarat was different; it was the beneficiary marginal farmers and agricultural labourers who possessed more milch animals than the non-beneficiary farmers. In Karnal, close correspondence was observed between the number of milch animals and the size of holding. Singh and Singh (1981) and, Birthal and Ravishankar (1999) reached similar findings from their study in Karnataka. The same researchers had found that the distribution of milch animals was less skewed than that of landholdings Several studies have found that only the relatively well-off sections of farmers maintain she-buffaloes, since buffaloes were costlier and their inter-calving period was longer than those of cows. (Singh 1975, Reddy *et al.* 1980, Chopra and Katyal 1980, Acharya and Pawar 1980). Evidence from Farm Management Studies and National Sample Surveys on Land holdings, have corroborated with this conclusion that the distribution of she-buffaloes was more skewed than that of cows. (Reddy *et al.* 1980, Gangwar and Bhatia 1980, Chopra and Katyal 1980, Srivastava and Singh 1975, and, Birthal and Ravishankar 1999).

A number of micro level studies conducted by individual researchers in different parts of the country have also provided data on the ownership of milch animals by households belonging to different landholding and social groups. Some of these studies have also looked into the specific role played by different poverty alleviation programmes in creating ownership of milch animals among poor households and the factors influencing the sustainability of this asset.

Prasad (1978) analysed the dairy scheme introduced in the tribal areas of Seethampeta and Salur blocks of Andhra Pradesh by the Girijan Development Agency. He observed that the animals distributed were of low quality and therefore their yield was lower than that had been estimated in the project. The tribals reported non-availability of concentrates in nearby local markets and lack of resources for purchasing them as reasons for poor feeding of concentrates to milch animals. The beneficiaries sold only 50 per cent of the milk production to the Dairy Development Corporation, the rest being sold in the local market for meeting daily expenses. Desai and Verma (1978) who carried out a study in Baroda and Padna taluks of

Gujarat found that beneficiary marginal farmers and agricultural labourers possessed more milch animals than non-beneficiaries, and that about one-fourth of the former groups had disposed of the milch animals for the purchase of which they had received loan assistance. Apte (1982) who evaluated the Integrated Dairy Development project at Warnanagar in Kolhapur District, Maharashtra state also found the same predicament for small farmers and agricultural labourers, due, reportedly, to the poor quality of milch animals. Also, since animals purchased under this scheme were from within the region itself the scheme did not add to its net cattle population. Nor was the scheme administrated in accordance with the stipulated guidelines. The National Bank for Agriculture and Rural Development (NABARD, 1987) evaluated the dairy development scheme in Quilon district of Kerala, implemented by the Kerala Co-operative Central Mortgage Bank. Financial assistance had been given to farmers for purchase of cross-bred cows and for construction of cattle sheds. Non-availability of green fodder in adequate quantity and the consequent heavy dependence on concentrate feeds raised costs of maintenance of the cows. Except for a few high-yielding animals, dairying became a losing proposition. This scheme also therefore failed to improve the economic conditions of the beneficiaries. Seabright (1989) examined the livestock investments made under IRDP in Tamil Nadu based on the evidence from two villages from Trichirapally district during 1985. He observed that the benefits to households, which invested in livestock through IRDP, were significantly lower than those to households, which purchased livestock on their own. Between a-third and more than half of IRDP beneficiaries had become in fact, worse off as a result of their availing of IRDP loans. It was also observed that the IRDP participants paid higher prices for their livestock and spent more on purchased feed and labour. Seabright (1991,1992) based on the same source of data, argued that investment in livestock under IRDP had been extremely unprofitable for many a participant household.

Singh and Das (1984) who evaluated the milch animal scheme of IRDP in Subarkantha district, Gujarat found that the average number of animals per household, the average milk production per animal per lactation, the average use of concentrate feed and veterinary medicine, the average quantities of milk sold and milk retained for consumption, the average price realised and the gross revenue from sale of milk, were all higher for the beneficiary households. The study highlighted the role played by the village milk producers' co-operative societies to realise such an impact from the scheme. Though the cost per litre of milk was higher for the beneficiaries than for the non-beneficiaries, a situation which they attribute to the better feeding of the animals by the beneficiaries, the cost difference was offset by the higher milk production per milch animal kept by the beneficiaries. The study also revealed that differences in natural and human resource endowments and basic infrastructural facilities across regions had a significant bearing on the performance of the programme.

Bowonder *et al.* (1987) attempted to examine the impact of the dairy development programme of the IRDP in three major States, viz. Karnataka, Andhra Pradesh and Maharashtra. The programme was found to have resulted in higher levels of income and consumption of milk and milk products as well as in higher food consumption among beneficiary households. It had resulted in higher milk yield, higher quantities of milk to be retained for own consumption and higher levels of income through sale of milk per household in all the four land-holding classes. The study also highlighted, however, the fodder shortage problem. Cattle distribution was not linked up with the fodder generation programme and the problem of fodder shortage was severe among landless labourers and marginal farmers in several dairy villages. Sharma and Singh (1994a) observed the existence of cross-bred cows and graded buffaloes, of higher number of dairy animals per household and higher milk production, and of higher consumption and marketed surplus in areas in which the cattle development projects were implemented, than in non-project areas.

In sum, the studies surveyed in this section indicate the influence of the draught power requirement in agriculture on the size of milch animal holdings, the superiority of she-buffaloes over she-cattle as milch animals, the influence of draught power in the diffusion of cross-breeding technology and the distributional bias of milch animals towards larger holdings. The review also reveals that the distribution of milch animals under anti-poverty programmes did not contribute to increase in the ownership of milch animals by poor households. We examine in the next section the trends and the determinants of milk production.

Milk Production and Consumption

Bhote and Jayaraman (1967) who studied the trends in milk production during 1951-61 based on data from Central Statistical Organisation for 18 states observed that milk production of both cow and buffalo had steadily increased. Singh and Sharma (1979) who analysed data published by F.A.O in its Production Year books, found that during 1965 to 1973 the milk production in India had increased at a much higher rate than in the world as a whole and that buffalo milk production had increased at a higher rate than cow milk production. Nair (1985) observed that the estimated milk production, which had been about 20 million tonnes during the 'sixties, had increased to 23 million tonnes by 1974 and further to 33 million tonnes by 1982. He also found that the proportion of buffalo milk to total milk production had been increasing; while the growth in milk production during the 'sixties was due mostly to increase in the population of milch animals, during the 'seventies, it was due largely to increase in the productivity of the stock. Increase in productivity was facilitated by the increase in the supply of feed made possible by the higher rates of agricultural growth from the mid-'sixties onwards. George (1985) attempted to decompose the aggregate state level milk production estimates into contributions by cows and buffaloes separately. His analysis of the sources of growth (George 1988) in milk production between 1961-72 and 1972-82 showed that growth in the production of cow milk was accomplished by improvements in breeding efficiency and average yield of animals in-milk, whereas the growth in buffalo milk production was due to a large extent, to increase in the milch animal population and only partly to improvements in breeding efficiency and productivity per milch animal. Based on official milk production figures, the growth pattern and compositional change in milk production between 1964 and 1983 were analysed by Singh, *et al.* (1986). They observed that she-buffaloes contributed a major share of milk production: that milk production was growing at a more rapid rate in the later decades, and that significant disparities existed in the production of milk across states.

The factors of growth of milk production varied from state to state. Mergos and Slade (1987), in their study with reference to Madhya Pradesh, observed that the increase in milk production was caused by improvements in yield without any substantial adoption of the cross-bred technology. The increase in yield was due to higher input use and greater technical efficiency. In Karnataka the growth was found to be due to changes in the composition of local and crossbred cows rather than yield developments (Alderman 1989). Birthal and Ravishankar (1999) observed that milk production in Karnataka more than doubled during a period of less than two decades from the mid-1970s and that the proportion of cow milk in total production remained unchanged at about 55 per cent; but the share of cross-bred cattle milk to the total cattle milk was increasing during the period. In Himachal Pradesh, the increase during 1951 to 1986 was accounted for more by increase in buffalo milk than by increase in cow milk (Sharma and Varsisht 1992). In Bihar, rapid increase was noted till the early years of the 1990s; since then the state has been experiencing relative stagnation.

The relationship between increase in feed availability and growth in milk production is best understood from a review of studies on feed availability and requirement as well as of response of milk yield to feed input. Estimates of feeds and fodder show that a wide gap existed between availability and requirement. The Nutrition sub-Committee of ICMR and ICAR (1964) estimated that the total supply of animal feeds was deficient by 30 per cent in respect of TDN and 70 per cent in respect of DCP. Based on the 1961 Livestock Census and crop-cutting experiments, Whyte and Mathur (1968) estimated a shortfall in the supply of green fodder, dry fodder and concentrates to the tune of 470.4 million tonnes, 727.9 million tonnes and 85.6 million tonnes respectively. Amble *et al.* (1965) estimated the deficiency of DCP at 30 per cent for animals in milk, 50 per cent for dry animals, 60 per cent for adult males and between 80 to 90 per cent for the young stock. The Committee on Livestock Feeds and Fodder estimated the quantity of straw and Kadbi estimated it in 1973 at 207 million tonnes (GOI 1974). According to the National Commission on Agriculture (1976), the total availability of green fodder, dry fodder and concentrates in India during 1976 was 219.55 million tonnes, 309.00 million tonnes and 11.50 million tonnes respectively. Studies carried out at the regional level also highlight the gap between the requirement and the availability of feed. Rajpurohit (1975) observed that during 1971-72, the availability-requirement ratios of both dry and green fodder in Karnataka were lower than one for all the districts. Nirman *et al.* (1982) estimated that the total production of dry fodder contributed by rice, wheat, jowar and bajra was 235 million tonnes in India for the year 1977-78; the production of fodder crops in Meerut and Karnal for the years 1972-73 to 1975-75, was estimated at about 1.8 million tonnes in Meerut and 2.1 million tonnes in Karnal (Prakash and Bokil 1983).

Some attempts have gone also into the relationship between feed input and milk yield. Mellor and Pontives (1964) in their study on demand for milk and concentrate feeds in India showed that as the input of concentrate feed per animal increased, its milk yield also showed an increasing trend thereby indicating the positive response of milk yield to feed input. Vaidyanathan (1989) analysed the trends in feed supply in terms of nutrients (viz., TDN and DCP,) for the Livestock Census Years 1951-1972, but he was not able to relate feed supply to productivity due to paucity of comparable data on milk yield. However, his analysis of cross-sectional data on feed input and milk yield of cows and she-buffaloes, (based on the data available from the IARS milk production surveys) indicated that as one moves from regions with low availability of feed per animal to regions with higher availability, the milk yield of animals also showed a rising trend. States with higher availability of feed per animal also seem to have had a larger proportion of animals in milk thereby indicating the positive effect of feed supply on the productivity of milch animals. It may be noted that the role of feed in milk production is very much determined by the relative price of feed and milk, the price of the latter being influenced by the level of its demand.

The demand for milk is expected to be influenced by size and composition of human population, per capita income, consumption pattern, price of milk, the relative prices of its close substitutes and the availability of supplies. The size of the population, which represents the size of the consumers' market in total, is expected to have a positive association with the demand for milk. The pattern and levels of milk consumption also vary across age, sex, religion, region and socio-economic and employment groups. When income increases, people consume more nutritious food (Gopalappa: 1996). The relationship between income and demand for milk is usually expressed through the concept of income elasticity of demand for milk. As it is easier to obtain more reliable data on expenditure than on income, expenditure elasticities are used as proxy for income elasticities. Several studies show that the value of the elasticity is greater than one and that its value is higher in rural areas than in urban areas. Using the data available from the Natioanl Sample Survey organisation, Bose 1960, Ganguly 1960, Roy and Laha 1960, Iyenger and Jain 1969, and Sinha and Giri 1989 estimated the expenditure and income elasticities of broad categories of food items, including milk and milk products. Jonas (1971) analysed the inter-temporal and inter-city variations in expenditure on milk and milk products and observed that the lowest level of expenditure elasticity was 1.08 and that the per capita expenditure on milk and milk products was the highest in Delhi. The National Council of Applied Economic Research (1972) observed that the expenditure on milk and milk products among middle class families was more sensitive to income changes as revealed by the high income elasticity coefficient.

Several other studies on expenditure elasticity of demand for milk and milk products conducted in different regions of India have shown significant variations among income and expenditure classes and locations (Singh 1981, Sharma and Ram 1991, Gandhi and Mani 1995, Birthal 1996, NCAER 1967, NCAER 1972, Patel *et al.* 1974, Kesavan 1982, Singh and Singh 1986, Parisot, 1990, Sardana *et al.* 1995). The sex-disparity in consumption of milk was studied by Jatrana and Sangwan (1996). They found higher levels of consumption among boys in all income groups than among girls. In general, children particularly below five years of age consumed more milk than others.

The per capita expenditure on milk and milk products was higher in farming, business and service categories than in the labouring groups. Various other state-level studies have also reinforced these general findings (Ram and Singh 1974, Prabhakaran and Sivaselvam 1986, Sharma and Kuber Ram 1991, Kumar *et al.* 1995, Singh *et al.* 1996 and, Keshari and Malik 1998). Longitudinal and cross section studies across regions and districts have also drawn similar conclusions (Jain and Kalla 1981, Jain and Patel 1987). Rural-urban differences in expenditure on milk and milk products were also observed to be high; in rural areas, the expenditure was in some cases almost double of that in urban areas (Lata and Ram 1986). Occupational status was found to be a major factor too.

The demand for milk is also influenced by the cost and availability of substitutes for milk. Raj (1969) identified edible oils and meat, fish and egg as close substitutes for milk fat and milk protein respectively. Vegetable oil is considered a close substitute for milk fat because it can be used for almost all the purposes for which butter is used. Meat, fish and egg are also considered close substitutes for milk protein (Vaidyanathan 1983 and Nair 1987). Using inter-state cross-section data for 1961-62, Nair and Vaidyanathan (1979) attempted to examine the extent to which these commodities are close substitutes for milk fat and milk protein. Their analysis did not conclusively show that these commodities are close substitutes for milk. Apart from the limitations of the data, Vaidyanathan (1982) underscored certain factors that limit the substitutability of these items for milk.

> "..........by estimating the separate relations for milk protein and milk fat, we are in effect ignoring the important fact that proteins and fat are joint products of milk and that their relative proportions in milk were highly variable across states. Moreover, the model ignores the effect of supply factors on consumption and relative prices, and views observed variations in intake wholly as adjustments of demand to given relative prices assumed, implicitly, to be governed by long-term supply conditions"(p. 110). Vegetarians do not consume meat, fish or eggs under any circumstances. It could also be that the substitution is limited to a certain part of the consumption, only milk fat taken in the form of ghee might be substituting for edible oil...." (Pp. 109 and 110).

The consumption of milk is also determined by its availability. During the past three decades the centre and the state governments have made large scale attempts to link the rural milkshed areas with the urban milk markets through investment in milk procurement, processing and marketing as part of their dairy development strategies. The efforts under the Operation Flood to expand co-operative dairying in the country have played a vital role in this process. There exists a vast literature that examines the impact of this intervention on the production and consumption of milk (see for instance, Research Team 1982, Singh and Katar 1984, Alderman 1987, Mascarenhas 1988, Doornbos and Nair 1990, Doornbos *et al.* 1990, Franco and Chand 1991, George 1985 and 1994). In general, these studies argue that (1) the commercialization of milk production through co-operatives has led to decline in milk consumption in rural areas; (2) since the price of milk in rural areas has gone up, milk consumption of rural producing households has declined, and (3) as the milk price has not increased in proportion to the prices of other commodities and feed inputs the price advantage has gone mainly to the urban population.

Conclusion

In the preceding sections, we have made an attempt to review the theoretical and empirical findings regarding the factors and the processes shaping bovine sex ratios in India. The principal insights emerging from this review are summarized as follows:

1. Apart from agro-climatic conditions, the density of work animals is determined by cropping pattern, size distribution of land holding and degree of technological change (agro-technology) in agriculture. The higher the density of work animals the higher will be the bovine sex ratio.
2. The bovine sex ratio would shift in favour of females with decline in the requirement of draught power in agriculture.
3. The shift in sex ratio in favour of females will be determined also by the demand for milk. The reduction in draught animal stock and the consequent release of feed thus raising the number of milch animals would result in shifts in size and composition of bovines in favour of females.
4. The species composition of milch animals is determined by the demand for milk and availability of feed supply. When demand for milk tends to increase and feed supply becomes larger, the species composition of milch animals would become weighted increasingly in favour of she-buffaloes because of their comparatives advantage over milch cows.
5. The diffusion and adoption of cross-breeding technology will be faster with reduction in draught power requirements in agriculture.
6. The number of milch animals per holding tends to increase with increase in the size of land holdings. This

relationship might not have undergone change due to the distribution of milch animals under various anti-poverty programmes.

7. The growth in milk production in recent years has been largely due to increase in the productivity of milch animals. The increase in the milk yield for reasons other than breed improvement appears to be due to increase in feed input per animal.
8. Milk has become an essential item of consumption and not at all a luxury as is reflected in the decline in expenditure elasticties. The level of milk consumption is determined, apart from income and other household characteristics, by cost and availability of substitutes for milk fat and milk protein.
9. The expansion of the commercialization of milk production appears to be resulting in increase in the disparity of milk consumption between rural and urban areas.

These propositions arising out of our survey of research will be explored in detail in the chapters that follow. As a prelude, we analyse in the ensuing chapter the inter-relationship between agricultural change and bovine holdings in Tamil Nadu for a major part of the 20th century.

3

BOVINES IN TAMIL NADU ECONOMY: A HISTORICAL PERSPECTIVE

Introduction

Livestock have had a significant place of importance in the rural economy of Tamil Nadu, right from ancient times. Cattle and other species of livestock remained an indispensable part of the society, particularly in the plains. "The early inhabitants of the plains were almost certainly immune to the Vedic interdictions against eating the cow. Certainly they regularly replenished their supplies by raiding one another's herds and pilfering other stock from the valleys; ...and the ritualised way to start a war between plain peoples was by seizure of the opponent's cattle" (Baker 1984, p. 35). The sport of *'jallikattu'* (bull-fight) is a reflection of the plain dwellers' involvement in a herding economy.

The farmer has been dependent for ages on cattle mainly for draught purposes. Bullock has remained practically the only source of power available to the cultivator; whether for ploughing, transportation or for the lifting of water for irrigation purposes. Cattle have also been essential for manuring the cultivated land, threshing operations and development of rural industries like oil pressing and sugarcane crushing. Though animals have been in use in all these operations, their utilization pattern has varied significantly across regions, with changes taking place over time. This pattern has begun to change in recent decades. The present chapter examines the role that bovines played in the Tamil Nadu economy during the first half of the twentieth century.

The discussion in this chapter is presented in the following order. First, the size and composition characteristics of bovines in the state are discussed. Thereafter the utilisation pattern of bovines and its changes during the period are presented.

Size and Composition of Bovines

According to the 1951 livestock census, Tamil Nadu had a total of 12.52 million bovine population, of which 82 per cent were cattle and the rest buffaloes. The very high proportion of cattle among the bovines was observed in each age group (Table 3.1). Though the number of adult male and adult female bovine stock are equally distributed, the species-wise analysis showed significant variation. Whereas in the case of cattle, adult males out-numbered adult females, for buffaloes, the reverse was the case, adult females out-numbering adult males. In terms of percentages, while 56 per cent of the total adult cattle were accounted for males among the cattle species, the corresponding proportion was only about 23 per cent in the case of buffalo, due presumably to the higher utility of the former as draught animals. Cows are maintained more for their male progeny than for milk. On the other hand, since buffaloes are considered better dairy animals, she-buffaloes are given more importance than he-buffaloes. The sex ratio was 1.19 in the case of cattle as against a mere 0.42 for buffaloes. Interestingly, in the case of cattle, sex ratios are found to increase with increase in age which in the case of buffaloes, declined with the rise in age, indicating that while the cattle stock grows in age, female stocks are progressively eliminated and the male stocks retained fully. On the other hand, in the case of buffaloes, males are eliminated and females retained with increase in age. Thus, it is the superiority of one species over the other in respect of draught power and milk production

Table 3.1
Distribution of Bovines by Species and Sex: Tamil Nadu, 1951

Group		*Cattle Number in '000*	%	*Buffalo Number in '000*	%	*Bovine Number in '000*	%
Adult Stock	Male	4370 (92.62)	42.73	348 (7.37)	15.19	4718 (100.00)	37.69
	Female	3504 (75.48)	34.26	1137 (24.52)	49.63	4641 (100.00)	37.07
Young Stock(1 to 3 years)	Male	765 (81.82)	7.48	170 (18.18)	7.42	935 (100.00)	7.47
	Female	753 (73.46)	7.36	272 (26.54)	11.87	1025 (100.00)	8.19
Young Stock(under 1 year)	Male	414 (72.38)	4.05	158 (27.62)	6.90	572 (100.00)	4.57
	Female	421 (67.15)	4.12	206 (32.85)	8.99	627 (100.00)	5.01
Total Stock		10227 (81.70)	100.00	2291 (18.30)	100.00	12518 (100.00)	100.00
Sex Ratios		*Cattle*		*Buffalo*		*Bovine*	
(a) Adult Stock		1.25		0.31		1.02	
(b) Young Stock (1 - 3 years)		1.02		0.63		0.91	
(c) Young Stock (< 1 year)		0.98		0.77		0.91	
(d) Total Stock		1.19		0.42		0.99	

Source: Livestock Census, Tamil Nadu, 1951.
Note: Figures in brackets indicate the percentages to total.

capacity that significantly influences bovine composition. Moreover, the higher proportion of cattle in total bovine population (in each sex and age group) indicates that farmers are concerned more about draught requirements for agricultural operations than about milk supply.

Changes in Size and Composition of Bovine Population

The bovine population in the state showed an increasing trend during the period between 1920 and 1951. In 1920, the total number of bovines in the state was 9.7 million. The number increased, albeit slowly, to 10.8 million in 1935. By 1951, the total bovine population had risen to 12.5 million (Table 3.2).

Table 3.2
Trends in Size and Composition of Bovine Population in Tamil Nadu (1920-1951)

Year	*Population in '000*			*Density*					
				Per 100 acres of Net Sown Area			*Per 100 Human Population*		
	Cattle	*Buffalo*	*Total Bovine*	*Cattle*	*Buffalo*	*Total Bovine*	*Cattle*	*Buffalo*	*Total Bovine*
1920	8101 (83.77)	1570 (16.23)	9671 (100)	60	12	72	32	7	45
1925	8018 (82.72)	1675 (17.28)	9693 (100)	61	13	74			
1930	7801 (78.87)	1590 (21.13)	9391 (100)	58	12	70	33	7	40
1935	8889 (82.22)	1930 (17.84)	10819 (100)	69	15	84			
1940	8632 (83.21)	1742 (16.79)	10374 (100)	66	13	79	33	7	40
1945	8892 (83.65)	1738 (16.35)	10630 (100)	68	13	81			
1951	10227 (81.70)	2291 (18.30)	12518 (100)	69	13	97	34	8	42

Source: Indian Agricultural Statistics, various years, and Indian Livestock Census, various years.

Though a general long-term increase is observed in the bovine population, population of the cattle and buffalo population registered a decline during the period 1935 and

1940. The trend in the density of bovines with respect to net sown area remained constant up to 1930 at around 70 animals, increased to 84 by 1935, declined to around 80 by 1940 and remained unchanged till 1945; but it rose to 97 in 1951. Such an increase in the density from the mid-thirties was partially due to the decline in cultivated area.

Interestingly, more than four-fifths of the bovines were cattle and the rest buffalo, a proportion, which remained almost unchanged in all the census years from 1920 to 1951.

The sex ratio of adult cattle remained at more than unity in all these census years; in the case of buffaloes the corresponding figures were less than unity (Table 3.3). There were however some changes taking place in the sex composition within each species. It appears that in Tamil Nadu, there happened a tilt towards production of milk from the mid-thirties onwards, as evidenced by the decline in the sex ratio of cattle during 1935 to 1945.

Table 3.3
Trends in Sex Ratio of Adult Stock by Species: Tamil Nadu, 1920-1951

Species	*Number of adult males per adult females*						
	1920	*1925*	*1930*	*1935*	*1940*	*1945*	*1951*
Cattle	1.24	1.29	1.30	1.14	1.14	1.17	1.25
Buffalo	0.42	0.38	0.31	0.34	0.25	0.24	0.31

Source: The same as for Table 3.2.

The growth pattern and the changes in the sex ratio of bovine stock shows that (i) there was an overall growth in both males and females during the period under reference, (ii) up to 1930, the adult male stock increased at a higher rate than female stock, (iii) in 1935, the growth rate of female stock increased and thereafter it remained comparable to that of the male stock, and (iv) the species-wise growth rates remained unchanged except for a decline in the adult male buffalo stock from the 'thirties onwards.

From 1935 onwards, the density of bovines increased, the sex ratios were reversed, the growth rate of adult females increased more rapidly and both male and female stock increased. Interestingly, the increase of both the female and the male stock indicates that the dairy sector as a whole was gaining in importance. For all these reasons, the period, 1935 to 1951 may be termed as the "transition period" in the bovine economy of Tamil Nadu.

In the ensuing section, we discuss briefly, the bovine use pattern and its changes in Tamil Nadu during the period.

Bovine Utilisation Pattern

Bovines render various services like draught power, milk, meat and manure. They are also essential for the development of traditional rural industries like oil-pressing and sugarcane-crushing. Historically, cattle were considered 'beast for work' and buffaloes 'beast for milk' (Oliver 1943). Bullocks were used for various agricultural operations like tilling, lifting water for crops, separating grain from straw and transporting produce to the market. Cows were valued for their male progeny that supply animal power for agriculture. While certain breeds of cows were known for their efficiency in producing high-class bullocks, there existed certain exotic and cross breeds too which were kept for milk production and for producing efficient milch cows. In fact, there was a third category, which were dual-purpose animals-both good for producing work animals and for milk production. She-buffaloes were commercial dairy animals, known for the high fat content of their milk and their high yield potential. Male buffaloes were used for work in agriculture in certain areas, but to a small extent (TIVJ 1938).

A detailed discussion of the utilisation pattern of bovines in Tamil Nadu during the first half of the twentieth century is made in the following sections.

Bovines for Work

Bovines for Cultivation Purposes

Draught animals are used in the state to carry on a variety of cultivation activities. Given the magnitude of rainfall and its seasonality, it was necessary for farmers to own work animals to carry on their cultivation operations in time. But, there are no reliable data on the total number of animals used, by agricultural activity. Changes in the requirement of work animals must have played an important role in shaping the size and composition of bovines.

A useful way of looking at changes in the availability of draught animal power in agriculture is in terms of their numbers per unit of net sown area (NSA). Estimates of the density of work animals per 100 hectares of NSA varied between 28 and 31 during the period 1920 to 1945, but sharply increased thereafter[1]. In 1951, the density of work animals per unit NSA was 37.

Though the work animal stock increased, the cultivators found the stock inadequate for agricultural operations. The eighth round of the National Sample Survey conducted for the year 1953-54 provided details about the farming conditions and practices in rural areas (Table 3.4). Nearly five to six per cent of the agricultural households reported inadequacy of local animal labour for all the three major agricultural operations in the state, indicating thereby a year-round permanent, shortage.

Table 3.4
Percentage of Agricultural Households Engaged in Agricultural Operations in Rural Areas Reporting on Adequacy of Local Animal Labour by Operations: Tamil Nadu, 1953-54

Category	*Animal Labour*		
	Land Preparation	*Sowing*	*Harvesting*
Adequate	92	89	88
Not adequate	6	5	5
Not recorded	2	6	7
Total	100	100	100

Source: GOI: (1962).

It has been estimated that the shortage of work animals came to about 5.2 lakh in 1920 (about 12 per cent), 6.2 lakh (13.3 per cent) in 1945 and 11.4 lakh (19.1 per cent) in 1951 (Table 3.5).

Table 3.5
Trends in the Work Animal Stock Shortages for Cultivation: Tamil Nadu, 1920-1951

Years	*No. of working bovines '000*	*No. of ploughs '000*	*No. of animals required '000*	*Shortage of work animals '000*	*Percentage of shortage*
1920	3837	2180	4360	523	12.00
1925	3937	2120	4240	303	7.15
1930	3843	2117	4234	391	9.23
1935	3826	2201	4402	576	13.08
1940	3815	2281	4562	747	16.37
1945	4062	2342	4684	622	13.28
1951	4838	2991	5982	1144	19.13

Note: Number of animals required is estimated by multiplying the number of ploughs by two.

Source: The same as for Table 3.2.

The effect of shortages in draught animals supply was also getting reflected in their prices. From the early 'twenties, the prices of draught animals kept on increasing at a more rapid rate than grain prices (Table 3.6). In consequence, the capital cost of work animals was growing fast.

One of the major factors responsible for the shortage of work animals and their rising cost was the shortage of feeds and fodder[2]. The magnitude of the fodder problem in the Madras Presidency (including our study region) is evident from the following statement.

> "The scarcity and the deficit areas comprise more than half of the Province with half of the cattle population. The fodder is just sufficient for a satisfactory ration only in 30 per cent of the total area. Even here, the satisfactory balance may be upset by an adverse season. The regions of surplus and abundance constitute only a fraction of the total area of the Province and the cattle population in them is less than one-sixth of the total cattle population of the Province. Neither are these surplus and abundant areas useful to meet the requirements of the scarce or deficit areas, as it is impossible to transport bulky fodder over long distances. Therefore between these three categories which represent 80 per cent of the Presidency area, the fodder supply position cannot be viewed with equanimity" (Krishnaswami 1947, p. 194).

Table 3.6
Index of Prices for Certain Grains and Plough Animals: Tamil Nadu

(Base: 1913-14 = 100)

Year	*Rice*	*Cholam*	*Cumbu*	*Ragi*	*Plough Animals*
1913-14	100	100	100	100	100
1914-15	94	93	93	95	100
1915-16	93	89	89	91	100
1916-17	96	98	96	96	100
1917-18	101	112	103	101	100
1918-19	136	171	150	161	100
1919-20	167	215	207	211	286
1920-21	145	174	177	174	301
1936-37	71	81	83	81	417
1937-38	73	82	81	77	333
1938-39	74	82	83	80	333
1939-40	80	89	91	93	333
1940-41	91	90	92	93	333
1941-42	85	102	101	101	283
1942-43	154	179	183	181	366
1943-44	184	247	259	268	433

Source: GOI: (1938 and 1956).

Owing to increasing population pressure, the average size of holding per household was steadily on the decrease; in consequence, the competition for land for cultivation of foodgrains and fodder was also becoming increasingly intense. Though reliable data on size of land holdings for the study period are not available, the *patta* data with all their limitations did show a sharp decline in the average size of holdings in all the districts, from 4.16 acres to 3.08 acres between 1920-21 and 1950-51. The observed decline in the average size of land holding[3] would have undoubtedly acted as a barrier to the growth of the bovine population.

In a survey conducted by H.C. Sampson, it was remarked that in certain districts, the supply of cattle hardly meets the demand and pointed out the rise in the price of cattle (Low 1912, The Agriculturists 1914a).

In the districts of Coimbatore and Salem, the ryots reared young male cattle up to 2 or 3 years of age and disposed them of in the cattle markets, from where they were brought to

Trichy, Madurai, Ramnad and other southern districts. The additional requirement of work animals in the southern districts was thus met from supply of animals originating from Salem, North Arcot, Coimbatore and Mysore through cattle markets and movement of cattle from one region to another.

Cattle were sold at various sites - farms, open fields, road-sides, private premises, village commons, fair grounds and weekly markets. There were four types of cattle sale centres[4], fairs, hatts, weekly markets and daily markets. Cattle fairs were held annually, half-yearly, and, in a few cases, quarterly and monthly. They were held in general, in conjunction with religious festivals and during post-harvest seasons when cultivators are free from work. The duration of a fair varied from a day to three months, but usually lasted for about a week. Cattle *hatts, shandis or bazaars* were weekly or bi-weekly markets held generally for a day. Daily markets were found in towns and cities, where milch and draught cattle were sold in stockyards. The demand for cattle (work animals) in rural areas was met mostly from neighbouring fairs and *hatts*; while the requirements of milch, cart and slaughter cattle for urban centres were met through daily markets.

The prevalence of cattle trade and the movement of cattle[5] from one place to other were discussed by Randhawa (1958) and others.

> The average farmer usually brings up the nondescript male offspring of his cows for ploughing or for draught. Some go in for animals from outside from time to time and the supply is made by professional drovers who buy them in their native tract and drive them round to the various cattle fairs in different districts. There are well-known routes along which the drovers travel; those from the Kangayam area drive their cattle to the big cattle fair at Uppidamangalam and from there to Manapparai and then proceed to Pudukottai-all in Tiruchirapalli district. Other dealers proceed along the north bank of the Caveri beginning with the cattle fair at Shevapet in Salem; they attend the big fairs at Nainamalai, Turaiyur and Ariyalur. There are many other big cattle fairs in places like Perundurai, Samayapuram, Tiruvannamalai where

> animals from different places are brought by the professional cattle dealers. (Randhawa 1958, pp. 116-117).

> "A farmer would buy them (cattle) just before the cultivation season began and resell them immediately his work was over at a low price. The buyer in turn employed them for his cultivation and then sold them at a still lower value and so on." (Raju 1941, p. 109)

The practice of buying animals for the purposes of ploughing and other cultivation operations was narrated in the village resurveys conducted in various parts of Tamil Nadu (see Thomas and Ramakrishnan 1940, pp. 17, 165 and 194).

Thus, these resurveys indicated the practice of trade of animals, movement of animals from one place to another, the practice of buying animals for specific operations and selling them once the use were over. Moreover, they also highlighted the development of cattle trade and farmers' growing dependence on cattle markets for purchase and sale of animals.

The practice of farmers of meeting their draught requirements by using female cattle (cows) also played a positive role. Sampson observed this practice during his investigation conducted during the beginning of the twentieth century itself. He indicated that while there existed shortages of work animals in certain districts the supply of animals required for draught and agricultural purposes was augmented by supplementing the use of cows. He also stated that the use of cows for ploughing was in practice in the Salem district extensively (Indian Agriculturist: 1914b).

Krishnaswami also indicated in 1947 the practice of using cows for work to meet the shortage of work animals in some parts of the Madras Province

> "The number of cattle maintained per 100 acres of net sown area in Madras is 69..... In Madras for the total cropped area of 37 million acres 3.7 million pairs of cattle are required for cultivation at one pair for every 10 acres, whereas, according to census figures there are only 3 1/4 million pairs of cattle. The deficit is made up by working cows and buffaloes in their dry period." (Krishnaswami: 1947 pp.195).

The survey conducted during the mid-thirties in the Ongole tracts of the Madras Province by the Imperial Council of Agricultural Research (GOI 1939) observed not only the fact that females (both cattle and buffaloes) were used for work, but also quantified the magnitude of the use of female stock ; see Table 3.7.

Table 3.7
Estimated Number of Working Animals: Madras Province, 1936-37

Cattle		*Buffaloes*		
Working Bullocks	*Cows used for work*	*Working Males*	*Females used for work*	*Total*
61,76,509	11,29,305	11,16,701	2,71,235	86,97,750

Source: GoI: (1939).

The practice of using female cattle for work[6] was reported also in the Livestock Censuses. According to the Livestock Census 1951, the total number of female bovines used for work was about 7.23 lakh. Of the total female animals used for work, cattle alone accounted for about 90 per cent and buffaloes, the rest 10 per cent.

The practice of hiring in and out of animals during times of need would also have enabled the cultivators to meet their work animal requirements for completing the various cultivation operations. The available data obtained from the eighth round of the National Sample Survey (NSS) provided information about the percentage distribution of agricultural households by the main sources and patterns of utilisation of animal labour and implements for different agricultural operations in the state (Table 3.8).

A larger proportion (53 to 57 per cent) of the cultivator households depended exclusively on own animals; about 12 to 14 per cent of the households on hired animals alone; and, 24 to 27 per cent of households on both owned and hired animals. This implied that (a) not every cultivator possessed work animals to meet his cultivation operations; (b) animal-owning households too hire-in animals to meet their requirements; and (c) the practice of hiring-in of animal labour was observed for all the agricultural operations and particularly so, for land preparation and harvesting activities.

Table 3.8
Percentage of Agricultural Households Engaged in Agricultural Operations in Rural Areas by Sources and Uses of Animal Labour and Implements for Different Operations: Tamil Nadu, 1953-54

	Animal Labour Operations			*Household Implements Operations*		
	Preparation of land	*Sowing*	*Harves-ting*	*Preparation of land*	*Sowing*	*Harves-ting*
A. Source						
Owned	57	56	53	61	61	56
Hired in	14	12	12	11	10	11
Owned and hired in	27	24	26	27	25	30
Not recorded	2	8	9	1	4	3
Total	100	100	100	100	100	100
B. Utilisation Pattern						
Own cultivation	78	75	75	87	84	87
Hired out	0	0	0	0	0	0
Own cultivation & hired out	9	8	9	6	6	6
Not recorded	13	17	16	7	10	7
Total	100	100	100	100	100	100

Source: GOI: (1962).

The data on the use pattern of animal labour and implements by households have also provided further insights into the hiring practices of animals for work. It was estimated that only about 75 per cent of the households used animal labour exclusively for own cultivation. About 9 per cent of the households used the animals for own cultivation and hiring out for others. Interestingly, no household was found practising hiring-out of animals (exclusively) as a commercial activity. The extent of hiring out along with own household use of animal labour was estimated to be higher than that of household implements. This indicated that maintenance of animals had become costlier than of implements on the one hand and that the shortage of animals and the consequent demand for work animals for short intervals to undertake specific operations on hire on the other, led to the emergence of hiring out practices of household animal labour, on the other.

The existence of the practice of hiring in animals for work had been highlighted in an early study conducted during the mid-thirties in the sugarcane and cotton tracts of Tamil Nadu. In this study, the number of hired bullocks employed in six villages of Coimbatore district during the years 1934-35 to 1935-36, was estimated (see Table 3.9). The estimates of bullock days employed revealed that the hiring-in of animals had been in practice even prior to the 'thirties and that the extent of hired animals under use varied significantly across regions. There were villages in which hired animals were employed more than own animals, while in some other villages no hired animals were used at all. The extent to which farmers depended on hired animals was influenced very much by the availability of own stock, animal power requirement and the socio-economic background of the farmers. Possession of working animals was basically determined by possession of land (GOI 1938, p. 12).

Table 3.9
Extent of Hired Bullocks
Employed in Coimbatore Districts: 1933-34 to 1935-36

Village	*Number of bullock days*					
	1933-34		*1934-35*		*1935-36*	
	Owned	*Hired*	*Owned*	*Hired*	*Owned*	*Hired*
Annur	3251	7	3885	235	3363	-
	(99.79)	(0.21)	(94.30)	(5.70)	(100)	
Budinatham	2487	213	4616	463	2363	175
	(92.11)	(7.89)	(90.88)	(9.12)	(83.26)	(16.74)
Athipalayam	227	150	111	201	204	270
	(60.21)	(39.79)	(35.58)	(64.42)	(43.04)	(56.96)
Anthiyur	136	227	20	125	48	175
	(37.47)	(62.53)	(13.79)	(86.21)	(21.52)	(78.48)
Perumanallur	1712	-	3381*	-	2338	-
	(100)		(100)		(100)	
Vellakinar	1120	834	2635	32	2078	44
	(57.32)	(42.68)	(93.80)	(1.10)	(97.93)	(2.07)

*The high figures in 1934-35 are due to the bullocks having to lift more water from wells to irrigate the crops owing to defective rainfall.

Source: Government of India: (1938).

The density of work animals as a whole had shown an increasing trend in all the districts from 1940 onwards, though there were wide variations in the trend across districts. There were shortages in the work animal stock, but they were met by movement of animals through the cattle markets, by supplementing male stock with female stock for work and by hiring-in work animals.

Bovines for Non-Agricultural Purposes

The work animals were also used as a source of motive power in various non-agricultural activities such as rural industries (sugarcane-crushing and oil-extraction) and rural transport services (cart).

The rural industries, both sugarcane-crushers and oil *ghanis,* depended to a great extent on animal energy right from the time these industries began. They emerged initially as cottage industries operating on a very small scale.

As far as the sugarcane-crushing units were concerned, the motive power for their operation was derived either from animals or from electricity. While the major sugarcane industries (which were small in numbers but the scale of operation of which was large) were purely run by electrical power, the medium and small-scale industries basically depended on animal power. The small scale crushing units functioned only seasonally and the level of their capacity utilisation was influenced by crop and season. Since these units did not work throughout the year, the demand for animals in these industries was also seasonal; therefore, work animals were hardly maintained exclusively for service in crushing units. The requirements were met either by animals purchased from the market at times or using animals mainly kept for agricultural operations. It could be argued that the increase in the demand for work animals did not arise exclusively or mainly from these industries.

Table 3.10 provides the trends in the number of sugarcane crushers and their break-up by source of power during 1920-1951. In 1935, the total number of crushers using bullock power in the state was 7,294; it increased to 17,144 by 1951 an increase of 135 per cent within 15 years! During this period, the number of crushers operated by power increased from 230 to 1,644 an increase of more than 6 times. The share of units operated by bullocks declined from 97 per cent in 1935 to 91 per cent by 1951. Though crushing units operated by bullock continued to occupy the dominant share, their importance was slowly on the wane.

Oil extraction, one of the traditional rural small-scale industries, was carried out as a cottage industry using either animal or electricity as energy input. The units operated by animal power were known as 'oil *ghanis*' and those by electric motor as 'oil mills'. Though the production of the basic inputs (oil seeds) was seasonal in nature, the *ghanis* functioned all the year round. Moreover, the *ghanis* were of different sizes, conditioned by factors like climatic conditions, size of draught animals and seed quality and variety. In areas in which rains were plentiful, *ghanis* had to be run indoors. Therefore, they were necessarily small sized, single bullock *ghanis*. In areas where rain was scanty, bigger *ghanis* installed in open yards, and drawn by a pair of bullocks were in use. Similarly, where strong and sturdy bullocks were available, big *ghanis* were operated; but in areas where the animals were weak, only relatively small *ghanis* were run. (Patel 1958). According to the 1951 Livestock Census, the total number of oil *ghanis* in the state was 21,734 of which 70 per cent were of more than 5 seers capacity and the remaining 30 per cent of less than 5 seers capacity. Krishnaswami had pointed out in 1947 that oil-pressing was an important industry which served a large section of the population (Krishnaswami 1947, p. 297).

The declining phase of the oil pressing units was observed in Gangaikondan village of Tirunelveli district by Natarajan (1940). According to him:

> "The reason stated by the oil mongers for the decay of the industry is that it is not paying at present owing to the competition of oil crushed in mills in towns. They have to take to other professions, chiefly trade." (Natarajan 1940, p. 99).

Table 3.10
Trends in Sugarcane Crushers and Oil *Ghanis*:Tamil Nadu, 1935–1951

Sugarcane Crushers								*Oil Ghanis*	
1935		*1940*		*1945*		*1951*		*1951*	
Power	*Bullock*	*Power*	*Bullock*	*Power*	*Bullock*	*Power*	*Bullock*	*>5 seers*	*<5 seers*
230 (3.06)	7294 (96.94)	371 (4.76)	7419 (95.24)	769 (6.55)	10975 (93.45)	1644 (8.75)	17144 (91.25)	15166 (69.79)	6568 (30.31)

Note: 1. Figures in brackets are percentages.
2. The figures are exclusive of Madras and Nilgris data.

Source: Livestock Census (various issues)

Thus, we find that the role of the oil *ghanis* was on the decline and that competition between oil mills and oil *ghanis* was driving the *ghanis* out. As the oil crushing units operated by animals entered a declining phase, the demand for animals for this purpose also started declining.

The other major area of non-agricultural activity in which work animals were extensively in use was transport. Animals were used to draw carts (called bullock carts) of two types: single-animal driven and double-animals driven. The small and marginal farmers kept the carts driven by single bullock. Since the load drawn by the single bullock carts was relatively small, the animals used on these carts were also generally poor in quality and strength. The double-animals driven carts were relatively sturdy and strong they being used to transport heavy loads over long distances. They were used for both own and hired purposes. The carts that were used exclusively for the villagers' own and hired travel purposes were well maintained with extra fittings and gadgetry on the cart. For hiring, charges were made based on the distance of travel, nature of the path to be travelled and the nature and quantity of the items carried. The role of bovines in providing transportation support, the importance given to bullock carts in transportation in the rural areas and the quality of animals used for carting were revealed in several studies of the 1940s.

The total number of carts in use in the state was about 4.8 lakh in 1920; the corresponding figure for 1930, 1940 and 1951 were 5.3 lakh, 5.7 lakh and 6.8 lakh respectively (Table 3.11). The trend was positive, but the rate of increase was low.

Table 3.11
Trends in Bullock Carts: Tamil Nadu, 1920-1951

Years						
1920	*1925*	*1930*	*1935*	*1940*	*1945*	*1951*
4,79,131	4,90,169	5,28,451	5,23,538	5,72,594	5,84,444	6,80,054

Note: The state figure excludes the Madras and Nilgris data.
Source: Livestock Census (various years).

The Directorate of Marketing and Inspection, Government of India, pointed out in 1956 that oil-crushing had been gaining momentum as an economic activity during the 1940s, that *ghanis* were being progressively replaced by mills and that public carriers were slowly driving bullock carts to the background (GOI 1956).

Bovines for Milk

It was stated earlier on that female cattle were maintained primarily for their male progeny and female buffaloes for the production of milk. However, milk obtained from cows was also an important contribution to household consumption.

In a traditional system of dairying, milk was considered primarily to be an item of home consumption, seldom a commodity for exchange. Dairy animals, particularly cows, were low milk producers. Since the yields of the milch animals were very low, calves were usually allowed to drink the entire quantity of milk. Farmers, who required milk for home consumption, maintained cows, which could yield higher quantities of milk. The farmers who produced milk for commercial purposes, maintained buffaloes being better yielders of milk with higher S.N.F and Fat contents than cow milk. If the milk produced was in excess of the household requirement, the excess were converted into milk products (Krishnaswami 1947, Naidu 1948).

Several studies have explained the logic underlying the practice of rearing cows as a breeding stock and of maintaining she-buffaloes for milk supply (Rao 1919, TIVJ 1938 and Krishnaswami 1947) and the growing importance of dairy animals (Rao 1919, Smith 1919, Iyer 1919, Matson 1922, Jamaluddin 1924, Ramakrishnan 1930, 1939, Fernandez 1939 and Krishnaswami 1947).

The survey conducted during 1936-37 to assess the actual position of cattle holdings, milk production and consumption of milk, by the Imperial Council of Agricultural Research, had provided information on the comparative performance o cows and buffaloes in milk production (Table 3.12). This survey suggested that in all the selected indicators, she-buffaloes were better as dairy animals than cows. While a major share of buffaloes (57 per cent) yielded 4-8 lbs of milk, the corresponding figures for a major share of cows (52 per cent) was only less than 4 lbs.

Table 3.12
Comparative Performance of Cows and She-Buffaloes: Madras Province, 1937-38

Particulars	*Cows*	*Buffaloes*
Average milk yield per day in lbs.	4.64	6.53
Average lactation length in months	9.54	11.3
Average dry period in months	9.47	6.99
Average calving interval in months	19.03	18.11
Average daily milk yield at peak of lactation in lbs.	6.7	8.3
Rate of decline in milk yield per month per 100 lbs	9.52	7.18
Ratio of any month's yield to that of preceding months	0.9048	0.9282
Estimated average lactation yield (for periods shown in 2 above) in lbs	1236.4	1903.4
Average daily milk yield between calvings in lbs. To	2.17	3.5
Percentage distribution of animals by milk yield per day: 0 – 4 lbs.	52.7	18.5
4 - 8 lbs.	37.4	57.3
8 - 12 lbs.	7.4	19.8
12 - 16 lbs.	2.2	3.9
16 - 20 lbs.	0.2	0.5

Source: GOI (1939):

Since she-buffaloes had been considered for long animals for milk due to their comparative advantages, since the time dairying gained importance as an economic proposition in the rural economy, they became the preferred animals to be maintained by milk producers. Such a species-specific preference began to get reflected in the price movements of dairy cows and buffaloes. It is observed that up to the early 'forties, the prices of both cow and she-buffaloes were almost equal; the price of cows increasing more rapidly than that of she-buffalo till the mid-forties; thereafter, the price of the she-buffalo began increasing at a much higher rate than that of the cow (Table 3.13).

Table 3.13
Price (Rs.0.00) of Milch Animals: Tamil Nadu, 1936-1950

Year	*Cow*	*Shebuffaloe*
1936	100	100
1937	100	100
1938	100	100
1939	100	105
1940	100	105
1941	110	110
1942	101	125
1943	159	200
1944	267	210
1945	350	250
1946	357	300
1947	392	350
1948	395	400
1949	395	500
1950	394	600

Note: Price of cow relates to Ongole breed animals in 2nd lactation yielding 4-6 seers of milk per day at Tiruvottiyur market. Price of she-buffaloe relates to country breed animals in 3rd lactation yielding 10 seers and above per day at Tiruvottiyur market.

Source: GOI: (1956).

Though cultivators carried dairying as a subsidiary source of income, the number of milch animals maintained by a household basically depended upon the size of their land holdings and economic status. This argument had been made even in studies conducted in the early decades of the century.

> "They (well-to-do cultivators) include in their herd a few milch buffalos which supply milk, curds, and ghee (clarified butter). The ryot does not keep more buffalos than he can find a use for, but a landlord owning 10 acres would probably have two or three buffaloes in milk, and the surplus milk generally goes to meet the needs of the town. The peasant proprietor, however, contents himself with only one, rarely two. The usual custom is to have two animals, one of which is always in milk"(Rao 1919, pp. 267).

It was referred in the earlier studies that the dairy industry directly benefited women who were involved in both production and marketing activities of milk and milk products. Marketing of milk products used to be carried out by several groups of Tamils (Goundans, Vellalas and Konaris) and Telugus (Gollas and Kammas). Ananda Rao had narrated their status and their involvement in the following words:

> "Konaris are professional traders in curds and ghee... The trade is entirely in the hands of the womenfolk. It keeps woman fairly independent of her husband for her daily necessaries, besides saving her from earning her livelihood as a day labourer". (Rao: 1919, pp. 267-8).

The benefits of dairying to women were narrated also by Krishnaswami.

> "The maintenance of milch animals for selling milk and other dairy products like ghee is an important rural industry, as it provides occupation to a large number of people, especially womenfolk, in rural areas..... The sale proceeds are generally the assets of the women folk and the savings are utilised for buying cattle food or replacing animals or in jewellery and cloths. In many cases this income makes the women folk independent in respect of running the household. Sufficient pocket money is always available to them to meet all odd and sundry expenses." (Krishnaswami: pp. 220-221; 1947).

During the 'thirties, a 'milk marketing survey' was conducted in the Madras Province. This survey covered various aspects of the milk economy which includeed, demand for milk in urban areas, rural-urban differences and regional variations in the levels of milk consumption, demand pattern of milk, price situation of milk and seasonal and regional price variations in the State. The survey revealed that about one half the output of milk of the province (Madras) was retained by the producers for conversion into milk products and the other half was sold as fluid milk[7]. Buffalo milk was in great demand for conversion into milk products and preference was always for cow's milk for fluid milk consumption. The survey also revealed that the price of milk in the same year did not fluctuate so often as was the case with the prices of other commodities[8]. At the same time, the price of milk varied across regions. In urban areas where the trade was better-organised, milk fetched higher prices. Moreover, the price of milk also varied according to the degree of its adulteration (TIVJ 1938).

Adulteration and poor quality of milk was a problem associated with milk marketing. Veeraraghavan, in his village resurveys reported "Milk and milk products are generally adulterated" in Eruvellipet, South Arcot District and "Ghee, oil and milk are generally adulterated" at Dusi, North Arcot district (Veeraraghaven 1940, pp. 172 & 200). Producers did not strain the milk, nor did they observe hygienic principles in the production and handling of milk. Adulteration of milk was a general practice followed throughout the Presidency. Therefore, a common practice in most towns was to have the cows taken from door to door for the purpose of milking; buffaloes were not, however readily amenable to this type of treatment. But, most of the milking was done in the open, exposed to the dirt and dust of streets (TIVJ 1938, Retnam 1943 and Natarajan 1950).

As the supply of milk was not growing in correspondence with the increase in demand for milk, several forms of malpractices[9] became common. The demand for milk in the state had been increasing due to improvements in the standard of living and changes in the consumption patterns. The consumption of tea and coffee with milk was rapidly growing in all the districts. Rural areas became drained of their milk to cater to urban requirements. Prices of milch cows were rising. The demand for milk for consumption remained small and stagnant in rural areas (Krishnaswami 1947, pp. 209-210, 217).

The increasing demand for milk, particularly in the urban areas led to developments in the organised marketing of milk and milk products (Ramakrishnan:1944 and Lucas: 1944). Soon cooperative supply societies and unions came to be established. As an effort towards organised milk marketing, a company on the joint stock principle had been formed during the beginning of the century. But the company failed as the method of its working was not business-like. Hence, cooperatives of producers began to be established from as early as in 1912.

But, the early attempts at cooperativisation also failed. In December 1927, the Madras cooperative Milk Supply Union began its operation with the main object of purchase and disposal of milk and milk products of its members, handled under sanitary conditions at reasonable rates to the residents of Madras. The union had at first 14 societies and 15 individuals as its members. By the end of the 'forties, the Union handled about 5000 measures of milk a day. However, this volume accounted for only 7 per cent of the total milk market in the city. A number of cooperative milk societies were established in subsequent years, but mostly in the 'forties. Though certain cooperative milk unions and societies had been successfully established and had performed progressively, they could replace only a negligible portion of the regular trade by petty dealers. The steady progress and performance of the Milk Supply societies and Unions in the Madras state during the 'forties is depicted in Table 3.14.

Thus we find that, though the cultivators of the state did not consider dairying a primary occupation, production of milk was gaining importance in the latter years of the first half of the twentieth century. In fact, dairying was constrained by various problems like low productivity, high cost of production, poor quality and lack of a marketing network. However, the demand for milk on the part of the non-milk producers, particularly of the urban residents, was increasing. Because of the excess demand for milk and the problems of distribution or marketing of milk, the milk suppliers and traders were able to carry out several malpractices like adulteration. Moreover, the development of the dairy industry particularly of the marketing of milk and milk products benefited rural women by providing them with both income and employment.

The increasing importance of dairying in the bovine economy of the State is clearly evident from the trends in the milch animal population (Table 3.15). The adult female stock had been increasing steadily in the State. In 1920, the total number of female bovines was 36.01 thousand; the number increased to 46.41 thousand by 1951. Among the female

Table 3.14
Progress of Milk Supply Societies and Unions: Madras State, 1941-42 to 1950-51

Year	*Milk Supply Societies*					*Milk Unions*			
	No. of Societies	*No. of Members*	*Paid up share capital (Rs)*	*Value of milk Sold (Rs)*	*Govt. loans issued (Rs)*	*No. of Unions*	*No. of Members*	*Value of milk purchased (Rs)*	*Value of milk sold (Rs)*
1941-42	59	3554	35698	536856	21766	12	2255	989995	1092625
1942-43	74	3105	40716	540034	21290	12	2352	1055232	1142711
1943-44	95	3690	82611	519085	62625	13	2482	1353713	1464504
1944-45	161	8731	102381	1217027	81906	14	2635	2771675	3285334
1945-46	197	16149	199006	2559735	178095	14	3067	4744715	5393535
1946-47	212	21140	268258	3820554	171585	14	3258	4608985	5094752
1947-48	234	19388	374808	3684083	343940	13	2585	4193755	4631921
1948-49	323	29167	474434	5609489	599262	17	2787	4546709	5712127
1949-50	351	37605	854542	8083862	552161	17	3139	5005048	6180199
1950-51	406	43781	894435	7390750	864859	19	4166	5330791	6561265

Note: The figures included that of S. Kanara and Malabar districts.
Source: GOI: (1950)

bovines, the share of female buffaloes had been increasing. Also, in both cows and buffaloes, the share of animals in milk had been increasing over time.

Table 3.15
Trends in Milch Animal Population: Tamil Nadu, 1920-1951

Species	*Population in thousand numbers*						
	1920	*1925*	*1930*	*1935*	*1940*	*1945*	*1951*
Cow	28.34	28.07	27.61	30.91	31.31	32.76	35.04
	(78.70)	(77.03)	(76.74)	(77.34)	(76.94)	(77.41)	(75.49)
Buffalo	7.67	8.37	8.37	9.06	9.38	9.56	11.37
	(21.30)	(22.97)	(23.26)	(22.66)	(23.06)	(22.59)	(24.51)
Total	36.01	36.44	35.98	39.97	40.69	42.37	46.41
	(100.00)	(100.00)	(100.00)	(100.00)	(100.00)	(100.00)	(100.00)

Source: The same as for Table 3.2.

Thus, the foregoing discussion indicated that the use of bovines for work and for milk purposes were species-specific and sex-based. The role of bovines as a supplier of draught power had been increasing. At the same time, the importance of bovines for milk production (dairying) had also been gaining significance towards the closing years of the first half of the twentieth century.

Conclusion

We have examined in this chapter the role of bovines in Tamil Nadu economy and its changes over time during the first half of the twentieth century. The conclusions drawn from the discussion are the following:

(a) Tamil Nadu was a cattle-dominated region. Farmers depended generally on cattle for draught purposes and on buffaloes for milk production. Therefore, cows were kept more for the production of their male progeny than for milk and she-buffaloes exclusively for milk production.

(b) Significant changes took place in the bovine economy of Tamil Nadu from 1935 onwards. They were: increase in the density of bovines, reversal of the sex ratio, rapid growth of adult females and simultaneous increase in the stock of work and milch animals.

(c) An increase in the density of work animals was observed in the state from 1940 onwards.

(d) There were shortages in the work animal stock, but they were met by the movement of animals through cattle markets and by supplementing male stock with female stock for work.

(e) Though the role of bovines as a supplier of draught power was predominant in the State, the importance of bovines for milk production (dairying) was increasing in the later years of the period under review.

Keeping this historical background in mind, we analyse in the ensuing chapters the size, composition and distribution of bovines during the period between 1956 and 1997 and the major factors underlying the observed trends.

Notes

1. See Appendix Table 3.1.
2. Across the regions in the state, there existed significant variations in the availability of feeds and fodder. The Provincial Fodder and Grazing Committee had identified surplus and deficit districts in livestock feed. The paddy growing regions like Tanjore, Chingleput, North Arcot and South Arcot were identified as deficit areas. On the other hand, Madurai, Tirunelveli, Salem and Coimbatore were regions with satisfactory feed supply position. In fact, some of the taluks of Madurai and Coimbatore were regions with surplus livestock feed. Interestingly, the feed situation in the region was more or less the same, as that had existed in the entire Madras Presidency. For further details on this aspect, refer, Low 1912, Clouston 1920, Leake 1923, Ramakrishnan 1930 and Kaura 1944.
3. The data related to trends in average size of landholdings is given in Appendix Table 3.2.
4. The list of major cattle fairs and hats in the state and certain details like the occurrence time and the areas from where animals come and go in1948-49 are given in Appendix Tables 3.3 and 3.4 respectively. It could be seen that the major fairs were conducted in districts such as Coimbatore, Madurai and Tirunelveli. More of such fairs were conducted in Tirunelveli district. It is also noted

that a major share of animals assembled in all these fairs were bullocks. In addition to the transactions done in these fairs, animals were also purchased from the fairs conducted in the Mysore state. The important fairs of Mysore state from where animals were imported to Tamil Nadu include Kolapalli, Honnenahalli, Nandi, Bakaleraj, Thornahalli, Hemogiri, Rampur, Tirumale of Magadi, Sugganahalli, harthikote, Nandigudi and Meswaraswami.

5. There was a large scale movement of animals across the southern states Andhra Pradesh (Hyderabad), Karnataka(Mysore), Tamil Nadu (Madras) and Kerala (Travancore). Cattle from the Kolar district (Mysore) moved to Palmaner(Chittoor) and Ranipet(Chingelpet) which also received animals from Cuddapah and Nellore district of Andhra Pradesh. From Ranipet, animals moved to Madras or to Mailam (South Arcot) for the fair held there in March. This fair supplied cattle as far south as the Kalugumalai Fair (Tirunelvelli) held twice in January-February and March-April. Cattle from Kolar and Bangalore districts went to the Tiruvannamalai Fair (North Arcot) held in November. Some proceeded to Madura via Tiruchirappally while others went to the Mailam Fair. Bangalore and Mysore districts also exported cattle to the Madras State via Palani or Dindigul (Madurai). On the way, they used to be presented for sale at various fairs, such as at Salem, Tirupur, Andiyur (Coimbatore) etc., from Madurai cattle moved southwards and attended the Kalugumalai fair, whence some went to Tuticorin (mainly for export to Ceylon) and to the Sivalaparai fair held in April-May. Buyers from Anchal, Omallur and Kottayam (Travancore) purchased a large number of cattle at these fairs. Cattle from the Mysore district went to Pollachi (Coimbatore) via Gundalpet (Mysore), Ootacamund and Coimbatore. Cattle for slaughter were mostly retained at Ootacamund. Coimbatore and Pollachi further supplied cattle to several villages in the Malabar district and Trichur (Cochin) respectively. Cattle from the Hassan district moved first to Mercara (Coorg) and then by the Mangalore road to villages in the South Kanara district and by the Cannannore road to villages in the Malabar district (The Agriculturists:1914).

6. The scope for increasing female bovines for work or dependence on female bovines for work has its limits. On realising the constraints of the use of females for work, steps were initiated to popularise dual purpose animals (females which could be used for milk and work).

7. The survey revealed that, "About one half of the output of milk of the province (Madras) is retained by the producers for conversion into milk products such as ghee and curd and the other half is sold as fluid milk. ..... Buffalo milk is in great demand for conversion in to milk products, as it contains 7 per cent of butter fat as against 4 per cent of cow milk. Preference is always for cow's milk where fluid milk is consumed as such." (IJVJ 1938, p. 92).

8. As per the survey, "The price of milk in the same year does not fluctuate so often as the other commodities. The highly perishable nature of milk leads to the necessity of finding a speedy sale on the part of the producers and this was the effect of keeping the price level fairly uniform. In urban areas, where the trade is better organised than in villages, milk fetches an enhanced price, and consequently the proximity to a town is a great impetus to the producers. ..... The price often varies according to the type of milk; cow's milk is dear at most places and cheap at few centres while both cow and buffalo milk is sold at the same rate at some other places.... The price of milk in many places also varies according to the degree of adulteration.

   Usually the producer's and consumer's prices is identical since the bulk of the fluid milk is retained by the producers themselves. Where milk passes through intermediary agencies, the producer secures about 75 per cent of the consumer prices" (IJVJ 1938, pp. 93).

9. "It is indeed a task to get pure and unadulterated milk from a milkman. The adulteration is done cleverly in many ways. The general thing is to add water to the milk without the knowledge of the consumer. To make diluted milk look thicker they add to it milk of ground wheat or mix fine wheat flour itself. Buffaloe□s milk is added with water and sold as cow's milk." Retnam 1943, pp. 240.

   B. Natarajan who studied the distribution of milk in the city of Madras argued as follows:

   "Adulteration is a practice widely prevalent in the milk trade; the penalties imposed by the Food Adulteration Act cannot fly in the face of economic facts of the situation... Statistics of samples tested ... in August show that out of 230 cases examined 164 cases or 70 % nearly, were adulterated. The proportion of water added to milk in the case of 164 samples examined varied from 4 to 70 % and the average percentage was about 22..... It cannot, however, be said that the entire quantity of milk produced is adulterated. Adulteration generally takes place only in respect of milk drawn in the milkmen's shed and sold to customers outside", Natarajan 1950, pp. 139.

APPENDIX

Appendix Table 3.1
Trends in the Density of Work Animals in Tamil Nadu, 1920-1951

Number of Work Animals per 100 acres of Net Sown Area						
1920	*1925*	*1930*	*1935*	*1940*	*1945*	*1951*
28	30	29	30	29	31	37

Source: Computed from Livestock Census (Various years).

Appendix Table 3.2
Trends in Average Size of Land Holdings

	Area in (0.00) acres		
Districts	*1920-21*	*1940-41*	*1950-51*
Chingleput	3.67	2.77	2.58
South Arcot	2.56	2.25	2.14
North Arcot	2.98	2.50	2.31
Salem	4.75	4.06	3.99
Coimbatore	8.75	7.93	7.05
Trichy	5.01	3.40	3.06
Tanjore	3.79	2.58	2.40
Madurai	4.08	3.32	2.90
Ramnad	3.50	3.11	3.18
Tirunelveli	4.40	3.37	2.98
Tamil Nadu	4.16	3.31	3.08

Source: Statistical Atlas of Madras Presidency, (Various years).

Appendix Table 3.3
Cattle Fairs, their Location, Occurance, Animals Assembled and their Movements: Tamil Nadu, 1948-49

District	Name of the fair (Location)	Occurrence	Number of Animals Assembled							Recognised Breeds	Animals come from	Animals go to
			Bulls	Bullocks	Cows	Calves	Hebuf faloes	Shebuf faloes	Total			
Tanjore	Neelatha-nallur	March April	4	13679	-	-	-	-	13683	-	Tanjore Trichy Mysore border	-
Madurai	Athicomkai	-	-	14000	-	-	-	-	14000	Kangayan Mysore Local	Madurai Trichy Coimbatore	-
	Vada-madura	April		15000					15000	do	do	
	Kanniseri	June		20000					20000	do	do	
	Kalugmalai	January	2370	10752	250	47	305		13724	Kangayan Alambadi	Mysore Ramnad Madurai	Southern districts
	do	March	298	11284	107	192	209		12090	do	Ramnad Machora	do

Contd...

District	Name of the fair (Location)	Occurrence	Number of Animals Assembled									
			Bulls	Bullocks	Cows	Calves	Hebuf faloes	Shebuf faloes	Total	Recognised Breeds	Animals come from	Animals go to
Tirunelveli	Tiruchendur	February	800	3600	500	20	200		5120	do	do	-
	Kilaran-ganauram	June	1320	5939	425	75	250		8009	do	do	-
	Swalpuri	April	502	14217	512		3083		18314	do	do	-
	Samkarankoil	August	1500	2500	500	103	529		5132	do	Southern districts Travancore	
	Kanrapuram	April May	12000	6000	500	1500	-	-	20000	Kangayan	Coimbatore Salem Trichy	Maduai
Coimbatore	Tirupur	May	-	-	-	-	-		12000	do	do	do
	Pudupalayam	August	2000	300	30	5000	-	-	7330	-	-	-
North Arcot	Thiruvannamalai	November	-	-	-	-	-	-	5000	-	-	-

Note: The fairs listed are where more than 5000 animals assemble.
Source: GOI: (1956).

Appendix Table 3.4
Details of Some of the Important Cattle Hats: Tamil Nadu, 1948-49

			Number of Animals Assembled						
District	*Name of the fair (Location)*	*Hat-day*	*Bulls*	*Bullocks* 700	*Cows* 20	*Calves* 10	*He-Buffaloes*	*She - Buffaloes*	*Total*
North Arcot	Pavitram	Friday					10	5	745
	Pudupet	Thursday							800
Salem	Payarmalai	Wednesday							3000
	Seshari	Monday							800
	Shervapet	Tuesday							750
	Muthuraikanpatti	Tuesday							1000
Combatore	Perundurai	Sunday	100	300	50	100	5	10	565
	Muianur	Wednesday	200	150		200	150		700
	Ravandanuady	Wednesday	450		50	100			600
	Andiyur	Monday		250	300	100		20	670
	Punjai	Thursday	40	620	105	165	20	50	1000
	Pollachi	Thursday		2460	1740	760			4960
	Tudiyalur	Monday							1000
Madurai	Usilempetti	Wednesday		300	250				550
	Melur	Monday	100	100	200	30	10	10	450
	Virupakasi	Thursday							550
Ramnad	Singanpunari	Thursday		300	200	50			550
Tiruchinapalli	Uppidiamoyalam	Sunday & half Monday		1000	300		500		1800
	Paramathi	Tuesday	400		100		150		650
	Manaparai	Wednesday	2000		100		60		2160

Contd...

District	Name of the fair (Location)	Hat-day	Number of Animals Assembled						
			Bulls	Bullocks 700	Cows 20	Calves 10	He-Buffaloes	She - Buffaloes	Total
Tanjore	Pattukettai	Monday	6500						6500
	Peruviur	Sunday	6000						6000
	Madhukur	Tuesday	6500						6500
	Aranthangi	Tuesday	6000						6000
	Tiruthurapundi		850						850
	Kariapatinam		850						850
	Muthuneet		800						800
South Arcot	Panruti	Thursday	1400						1400
	Kallakurichi	Thursday	950						950
	Kuthagudi	Friday	700						700
	Chettipalayam		800						800
	Chinnesalem	Friday	800						800
	Kutteripatti		800						800
	Madapatti		1000						1000
Kanyakumari	Nagercoil	Sunday & Tursday	50	200	10	40	50		350

Note: The hats listed are where the number of assembling are more than 50.
Source: GOI: (1956).

4

TRENDS AND DETERMINANTS OF BOVINE SEX RATIOS IN TAMIL NADU

Introduction

Following the historical analysis of the changes in the bovine stock and its pattern of utilisation in the first half of the twentieth century, in this chapter, we make an attempt to provide an empirical analysis of the different factors shaping bovine sex ratios during the second half of the century. As a prelude, we examine the changes in bovine stock in terms of its size, age-sex composition and survival rates during the past fifty years. The observed trends and patterns are examined in greater detail in the subsequently. The determinants of the work animal stock and the determinants of the milch animal stock are examined. The empirical testing of the relationships is done with the help of multiple regression models with work animal and milch animal densities as dependent variables and appropriate explanatory factors as independent variables.

Changes in the Size and Composition of the Bovine Stock

The total bovine stock in Tamil Nadu in the mid-'fifties was about 11.74 million; it increased to 13.42 million by the early 'sixties. In the subsequent years up to 1982, the bovine population remained at around 13.5 million. Since then, it showed a falling trend reaching 11.79 million by 1997. It is noted that the trends in the cattle population followed more or less the overall trend in the bovine stock until the early 1980s. However, the rate of increase in buffalo population was higher than that of the cattle population. In the subsequent years, the fall in the cattle population was much more rapid than that of the buffalo population. Consequent on these changes, the share of cattle in the total stock declined while that of buffaloes increased (see Table 4.1).

Interesting changes are also noted to have taken place in the composition of the cattle population. The proportion of adult males (mostly used for work) has declined sharply, from 46 per cent in the mid-'fifties to 25 per cent by 1997. In absolute numbers, the decline in the adult male population was from 4.2 million to 2.25 million; the number of adult female increased from 3.45 million to 3.8 million by 1977 and then stabilised at around 3.5 million in the subsequent years.

Among the young stock, the male population centred around 1 to 1.1 million throughout the period, and the female population increased from the early 'seventies from 1.17 million in 1974 to 2.4 million in 1997. As far as buffaloes are concerned, both the young and the adult male populations have shown a declining trend; the young female stock an increasing trend and the adult female stock a declining trend from the early 'eighties. The decline in the proportion of adult female stock in both the cattle and the buffalo populations is a clear indication of the increase in the rate of replacement of the adult stock by the young stock.

Adjustments in the size of the male and the female cattle populations have been taking place through different age-specific survival rates. We have estimated the survival rates[1] of males and females for both the species in the 0-1 and the 1-3 age groups; see Table 4.2. The estimates reveal a decline in the survival rates of male young stock (both cattle and buffaloes) and increase in the survival rates of females, especially from the early 'eighties.

Table 4.1
Trends in the Species Composition of Bovine Population: Tamil Nadu, 1956-1997

(in million)

Year	Cattle						Buffalo						Total Bovine stock	
	Male		Female				Male		Female					
	adult	young stock	adult	young stock	Total Cattle		adult	young stock	adult	Young-stock	TotalBuffalo			
1956	4.2 (46.18)	1.17 (11.19)	3.45 (32.98)	1.01 (9.65)	9.70 (100)	[82.62]	0.28 (15.77)	0.44 (16.92)	1.06 (40.77)	0.69 (26.54)	2.04 (100)	[17.38]	11.74	[100]
1961	5.08 (46.91)	1.06 (9.79)	3.65 (33.70)	1.04 (9.60)	10.83 (100)	[80.70]	0.46 (17.76)	0.41 (15.83)	1.29 (49.81)	0.43 (16.60)	2.59 (100)	[19.30]	13.42	[100]
1966	4.95 (45.58)	1.10 (10.13)	3.71 (34.16)	1.10 (10.13)	10.86 (100)	[79.97]	0.50 (18.38)	0.38 (13.97)	1.35 (49.63)	0.49 (18.02)	2.72 (100)	[20.03]	13.58	[100]
1974	4.64 (43.9)	1.10 (10.40)	3.66 (34.63)	1.17 (11.07)	10.57 (100)	[78.76]	0.40 (14.04)	0.41 (14.38)	1.48 (51.93)	0.56 (19.65)	2.85 (100)	[21.24]	13.42	[100]
1977	4.64 (42.96)	1.13 (10.46)	3.80 (35.19)	1.23 (11.39)	10.80 (100)	[77.81]	0.38 (12.34)	0.43 (13.96)	1.64 (53.25)	0.63 (20.45)	3.08 (100)	[22.19]	13.88	[100]
1982	3.94 (37.99)	1.26 (12.15)	3.49 (33.66)	1.68 (16.20)	10.37 (100)	[76.36]	0.30 (9.35)	0.37 (11.53)	1.72 (53.58)	0.82 (25.54)	3.21 (100)	[23.64]	13.58	[100]
1989	3.30 (35.25)	1.01 (10.79)	3.30 (35.33)	1.74 (18.63)	9.35 (100)	[74.94]	0.21 (6.64)	0.29 (9.33)	1.67 (53.49)	0.96 (30.54)	3.13 (100)	[25.06]	12.48	[100]
1994	2.76 (30.33)	0.97 (10.66)	3.36 (36.92)	2.01 (22.09)	9.10 (100)	[75.64]	0.19 (6.49)	0.31 (10.58)	1.56 (53.24)	0.87 (29.69)	2.93 (100)	[24.36]	12.03	[100]
1997	2.25 (24.83)	1.13 (12.49)	3.53 (39.01)	2.14 (23.66)	9.05 (100)	[76.76]	0.18 (6.58)	0.33 (11.89)	1.39 (57.24)	0.85 (30.87)	2.74 (100)	[23.24]	11.79	[100]

Source: Report on Livestock Census -Tamil Nadu, 1966, 1977, 1982, 1989, 1994 and 1997.

The manner in which age specific survival rates affect the sex ratios in both the species is evident from Table 4.3. It shows a sharp fall in sex ratios of both the species, in all the age groups during the period (Table 4.3).

Table 4.2
Trends in Age-Specific Survival Rates by Bovine Species: Tamil Nadu, 1956-1997

Year	*Cattle*				*Buffalo*			
	Animals of <1 year		*Animals of 1-3 years*		*Animals of <1 year*		*Animals of 1-3 years*	
	Male	*Female*	*Male*	*Female*	*Male*	*Female*	*Male*	*Female*
1956	0.94	0.92	0.42	0.43	0.70	0.88	0.19	0.28
1961	0.95	0.91	0.44	0.44	0.79	0.82	0.28	0.31
1966	0.96	0.96	0.44	0.45	0.69	0.84	0.22	0.31
1974	0.87	0.90	0.41	0.44	0.66	0.84	0.19	0.29
1977	0.87	0.93	0.40	0.45	0.64	0.88	0.20	0.30
1982	0.69	1.00	0.43	0.53	0.46	0.92	0.15	0.38
1987	0.50	1.00	0.30	0.45	0.32	1.00	0.10	0.36
1994	0.46	1.00	0.21	0.39	0.37	1.00	0.11	0.32
1997	0.50	1.00	0.25	0.44	0.39	1.00	0.14	0.36

Source: Computed from, Livestock Census, Tamil Nadu, 1966, 1977, 1982, 1989, 1994 and 1997.

Table 4.3
Trends in Sex Ratios By Species and by Age Group: Tamil Nadu, 1956-1997

Species	*Age Group*	*Sex Ratio (Male/Female)*								
		1956	*1961*	*1966*	*1974*	*1977*	*1982*	*1989*	*1994*	*1994*
Cattle	Under 1 year	1.03	1.05	1.00	0.96	0.94	0.69	0.50	0.42	0.50
	1 to 3 years	0.99	0.99	0.99	0.93	0.89	0.81	0.67	0.56	0.57
	Over 3 years	1.23	1.39	1.33	1.27	1.22	1.13	1.00	0.82	0.64
	Total	1.18	1.31	1.26	1.19	1.15	1.01	0.85	0.69	0.60
Buffalo	Under 1 year	0.79	0.97	0.83	0.79	0.72	0.50	0.32	0.38	0.39
	1 to 3 years	0.24	0.90	0.70	0.65	0.65	0.40	0.29	0.33	0.38
	Over 3 years	0.27	0.36	0.37	0.27	0.23	0.17	0.12	0.12	0.13
	Total	0.33	0.51	0.48	0.40	0.36	0.26	0.19	0.21	0.21
Bovine	Under 1 year	0.95	1.02	0.94	0.90	0.86	0.62	0.43	0.41	0.46
	1 to 3 years	0.91	0.97	0.91	0.85	0.82	0.68	0.54	0.49	0.52
	Over 3 years	1.00	1.12	1.08	0.98	0.93	0.81	0.70	0.60	0.49
	Total	0.98	1.09	1.04	0.95	0.90	0.76	0.63	0.54	0.49

Note: For the period from 1982, the cattle are classified as under 1 year, 1 2.5 Years and 2.5 years & above.

Source: The same as for Table 4.2.

The shifts in the relative importance of adult male and female stocks and the changes in their age composition indicate that adjustments were carried out by farmers for managing their herd size and composition in accordance with changing requirements. The size of the work animal population[2] is influenced by a number of factors such as land use, pattern[3], irrigation[4], size of landholding[5], intensity of agricultural mechanisation[6] and cropping pattern[7]. The relative contributions of these factors do vary across regions and over time. The relationship between these variables and their influence in shaping the work animal population in Tamil Nadu since independence are examined in section 4.3. In order to capture precisely the influence of these variables on the work animal stock, we have excluded the buffalo species from the work animal category. As was discussed earlier, buffaloes are valued more as a milk-producing animal rather than as a work animal. Moreover, the proportion of buffaloes used for work is also very small.

Factors Determining Trends in Work Animal Population

The relationship between work animal population and land use pattern needs to be examined from both the demand and the supply sides. On the demand side, gross cropped area is an important factor that determines the requirement of work animals. If the scope for agricultural expansion were high one would expect the demand for work animals to go up. From the supply point of view, to sustain the work animal stock, adequacy of feed supply is crucial. Since the area of non-agricultural land for grazing has been declining, the increase in feed requirement had to be met from the principal products and by-products of crops and by cultivating fodders. One would expect a strong relationship between agricultural expansion and the requirement of draught animals. The intensification of cultivation that normally follows agricultural expansion would further add to the requirement of work animals. However, if the cropping intensity facilitates the intensive use of work animals (by using the animals more hours efficiently), it may not increase the density of work animals, (a measure of the availability of draught animal power per unit of land) even though the total farm power requirement increases.

The expansion and intensification of agriculture is strongly influenced by agro-climatic conditions and the extent and quality of irrigation. The agro-climatic conditions, particularly the soil condition and the intensity and seasonal distribution of rainfall, have significant influence on the density of work animals and the pattern of their utilisation. The cultivation operations in rain-fed areas are heavily dependent on the quantum of rainfall and its seasonal concentration. In general, summer is generally hot and the soil becomes very dry and hard. Hence, with onset of monsoon[8] by June, the land has to be ploughed and made ready for cultivation within a short span of time so that timely sowing and crop growth could be ensured. In this context, the ownership of work animals provides enough strength and flexibility for the cultivators for the timely completion of their cultivation operations. Though animals are not used during some parts of the year, they serve as an 'energy gate' that can be drawn as and when needed.

Given the agro-climatic conditions, irrigation is the most important factor that could mediate the number and utilisation pattern of draught animals[9]. When the extent and quality of irrigation is better, both net sown area and intensity of cropping would become higher, thereby leading to higher requirement of draught power. While the proportion of irrigated area to gross cropped area would provide a measure of the spread of irrigation, the proportion of adequately irrigated area to total irrigated area would be a suitable indicator of the quality of irrigation. Since well irrigation provides to a great extent assured irrigation and thereby a stable agriculture, it would lead also to more effective utilisation of work animals. This is not only through increased use of work animals in crop production, but also through use of animals for lifting water, in conditions in which the wells are not energised. It would also mean that mechanisation of irrigation could displace the animals used for irrigation purposes and thereby reduce the required work animal stock. Mechanisation of irrigation[10] has differential impacts on the work animal population. Electric pumpsets and oil engines might displace animals employed for lift irrigation. Energisation of wells leads to an increase in the volume of water lifted per unit of time, and thereby to an extension of cultivated area and rise in cropping intensity. Consequently, the requirement of draught power may increase for other operations like tillage, manuring, harvesting and threshing.

If mechanization of irrigation is followed by mechanization of land preparation and other cultivation operations like harvesting and threshing, it would result in the reduction of work animal stock. In this context, it may be useful to highlight the influence of the sequence of cultivation operations on work animal population. Cultivation operations could be broadly classified under (i) land preparation activities[11], (ii) sowing and/or crop planting activities[12], (iii) plant protection activities[13], (iv) harvesting or reaping activities[14] and (v) post-harvesting activities[15]. Generally, cultivation operations vary significantly across crops, regions, agro-climatic conditions, size class of farms and socio-economic background of the cultivators. However, in a particular region and a specific crop, cultivation operations remain almost unchanged. Cultivation operations vary significantly between food crops and non-food crops. For instance, non-food crops like groundnut and gingelly require similar cultivation operations, as is the case also in certain food grains. Within the food crops, the cultivation operations of foodgrains (cereals and pulses) are similar and they vary significantly from those of the other food crops such as condiments and spices, sugar crops, and fruits and vegetables including root crops. Cultivation operations influence, in turn, the use of agricultural implements[16] As the requirement of human and animal labour inputs would vary from crop to crop, the cropping pattern[17] is an important variable influencing the requirement of draught power. Agricultural operations can be done with human, animal or mechanical power, either alone or in combinations. While a few operations could be carried out either by human labour, most of the operations could be done either by animal or mechanical power. In fact, mechanical equipment[18] could substitute most operations carried out by humans and animals.

Though the relationship between the use of work animals and of mechanical equipments seems to be inverse, in reality, their relationship is complex. For instance, tractors can displace draught animals in land preparation, sowing, manuring and threshing. But, the influence of tractors[19] in reducing the work animal population is constrained by the scale of operation and fragmentation of land holdings. For a tractor to be economical, its scale of operation should be high and therefore, tractorisation is carried out in general only in large farms. Moreover, due to fragmentation of land holdings, the average size of landholding declines and the number of plots per household increases, a situation which raises constraints on tractorisation and the consequent displacement of work animals, particularly in small and marginal farms. To understand this phenomenon, it is necessary to analyse the major institutional changes, especially in the size and the distribution of landholdings[20]. This is important not only because of the positive association between the size of landholding and the spread of mechanisation, but also due to the relationship between the size of holding and the density of work animals, as postulated in Vaidyanathan *et al.* (1982).

We have discussed the various factors that have influence on the work animal population and its density. In order to explain the influence of these factors on work animal density and also to capture changes in the relative impact of these factors over time in Tamil Nadu, a set of indicators of agriculture, irrigation, agro-climatic conditions, economic, institutional and technological status, are correlated with the density of work animal population. The correlation coefficients are estimated for two sets of pooled district-level data of Tamil Nadu; the first set represents the period between 1956 and 1974, and the second set the period between 1977 and 1997. The periodisation is made due to the shift observed in the size and composition of bovines from the seventies. The results are given in Table 4.4.

The correlation coefficients indicated a significant association between the selected variables and the density of work animal population in both the periods. During 1956-74, the climatic factor is seen to have been highly associated with the density of work animals, followed by size of landholding, agriculture and irrigation. During 1977-1997, the order of importance of the association is observed to have changed: climate is followed by agriculture, land holding, technology and irrigation.

Table 4.4
Coefficient Correlation Between
Density of Work Animal Population and Selected Indicators

Indicators		*Correlation Coefficient*	
		1956-1974	*1977-1997*
Agriculture Indicators	GCA/NSA	0.295	0.234
	FP/NSA	0.421	0.500
Irrigation Indicators	GIA/NIA	0.111	0.090
	NIA/NSA	0.386	0.284
	WIA/NIA	0.024	0.133
	WIA/NSA	0.202	0.229
Climatic (Rainfall) Indicators	NSWR	0.558	0.451
	NNER	0.239	0.143
	NTR	0.310	0.234
	PNSWR	0.593	0.530
	PNNER	0.103	0.203
Institutional Indicators	NSA/CULT	0.470	0.492
	NSA/CULT2	0.426	0.429
Technological Indicators	NT/NSA	0.227	0.014
	NP/NSA	0.170	0.422
	MP/NSA	0.175	0.356
	PTP	0.008	0.385
	PPP	0.012	0.043
	PMP	0.013	0.204

Note: 1. WAP=Work Animal Population; NSA = Net Sown Area; GCA=Gross Cropped Area; GIA = Gross Irrigated Area; NIA = Net Irrigated Area; WIA = Well Irrigated Area; NSWR = Normal South West Rainfall; NNER = Normal North East Rainfall; NTR = Normal Total Rainfall; PNSWR = Percentage of Normal South West Rainfall; PNNER = Percentage of Normal North East Rainfall; CULT = Cultivators; NT = Number of Tractors; NP = Number of Pumpsets; PTP = Percentage of Tractor Power; PPP = Percentage of Pumpsets Power; FP = Farm Power; PMP = Percentage of Mechanical Power; MP = Mechanical Power.

2. Figures in bold denotes that they are significant at 5 per cent level.

It may be seen that the technology indicators were not significantly associated during the former period; but they became highly significant during the latter period. There has taken place a significant shift in the cultivation operation (from the use of animal -operated implements to tractor-operated implements, from animal and human power based cultivation to tractor and electrical power based cultivation pattern and from traditional to modern cultivation) in the state and the shift has been sharp from the late 'seventies.

The cropping intensity (GCA/NSA) is observed to be positively related in both the phases, but not significantly. This indicates that even if cropping intensity increased, it did not lead to any significant increase in work animal density. To explain the reason behind this non-change, one has to understand the animal use pattern across various seasons in a year. It has been argued earlier that the possession of animals is conditioned not just by their energy power, but also by the flexibility of their availability. As work animals are relatively under-utilised, intensification of cultivation leads to greater utilisation of work animals and without any direct increase in the work animal stock. The growing contribution of farm power by mechanical equipment would also meet increased draught power requirements in agriculture arising from improvements in cropping intensity.

The association between farm power (FP/NSA) and density of work animals (WAP/NSA) per unit of cultivated area is positive and significant. In fact, the association between these variables has increased from 0.421 to 0.5 during the period from phase-I to phase-II. In areas where the farm power requirement per cultivated area is higher, the animal density is also higher and vice-versa. The farm power per unit of cultivated area, which represents the total agricultural performance in the context of draught power requirements, is contributed by animal power, electric power and mechanical power. It has been observed that the contribution of electric and mechanical power has been increasing in the state. In this context, the significant positive association observed between farm power per unit area and density of work animals indicates that animal power still occupies a significant position in Tamil Nadu agriculture.

Among the irrigation factors, only the proportion of irrigated area to total cultivated area (NIA/NSA) was positively and significantly correlated in both the phases. This indicates that when well irrigation improves it would lead to better use of land for agriculture and that it further increases the work animal density. But the association between the share of well-irrigated area to the net irrigated area (WIA/NIA) and to the net sown area (WIA/NSA), which was positive, but not significant in both the phases, needs to be explained. The insignificant contribution of well irrigation to work animal stock could be attributed to the energisation of wells by pumpsets and oil engines, only to mechanisation of well irrigation. The increase in well-irrigated area has not raised the work animal population proportionally.

The South-West rainfall (NSWR) and the seasonal concentration of South-West Rainfall (PNSWR) were found to be significantly associated with the density of work animals, indicating that in areas where the south-west rainfall and the seasonal contribution of south-west monsoon are high, work animal density is also high and vice-versa.

The average size of land holdings measured by the net sown area per cultivator (NSA/CULT) was found to be negatively and significantly associated with the density of work animals. When population pressure on agricultural land increases, the NSA/CULT declines. In otherwords, the average size of land holdings per cultivator declines over time. In such a situation, the possession of work animals for cultivation purposes becomes crucial. As animals are indivisible in nature and their services are sharable only to a limited extent due to the critical nature of farming and cultivation operations, the number of animals per household or farm increases when the size of land holdings declines or the fragmentation of landholdings increases. However, this relationship would exist only upto a critical limit at which farmers would find it difficult to maintain work animals due to reasons of economic viability and productive efficiency or production pattern. Therefore, decline in the size of landholdings beyond a limit, leads to a decline in work animal density. This is evident from the square of the size of land holdings that is associated with the density of work animals significantly, indicating the non-linear association, as argued by Vaidyanathan (1988).

Among the technological factors, a different type of association could be observed. The density of tractors (NT/NSA) was negative but not significant, in both the phases indicating thereby that though tractorisation has a negative impact on work animal population, its individual effect is insignificant. Although the employment of tractor may displace the use of work animals directly, it is possible only if the landholding patterns and the operation of the economies of scale are conducive. The densities of pumpsets (NP/NSA) and of mechanical power per cultivated area (MP/NSA) were positively associated with the work animal density; but the coefficients were significant only during phase-II. The percentage shares of tractor power (PTP), pumpset power (PPP) and mechanical power (PMP) to the total farm power, were positively associated during phase-I (though not significantly), but became negatively associated in phase-II. During phase-II, the share of tractor power to total farm power (PTP) alone was observed to be significantly associated with work animal density, indicating that while the share of tractor power increases, the work animal density declines and vice-versa. It is important to observe that the trends in tractorisation, which gained importance in the 'eighties and the 'nineties, had significantly influenced work animal density negatively.

Although on a one-to-one basis many variables provided significant relationship, they were inter-related among themselves. For instance, the FP/NSA was significantly associated with the MP/NSA and NP/NSA. As the correlation coefficient between FP/NSA and WAP/NSA was found relatively high, FP/NSA is considered for the regression exercise.

Based on the procedure discussed above, two regression exercises are made, one representing phase I (1956-1974) and the other phase II (1977-1997). Phase I basically represents the period when mechanisation in agriculture had been at the early stages and phase II represents the period when mechanization (both energisation of irrigation and tractorisation) was at a relatively high level. A comparison of the results between these models would highlight the changes that have taken place in the relative contribution of these factors over time. The regression models are explained below:

Model-I

WAP/NSA =f {NIA/NSA, PNSWR, NSA/CULT, NSA/CULT2, FP/NSA}

where, WAP/ NSA = Work Animal Population per Net Sown Area;
NIA/NSA = Net Irrigated Area per Net Sown Area,
PNSWR= Percentage of Normal South West Rainfall;
NSA/CULT = Net Sown Area per Cultivators,
NSA/CULT2 = Square of Net Sown Area per Cultivators,
FP/NSA = Farm Power per Net Sown Area.

Model-II

WAP/NSA =f {NIA/NSA, PNSWR, NSA/CULT, NSA/CULT2, PTP, FP/NSA}

where, WAP/ NSA = Work Animal Population per Net Sown Area;
NIA/NSA = Net Irrigated Area per Net Sown Area,
PNSWR= Percentage of Normal South West Rainfall;
NSA/CULT = Net Sown Area per Cultivators,
NSA/CULT2 = Square of Net Sown Area per Cultivators,
PTP = Percentage of Tractor Power to the total Farm Power;
FP/NSA = Farm Power per Net Sown Area.

The regression results are given in Table 4.5.

Table 4.5
Regression Results of Selected Variables on Density of Work Animal Population

		Indicators								
		Constant	*NIA/ NSA*	*PNSWR*	*NSA / CULT*	*NSA / CULT2*	*PTP/ FP*	*FP / NSA*	*R2 value*	*N*
1956-74	β -values	77.873	0.804***	1.339***	-0.839	0.002	– –	0.084	0.712	47
	t- values	1.951	5.765	3.973	-1.549	1.013	– –	1.375		
1977-97	β -values	99.802	0.719***	0.855***	-1.304***	0.004***	-1.966***	0.078**	0.674	67
	t- values	3.747	5.082	2.912	-3.589	3.272	-4.616	2.042		

*** indicates significance at 1 per cent level
** indicates significance at 10 per cent level.

The regression results for phase-I revealed that the seasonal concentration of rainfall and the proportion of irrigated area to the total cultivated area were the two significant factors that influenced work animal density. The model explained 71 per cent of the variations in the density of work animals. The contribution of seasonal rainfall was observed to be the maximum (1.333), followed by the proportion of irrigated area to total cultivated area (0.804). Though the size of landholding negatively contributed to work animal density, the contribution was not significant. Farm power per cultivated area contributed positively, but its influence, not significantly. The signs of the coefficients for the variables obtained in this exercise are in the expected direction. However, the insignificant contributions made by size of landholding and farm power per unit area indicated that though these factors were contributing individually, their combined effect was not significant due to the dominant role played by climatic and irrigation factors.

During Phase-II, all the variables included in the model significantly contributed towards work animal density and the model explained 67 per cent of the variations in the density of work animals. Among these variables, the contribution of the share of tractor power was dominant and had negatively contributed to the work animal density (-1.966). The next major contribution was made by size of landholding and that too negatively (-1.304). The relationship between work animal density and size of land holdings is observed to have been non-linear, and is supported by the significant coefficients of the square of the size of land holdings. This means that when the size of land holding declines, the work animal density increases initially and beyond a limit, there exists a positive association between them. The contributions of seasonal rainfall and the proportion of irrigated area were positive and almost equal (0.855 and 0.719 respectively). Farm power availability per cultivated area, which represents the total agricultural power requirement, contributed positively (0.078).

The regression results obtained for Phase-II provide significant insights into the relative importance of various factors influencing work animal density and help us draw the following inferences. The contribution of tractorisation has become dominant in influencing the density of work animals negatively indicating that tractorisation has played a significant role in the displacement of work animal population in recent years. The phenomenal increase in the number of tractors and power tillers from the' eighties corroborates this observation. As the pumpset revolution that began by the' seventies would have displaced work animals that had been in use for lifting water for irrigation purposes, the mechanisation of cultivation and other farm activities[21] by the use of tractors, would have made the displacement of work animals easier. It seems this sequence would have been under operation, a fact reflected in the regression results, as tractorisation is seen to have contributed the maximum part.

The observed influence of the average size of land holding on work animal density supports the density-dependent hypothesis. It may be seen that the contribution of both climatic factor and irrigation significantly declined during phase-II, while these two factors had contributed the maximum during phase-I. While agro-climatic and irrigation factors had played a major role in shaping the work animal density during the period prior to the mid 'seventies, technological, economic and institutional factors played a major role in more recent years.

In addition to these factors, there could have been other variables too that influenced the work animal population. Changes in the dairy economy, such as growth in milch animal population and its competitive nature, would also significantly influence it. Keeping these aspects in mind, a discussion of the factors determining milch animal population is undertaken in the next section.

Factors Determining Milch Animal Population

Both economic and non-economic forces determine the growth of milch animal population.[22] In simple terms, it may be argued that milch animal population increases when there is demand for milch stock[23] caused by increase in demand for calves and milk and milk products. Though this argument is technically accepted, the role of cows as producer of male calves that are reared as work animals must have been undergoing significant change in Tamil Nadu. It is worthwhile to examine the factors that determine the density of breeding cows in the context of the declining work animal densities. Vaidyanathan (1988) argued that the relation between the number of cows and the size of the bullock herd is conditioned by factors such as mortality rates of bullocks, rates of growth of bullock herds, mortality rates of male calves from birth to adulthood and rates at which cows produce calves. He examined the relative influence of these factors, using the cross-sectional data for 1972, based on a multiple regression model given below:

BC = f (AMC, CR, SRm, YSMC/AMC) where,

BC	=	breeding cows[24] per net sown area
AMC	=	adult male cattle per net sown area
CR	=	calving rate[25]
SRm	=	survival rate of males
YSMC/AMC	=	young stock male cattle per adult male cattle

His analysis based on cross sectional data of both districts of southern and northern states revealed that the density of breeding cows is an increasing function of AMC and YSMC/AMC and a declining function of CR and SRm. Though this argument sounds theoretically strong, one would expect significant changes in the relative influence of the determining factors over time and across regions. Keeping this aspect in mind, an attempt is made to examine the factors influencing milch cow population in Tamil Nadu. For the purpose of our analysis, district-level data were pooled for the periods 1956-1974 and 1977-1997. For the purpose of estimation, we have used the model formulated by Vaidyanathan (1988). The variables used in the estimation are the following:

1. Density of breeding cows (BC/NSA)
2. Density of adult male cattle (AMC/NSA)
3. Calving Rate (CR)
4. Survival Rate of males (SRm)
5. Replacement rate of males (RRm=YSMC/AMC)

As a first step towards our analysis, a correlation matrix was estimated to identify the variables that are associated with density of breeding cows and to understand the inter-relationship between the independent variables. The correlation matrix is presented in Table 4.6.

Table 4.6
Correlation Matrix

	Variables	*BC/ NSA*	*AMC/ NSA*	*CR*	*SRm*	*RRm*
Period I (1956–1974)	BC/NSA	1.000				
	AMC/NSA	.0710**	1.000			
	CR	-0.332*	-0.576**	1.000		
	SRm	0.330*	0.473**	-0.370*	1.000	
	RRm	0.085	-0.531**	0.717**	-0.156	1.000
Period II (1977–1997)	BC/NSA	1.000				
	AMC/NSA	.0716**	1.000			
	CR	-0.185	-0.409**	1.000		
	SRm	0.494*	0.602**	-0.385*	1.000	
	RRm	0.047	-0.446**	0.356**	-0.379	1.000

The density of breeding cows (BC/NSA) is found to be positively associated with the density of work animals (AMC/NSA), the survival rates of males (SRm) and the replacement rates of males (RRm) and negatively associated with calving rate (CR). The positive association was statistically significant with the density of work animals (AMC/NSA) and survival rate of males (SRm), in both the periods, and the negative association was statistically significant with the calving rate (CR) during period-I. Thus it is seen that the density of work animals, the calving rate and the survival rate of males influence the density of breeding cows.

The correlation matrix also clearly revealed significant association among the independent variables. That is, the density of work animals is significantly associated with survival and replacement rates of males. Similarly, the survival rate of males is significantly associated with the calving rate. As the determining factors are said to be complementary variables, such associations are inevitable. Keeping this aspect in mind, the regression analysis carried out and the results observed therefore are given in Table 4.7.

The regression results revealed that in both the periods, the density of work animals is the dominant and determining factor of the density of breeding cows. In Period-I, the model explained about 90 per cent of variations in the density of breeding cows and in period-II, it was only about 68 per cent (refer the adjusted R-2 figures). This result indicates that the influence of other (unexplained) factors has been gaining importance in recent years.

It may be observed that while all the observed variables showed significant influence on the population of breeding cows during period-I, the variable of calving rate became insignificant during period-II. Moreover, in period-I, the density of breeding cows was positively influenced by density of work animals and replacement rate of work animals and negatively influenced by calving rate and survival rate of males. This result reveals that (i) the density of breeding cows remains at lower levels during periods when the survival rates and calving rates are at high levels and vice-versa, and that (ii) the density of breeding cows remains at high levels in situations in which the density of work animals and replacement rate of males are at high levels and vice-versa. These findings go well with our theoretical position.

During period-II, the relationships have changed significantly. The calving rate has become an insignificant factor though its influence has become positive. Moreover, the survival rate influenced cow density positively, indicating that in regions where the survival rates of males are higher, the density of breeding cows is also higher. The observed shift could have been due to changes in the work animal requirements in recent years.

Thus, the discussion on the determinants of cow density reveals that the density of work animals though is the dominant determining factor of the density of breeding cows, its influence has been declining over time, and that of other (unexplained) factors have been gaining importance in recent years.

Table 4.7
Results of the Multiple Regression Analysis-Determinants of Density of Breeding Cows

Period-I

reg BC/NSA AMC/NSA CR RRm SRm, beta

Source	*SS*	*df*	*MS*			
				Number of obs	=	47
Model	0.8746	4	.2187	F(4, 42)	=	103.64
Residual	0.0886	42	.0021	Prob > F	=	0.0000
				R-squared	=	0.9080
				Adj R-squared	=	0.8992
Total	0.9632	46	.0209	Root MSE	=	.04593

BC/NSA	*Coef.*	*Std. Err.*	*t*	*P>|t|*	*Beta*
AMC/NSA	0.5626*	0.0351	16.023	0.000	1.0193860
CR	-1.1979*	0.1777	- 6.743	0.000	-0.4971715
RRm	1.4444*	0.1077	13.416	0.000	0.9533406
SRm	-0.4691*	0.1385	- 3.388	0.002	-0.1881296

Contd..

Period-II

reg BC/NSA AMC/NSA CR SRm RRm, beta

Source	*SS*	*df*	*MS*		
				Number of obs =	67
				F(4, 62) =	36.74
Model	1.9512	4	0.4878	Prob > F =	0.0000
Residual	0.8232	62	0.0133	R-squared =	0.7033
				Adj R-squared =	0.6842
Total	2.7744	66	0.0420	Root MSE =	.11523

BC/NSA	*Coef.*	*Std. Err.*	*t*	*P>|t|*	*Beta*
AMC/NSA	0.5757*	0.0634	9.052	0.000	0.8344991
CR	0.0697	0.0867	0.804	0.424	0.0632288
SRm	0.2786*	0.1279	2.179	0.033	0.1937010
RRm	0.7342*	0.1246	5.894	0.000	0.4694870

Note: * indicates significance at 1 per cent level

Conclusion

The foregoing discussion of the trends in the bovine size, composition and sex-ratios in Tamil Nadu during the period between 1955 and 1997 showed a differential pattern. The total bovine population increased up to the early 'sixties, remained unchanged up to the early 'eighties and thereafter declined slowly. The composition of bovines is getting increasingly oriented towards cattle stock, particularly, towards cows from the early 'eighties. The reversal of sex ratios from the early 'sixties indicates that the importance of milch animals that gained momentum during the 'thirties got accelerated. The analysis of the factors and the processes that were shaping work and milch animal densities showed that the density of work animals per hectare of gross cropped area had been increasing during the 1950s, remaining unchanged till the mid-1960s, and declining thereafter. The decline in density was the sharpest and the most significant from the 1980s. The density of work animal stock is influenced by a large number of factors, which were examined using a regression model. The contribution of tractorisation has been significant in the displacement of work animal population in recent years. The pumpset revolution that began by the 'seventies would also have displaced work animals from irrigation activities. Subsequently, tractorisation and mechanisation of farm activities would have displaced work animals from cultivation activities from the early 'eighties. The observed influence of the average size of land holding on work animal density supports the density-dependent hypothesis. The contribution of both climatic and irrigation factors has significantly declined in recent years; while agro-climatic and irrigation factors had played a major role in shaping work animal density prior to the mid-'seventies, it is technological, economic and institutional factors that played major roles in more recent decades.

The role of cows as a producer of male animals for work has undergone change over time, in the context of declining work animal requirements. It was observed that the density of work animals was the dominant determining factor of the density of breeding cows; but the influence of this consideration has been declining over time; the influence of the other (unexplained) factors has been gaining importance in recent years, implying thereby that the both price and non-price factors, including technological factors, have played a significant role in determining the density of breeding cows.

In short, the demand for milk and the commercialization of milk production could have been important factors, which played major roles in influencing the milch animal population, a proposition we examine in chapter 6. It would be necessary however to examine first the extent of the observed trends in deciding the work and milch animal population as reflected in the distribution of bovine holdings across size classes of landholdings. If there is reduction in the work animal population, is it happening among all size categories? The same issue has to be examined in the context of milch animals too. The answers to these questions have implications for the future development of the livestock sector in the state. Against this backdrop, the ensuing chapter examines changes in the distribution of work and milch animal stocks in the Tamil Nadu economy.

Notes

1. The survival rates of animals are estimated based on the assumption that the sex ratio at birth is 1:1. Accordingly, the total birth at the census year is assumed to be equal to the number of animals in milk or double the size of the young male or females of the age group 0-1; and, the number that is the maximum is treated as the animals born in a year. Keeping this as the base year stock, the population for the inter-census years is extrapolated and based on that the survival rate is calculated. For details, refer Nair (1981) and Vaidyanathan (1988) .
2. The trends in work animal population and its density in Tamil Nadu is given in Appendix Table 4.1.
3. See Appendix Table 4.2, for details of land use pattern in Tamil Nadu.
4. Trends in irrigation pattern by sources in Tamil Nadu are given in Appendix Table 4.3.
5. For details on trends in average size of operational landholdings in Tamil Nadu, see Appendix Table 4.4.

6. Trends in animal, tractor and power operated implements in Tamil Nadu is given in Appendix Table 4.5.
7. For details of cropping pattern changes in Tamil Nadu, see Appendix Table 4.6.
8. Though both the monsoon periods, South-West and North-East, are important sources of rainfall in Tamil Nadu, the monsoon just after the hot summer assumes importance as far as cultivation is concerned. It may be seen that these two monsoons together accounted for more than 82 per cent of the total rainfall in the state. (See Appendix Table 4.7).
9. According to the FMS conducted in Coimbatore, the average employment of bullock pair days per hectare varies significantly across crops in both irrigated and rain fed situations. In the case of irrigated crops, the maximum number of bullock pair days (23 days) was employed for paddy; for all the other selected crops it was less than 16 days. For certain commercial crops like cotton and tobacco and oil seeds like gingelly, the animal input was less than 10 bullock pair days. The animal labour input was observed to be much higher in the case of rain-fed crops than of irrigated crop. Almost 50 per cent less of animal labour was used for rain-fed crops than for irrigated ones.
10. The growth of mechanization of irrigation contributed significantly to the increase in the availability of draught power in agriculture. With the rapid increase in the number of pumpsets and oil engines, mechanical draught power per hectare of gross cropped area has increased significantly. (See Appendix Table 4.8).
11. Land preparation activities include, ploughing, levelling, bedding and manuring.
12. Planting activities include sowing/planting of seeds or planting of cuttings and growing and transplanting nurseries.
13. Plant protection activities include control of weeds, application of manures, irrigation and application of pesticides.
14. Harvesting includes separation of the output from the crop either by cutting, plucking or stripping.
15. Post-harvest activities include threshing, separation of shells, crushing and transportation.
16. The list of implements grouped by power used for various cultivation activities is given in Appendix Table 4.9.

17 The cropping pattern may be seen as 'Food vs Non-food crops', from the view point of 'use'; as commercial vs non-commercial, from the view of 'market value'; as 'short vs long duration crops', from crop life point of view; as 'irrigated vs unirrigated/ rain fed' from the angle of 'irrigation type' adopted; etc.,. From the point of animal labour input, the cropping pattern could be examined as 'High vs low/nil animal labour input use crops'. The cropping pattern in Tamil Nadu has been changing towards crops that requires low or nil animal power from crops that require high or medium animal power. The share of the area of crops that require 'nil' DAP has been showing a steady increase throughout the reference period, from 3.1 per cent by mid' fifties to 12 per cent by 2000-01 (See Appendix Table 4.6).

18. There has taken place a significant decline in the use of animal operated agricultural implements in Tamil Nadu, particularly from the mid' sixties and the decline was sharp from the' Eighties. The number of tractors and power operated implements also showed significant increase in recent years. Thus, the trends in the use of agricultural implements provides a clear indication that significant shifts are taking place in the cultivation pattern (a shift from the use of animal -operated implements to tractor and power operated implements, animal, and human- power-based cultivation, to tractor, and electrical- power- based cultivation pattern) in the state and that the shift has been sharp from the late' Seventies onwards (See Appendix Table 4.5).

19. The number of tractors, in terms of absolute numbers and number per GCA, showed a steady increase since independence in Tamil Nadu. However, their availability is still very low, about 17 tractors per thousand hectares by the late'nineties. In 1997, tractors contributed to only about 29 per cent of the total farm power available in the state. See Appendix Table 4.10.

20. According to the Agricultural Census data for the past three decades there were significant changes in the number and area of land holdings, the average size of land and the distribution of land across size classes of farms in Tamilnadu. The number of holdings which was about 53 lakh during the early 'seventies, increased to 72 lakh and further to 80 lakhs by the'nineties (see Appendix Table 4.4). In contrast to the trend in the number of holdings, the area of land has shown a declining trend. In this situation where the number of holdings increases and the area of holdings remains unchanged or declines, the average size of land

holdings declines. Accordingly, the average size of holdings, which were 1.45 hectare during early 'seventies, declined to 1.07 hectare by early 'eighties and then to 0.9 hectare by the mid 'nineties. The estimates based on the input surveys for the period 1976-77 to 1986-87 also indicate steady decline in the average size of operated landholdings and the increase in the share of marginal and smallholdings. (See Appendix Table 4.11).

21. The shift in energy use pattern for various farm activities is evident from the latest 59th round of NSS. (See Appendix Table 4.12).

22. According to the 1956 Livestock Census, the total stock of milch animals in Tamil Nadu was about 3.71 million which increased to 4.08 million by the mid-'sixties. In subsequent years, while showed an increasing trend, a marginal decline is observed in the 'nineties. The present position (1997) is almost a 28 per cent increase in the milch animal stock over that of the early 'sixties. (See Appendix Table 4.13).

23. Milch animals provide milk and calves, but the relative importance of these outputs is species-biased. Buffaloes are considered milk-producing animals and as such they are reared primarily for production of milk. On the contrary, cattle are kept primarily for producing male calves and milk out put has been considered as secondary.

24. Breeding cows refer to the adult female cattle which are used for reproductive purposes.

25. Caving rate refers to the number of caves born per breeding cow. It is calculated by doubling the number of males or female stock which ever is higher, belonging to less than 1 year and divide it by number of breeding cows.

APPENDIX

Appendix Table 4.1
Trends in Work Animal Population, its Composition and Density: Tamil Nadu, 1956-1997

Particulars		*1956*	*1961*	*1966*	*1974*	*1977*	*1982*	*1989*	*1994*	*1997*
Size of Work Animal Population										
Total Work Animals (in million Nos.)		5.24	5.88	5.75	5.38	5.36	4.39	3.71	2.99	2.18
Total Animal Power (in lakh HP)		20.96	23.50	23.00	21.51	21.45	17.54	14.85	11.94	8.72
Annual growth rate (%)		-	2.43	0.43	0.81	0.10	3.64	2.21	3.89	8.97
Share to the total Bovines (%)		44.64	43.78	42.33	40.06	38.63	32.30	29.76	24.82	18.51
Share to the total adult Bovine(%)		58.17	56.07	54.73	52.80	51.25	46.39	43.70	37.95	29.71
Density of Work Animal Population										
Animals per Gross Cropped Area		0.76	0.81	0.80	0.75	0.71	0.66	0.56	0.44	0.33
Composition of Work Animal Population (%)										
By Sex	Male	84.85	87.25	87.44	87.69	87.49	85.75	84.87	88.80	N.A
	Female	15.15	12.75	12.56	12.31	12.51	14.25	15.13	11.20	N.A
	Total	100	100	100	100	100	100	100	100	N.A
By Species	Cattle	93.65	92.02	92.24	92.69	92.95	94.17	95.02	94.22	93.60
	Buffalo	6.35	7.98	7.76	7.31	7.05	5.83	4.98	5.78	6.40
	Total	100	100	100	100	100	100	100	100	100

Contd...

Particulars		*1956*	*1961*	*1966*	*1974*	*1977*	*1982*	*1989*	*1994*	*1997*
By Function	Work Only	84.85	75.32	75.43	79.42	78.87	77.46	81.26	85.24	N.A
	Work +Breeding	0.00	11.93	12.00	8.27	8.61	8.29	3.61	3.57	N.A
	Work+Milk	15.15	12.75	12.56	12.31	12.51	14.25	15.13	11.20	N.A.
	Total	100	100	100	100	100	100	100	100	N.A
Composition of Farm Power (%)										
By Source	Animal Power	87.88	76.77	63.04	31.14	27.99	22.13	19.06	15.11	9.14
	Mechanical Power	12.12	23.23	36.76	68.86	72.01	77.87	80.94	84.89	90.86
	Total Farm Power	100	100	100	100	100	100	100	100	100

Note: Total farm power includes the energy supplied by mechanical and electrical equipments and animals. It is assumed that tractors supply about 25 horse power (HP), pumpsets and oil engines about 5 HP each and work animals about 0.4 HP each per day.

N.A = Not Available.

Source: 1. Livestock Census, Tamil Nadu, (various issues)

2. Season and Crop Reports of Tamilnadu, Chennai, (various issues).

Appendix Table 4.2
Trends in Land Use Pattern: Tamil Nadu, 1956-1997

Year	Forest	Land not available for cultivation	Total Cultivable Waste	Total Current Fallow	Net Sown Area	Gross Cropped Area	Total Occupied Area	Total Arable Area	Total Reported Area
Area of Land in hectares									
1956	1788432	2251862	1410601	1674477	5833141	6938563	7507618	8918219	12958512
1961	1871908	2224334	1323596	1621095	5970552	7211076	7591648	8915243	13011485
1966	1902819	2225836	1293049	1575581	6016283	7181986	7591864	8884913	13013567
1974	1994066	2310196	904863	1786697	6020192	7329239	7806889	8711752	13016014
1977	1998620	2289450	750819	1863047	6097049	7383492	7960095	8710914	12998985
1982	2025705	2348215	704917	2470088	5453055	6469784	7923142	8628059	13001979
1989	2137641	2348940	568845	2302425	5662380	6667238	7964805	8533651	13020231
1994	2146407	2390231	657610	1983552	5834676	7083890	7818228	8475838	13012476
1997	2140300	2432700	698342	2145427	5580786	6795318	7818228	8424555	12997555
Percentage Share to the Total Reported Area									
1956	13.80	17.38	10.89	12.92	45.01	53.54	57.94	68.82	100.00
1961	14.39	17.10	10.17	12.46	45.89	55.42	58.35	68.52	100.00
1966	14.62	17.10	9.94	12.11	46.23	55.19	58.34	68.27	100.00
1974	15.32	17.75	6.95	13.73	46.25	56.31	59.98	66.93	100.00
1977	15.38	17.61	5.78	14.33	46.90	56.80	61.24	67.01	100.00
1982	15.58	18.06	5.42	19.00	41.94	49.76	60.94	66.36	100.00
1989	16.42	18.04	4.37	17.68	43.49	51.21	61.17	65.54	100.00
1994	16.49	18.37	5.05	15.24	44.84	54.44	60.08	65.14	100.00
1997	16.47	18.72	5.37	16.51	42.94	52.28	60.15	64.82	100.00

Source: Season and Crop Reports, (various years).

Appendix Table 4.3
Trends in Irrigation Pattern by Sources: Tamil Nadu, 1956-1997

	Canals	*Tanks*	*Wells*	*Other Sources*	*Total (Net Irrigated Area -NIA)*	*Gross Irrigated Area (GIA)*	*Irrigation Intensity (GIA/ NIA)*
Area in Hectares							
1956	770608	869482	457515	57463	2155068	2957606	1.37
1961	861707	875705	554156	39967	2331535	3052535	1.31
1966	850542	920164	632674	41508	2444888	3236227	1.32
1974	918337	824505	914708	32126	2689676	3459946	1.29
1977	837623	819916	884179	35067	2576784	3366741	1.31
1982	851482	615083	1023563	21311	2511439	3150387	1.25
1989	815034	565133	1209310	15976	2605453	2954265	1.13
1994	836597	657086	1290082	16444	2800209	3505574	1.25
1997	837908	675495	1403756	18740	2944740	3518943	1.19
Percentage Distribution							
1956	35.76	40.35	21.23	2.67	100	–	–
1961	36.96	37.56	23.77	1.71	100	–	–
1966	34.79	37.64	25.88	1.69	100	–	–
1974	34.14	30.65	34.01	1.19	100	–	–
1977	32.51	31.82	34.31	1.36	100	–	–
1982	33.90	24.49	40.76	0.85	100	–	–
1989	31.28	21.69	46.41	0.61	100	–	–
1994	29.88	23.47	46.07	0.59	100	–	–
1997	28.45	22.94	47.04	0.64	100	–	–
Annual Percentage Change							
1956-1961	2.36	0.14	4.22	6.09	1.64	0.64	-0.92
1961-1966	0.26	1.02	2.83	0.77	0.97	1.20	0.22
1966-1974	1.00	1.30	5.57	2.83	1.25	0.86	-0.35
1974-1977	2.93	0.19	1.11	3.05	1.40	-0.90	0.52
1977-1982	0.33	5.00	3.15	7.85	0.51	-1.29	-0.80
1982-1989	0.61	1.16	2.59	3.58	0.53	-0.89	1.37
1989-1994	0.53	3.25	1.34	0.59	1.49	3.73	2.08
1994-1997	0.05	0.93	2.84	4.65	1.72	0.13	-1.60

Source: Season and Crop Report, (various years).

Appendix Table 4.4
Trends in Number, Area and Average Size of Operational Holdings in Tamil Nadu

Particulars	*Year*	*Marginal*	*Small*	*Semi-Medium*	*Medium*	*Large*	*Total*
Number of Holdings (in '000)	1970-71	3125	1109	696	325	59	5314
	1976-77	3951	1126	683	306	46	6112
	1979-80	5015	1209	658	269	40	7191
	1985-86	5498	1260	649	261	39	7707
	1990-91	5848	1274	618	228	31	7999
	1995-96	5951	1234	601	200	26	8012
Area of Holdings (in '000 hect.)	1970-71	1321	1578	1914	1893	1003	7709
	1976-77	1607	1587	1876	1763	795	7628
	1979-80	1907	1710	1822	1555	714	7708
	1985-86	2018	1772	1778	1508	720	7796
	1990-91	2118	1795	1687	1301	574	7475
	1995-96	2210	1721	1623	1135	614	7303
Average Size of Holdings (in hect.)	1970-71	0.42	1.42	2.75	5.82	17.00	1.45
	1976-77	0.41	1.41	2.75	5.77	17.36	1.25
	1979-80	0.38	1.41	2.77	5.78	17.85	1.07
	1985-86	0.37	1.41	2.74	5.78	18.46	1.01
	1990-91	0.36	1.41	2.73	5.71	18.52	0.93
	1995-96	0.37	1.39	2.70	5.68	23.62	0.91
Distribution of Number of Holdings	1970-71	58.81	20.87	13.09	6.12	1.11	100.00
	1976-77	64.65	18.42	11.18	5.00	0.75	100.00
	1979-80	69.74	16.81	9.15	3.74	0.56	100.00
	1985-86	71.34	16.35	8.42	3.39	0.51	100.00
	1990-91	73.11	15.93	7.73	2.85	0.39	100.00
	1995-96	74.28	15.40	7.50	2.50	0.32	100.00
Distribution of Area of Holdings	1970-71	17.14	20.47	24.83	24.55	13.01	100.00
	1976-77	21.07	20.80	24.59	23.11	10.43	100.00
	1979-80	24.74	22.18	23.64	20.17	9.26	100.00
	1985-86	25.89	22.73	22.81	19.34	9.24	100.00
	+1990-91	28.33	24.01	22.57	17.40	7.68	100.00
	1995-96	30.26	23.57	22.22	15.54	8.41	100.00

Note: Marginal = below 1.0 hect.;
Small = 1.0 - 2.0 hect.;
Semi-medium = 2.0 -4.0 hect.;
Medium = 4.0 - 10.0 hect.; and
Large = 10.0 hect. and above.

Source: Agricultural Census (various years).

Appendix Table 4.5
Trends in Animal, Tractor and Power Operated Implements: Tamil Nadu, 1956-1997

	Animal Operated Implements							
	Ploughs		*Carts*		*Ghanis*		*Sugarcane Crushers*	
Year	*Numbers*	*Annual % Change*	*Numbers*	*Annual % Change*	*Numbers*	*Annual % Change*	*Numbers*	*Annual % Change*
1956	2928071	-	639805	-	18075	-	15370	-
1961	3429902	3.43	664544	0.77	13293	5.29	16325	1.24
1966	3771672	1.99	627768	1.11	26661	20.11	14740	1.94
1974	3677359	0.31	594873	0.65	4791	10.25	11350	2.87
1977	3639832	0.34	630527	2.00	4719	0.50	10047	3.83
1982	3847386	1.14	579631	1.61	2784	8.20	11040	1.98
1989	2827884	3.79	477654	2.51	2471	1.61	3925	9.21
1994	2389978	3.10	441162	1.53	1718	6.09	6759	14.44
1997	1400255	-13.81	361994	-5.98	1794	1.47	8382	8.00
Tractor and Power Operated Implements								
Year	*Mould Board Plough*		*Power Tillers*		*Threshers*		*Trailers*	
1974	1921	-	3805	-	1084	-	3244	-
1977	3309	24.08	7480	32.19	1178	2.89	4651	14.46
1982	3542	1.41	8045	1.51	1283	1.78	7118	10.61
1989	5025	5.98	6802	2.21	1042	2.68	13908	13.63
1994	8994	15.80	10712	11.50	1943	17.29	27403	19.41
1997	19379	38.49	21022	32.08	21325	332.50	27458	0.07

Source: Livestock Census (various years).

Appendix Table 4.6
Trends in Cropping Pattern by Draught Power Requirements in Tamil Nadu

	Draught Power Requirements				
Period	*High*	*Medium*	*Low*	*Nil*	*Total*
Area of Crops (in hectares)					
1957-58	2285083	3639948	733176	212776	6870982
1960-61	2456820	3756685	769827	227458	7210791
1965-66	2605695	3678003	648604	249683	7181986
1970-71	2614493	3855518	644140	281485	7395636
1975-76	2361763	3766368	571936	307273	7007340
1980-81	2571250	3493409	621405	345991	7032054
1985-86	2242906	3520347	631225	410639	6805118
1990-91	1978948	3597513	737246	496641	6810348
1995-96	2117604	3104855	753272	607523	6583254
2000-01	2080010	2807222	694406	756471	6338109
Percentage Distribution					
1957-58	33.26	52.98	10.67	3.10	100.00
1960-61	34.07	52.10	10.68	3.15	100.00
1965-66	36.28	51.21	9.03	3.48	100.00
1970-71	35.35	52.13	8.71	3.81	100.00
1975-76	33.70	53.75	8.16	4.39	100.00
1980-81	36.56	49.68	8.84	4.92	100.00
1985-86	32.96	51.73	9.28	6.03	100.00
1990-91	29.06	52.82	10.83	7.29	100.00
1995-96	32.17	47.16	11.44	9.23	100.00
2000-01	32.81	44.29	10.96	11.94	100.00
Average Annual Percentage Change					
1957-58 to 60-61	2.51	1.07	1.67	2.30	1.65
1960-61 to 65-66	1.21	-0.42	-3.15	1.95	-0.08
1965-66 to 70-71	0.07	0.97	-0.14	2.55	0.59
1970-71 to 75-76	-1.93	-0.46	-2.24	1.83	-1.05
1975-76 to 80-81	1.77	-1.45	1.73	2.52	0.07
1980-81 to 85-86	-2.55	0.15	0.32	3.74	-0.65
1985-86 to 90-91	-2.35	0.44	3.36	4.19	0.02
1990-91 to 95-96	1.40	-2.74	0.43	4.47	-0.67
1995-96 to 2001	-0.38	-1.93	-1.57	4.87	-0.73

Source: Season and Crop Reports, Tamil Nadu, (various years).

Appendix Table 4.7
Rainfall Pattern by Monsoon Periods in Tamil Nadu, 2000-01

	Rainfall in m.m		
Season	*Normal*	*Actual*	*Percentage Contribution*
South-West Monsoon	322.8	314.5	40.05
North-East Monsoon	470.3	335.6	42.74
Winter	47.3	16.8	2.14
Hot-Weather Period	138.9	118.4	15.07
Total	979.3	785.3	100.00

Source: Season and Crop Report of Tamil Nadu (2002).

Appendix Table 4.8
Trends in Pumpsets and Oil Engines in Tamil Nadu (1956-1997)

Particulars	*1956*	*1961*	*1966*	*1974*	*1977*	*1982*	*1989*	*1994*	*1997*
Number of Pumpsets & Oil Engines (in 000)	53.73	60.80	251.34	915.62	821.51	1150.79	1128.10	1146.61	1185.75
Share of Electrical Power to the Total Farm Power	11.26	11.35	34.45	66.28	63.53	72.58	72.50	72.56	62.15
Number of Pumpsets per 1000 hect. of GCA	8	8	35	125	111	178	169	162	181

Source: The same as for Appendix Table 4.1.

Appendix Table 4.9
Agricultural Implements Grouped by Source of Power Used and by Cultivation Operations

Operations	*Animal & Human Operated Implements*	*Tractor & Power Operated Implements*
Land Preparation	Plough, Harrows, Pudallers, Levellers	Tractors, Disc Ploughs, Harrows, Tillers, Levellers
Sowing & Planting	Seed drillers	Seed drillers, Seed planters,
Plant Protection	Persian wheels, Sprayers and dusters	Pumpsets, Oil engines, Sprayers and dusters
Harvesting	Chaff cutters	Chaff cutters
Post Harvesting	Maize shellers, Animal carts, Ghanis, Crushers	Maize shellers, Threshers, Tractors, Ghanis and Crushers

Appendix Table 4.10
Trends in Tractors in Tamil Nadu, 1956-1997

Particulars	*1956*	*1961*	*1966*	*1974*	*1977*	*1982*	*1989*	*1994*	*1997*
Number of Tractors	822	934	3661	7107	8548	16780	26296	38949	109734
Annual Growth Rate (%)	-	2.73	58.39	11.77	6.76	19.26	8.10	9.62	60.58
Share of Tractor Power (%)	0.86	0.87	2.51	2.57	3.31	5.29	8.45	12.32	28.74
No. per 1000 hect of GCA	#	#	#	1	1	3	4	6	17

Note: # denotes less than one tractor per 1000 hectares.
Source: The same as for Table 4.1 and Season and Crop Report of Tamil Nadu (various years).

Appendix Table 4.11
Estimated Households and Operated Area in Tamil Nadu, 1976-77 to 1986-87

Particulars	*1976-77*	*1981-82*	*1986-87*
Estimated No of households	6100536	6494342	6997903
Estimated Operated Area (in hect.)	7568848	7775937	7479312
Average Area per Household (in hect.)	1.24	1.20	1.07
Share of Marginal and Small Households (%)	83.09	83.51	86.88

Source: Input Surveys (various years).

Appendix Table 4.12

Percentage Distribution of Farmer Households by Primary Sources of Energy for Different Farm Activities in Tamil Nadu, 2003

Activity	*Primary Sources of Energy*				
	Electricity	*Diesel/ Petrol / Kerosene*	*Animal Power*	*Others*	*Total*
Ploughing	1.7	67.9	30.4		100
Irrigation	72.4	27.3	0.3		100
Harvesting	8.3	78.6	13.1		100
Threshing	7.0	79.4	13.6		100
Cane Crushing	79.6	17.3	3.1		100
Transport	0.7	64.4	34.8	0.1	100

Source: GOI: (2005).

Appendix Table 4.13
Trends in Milch Animal Population in Tamil Nadu, 1956-1997

Particulars		*1956*	*1961*	*1966*	*1974*	*1977*	*1982*	*1989*	*1994*	*1997*
Total Milch Stock (in million)		3.71	3.86	4.08	4.23	4.53	5.21	4.77	4.64	4.75
Share of Milch Bovine to the Total Adult Females		82.38	78.21	8.72	82.29	83.35	100.00	95.73	94.42	96.65
Share of Milch Bovine to the Total Bovines		31.61	28.80	30.05	31.52	32.63	38.36	38.27	38.59	40.32
Density (Milch Animals/GCA)	Cattle	0.16	0.15	0.39	0.40	0.40	0.53	0.50	0.47	0.52
	Buffalo	0.06	0.06	0.17	0.19	0.20	0.26	0.26	0.21	0.21
	Bovine	0.22	0.21	0.56	0.59	0.60	0.79	0.75	0.68	0.72

Source: Livestock Census (various years).
Season and Crop Report of Tamil Nadu (various years).

5

CHANGES IN THE DISTRIBUTION OF BOVINE HOLDINGS IN TAMIL NADU

Introduction

Bovines are one of the major assets, the distribution of which is less skewed than the distribution of land. For a farmer, livestock is the major productive asset, next only to land. Moreover, bovine stock holdings are highly inter-linked with agricultural holdings. Since the major feed inputs for the bovines are obtained from land and the major outputs from bovines such as animal power, dung etc., are used for agricultural purposes, the relationship between bovine holdings and land holdings is strong and well-established Such inter-relationship may get altered, however, due to changes in the land holding pattern itself. In fact, compositional changes in bovines are significantly influenced by changes in the distribution of land.

Against this background, it is worthwhile to examine the changes in the distribution of bovines and its composition across size classes of land holdings, over time. The specific questions addressed here are: the pattern of distribution of bovines and their densities, the variations in the distribution of bovines by sex, age, species and function across land holding classes, the changes in the distribution of bovines over time and the factors that shaped the trends in the distribution of bovines, in Tamil Nadu.

For our analysis, the data provided by the National Sample Survey and the Agricultural Census (Input Survey) is extensively relied upon. However, to establish and support certain arguments, the findings of other primary studies and their data are cited at relevant places.

Changes in the Distribution of Bovines

In rural Tamil Nadu, the number of operational households showed an increasing trend; while the total operated area remained almost unchanged during the period between 1971 and 1991. The total number of holdings which had been 5.82 million in 1971, increased to 7.04 million by 1981 and further to 9.02 million by 1991. However, the total operated area which was about 4.48 million hectares in 1971; but it marginally declined to 3.91 million hectares by 1981 marginally increased to 4.11 million hectares by 1991. The immediate effect of the alarming increase in the number of land holdings is getting reflected in the decline in the average size of land holdings. The average size of land operated declined from 0.77 hectares to 0.46 hectares in 1991 (Table 5.1).

As far as the bovine population is concerned, there was a steady decline between the early 'seventies and the early 'nineties. The density of bovines (number of bovines per 100 hectares of operated area) showed a marginal increase from 213 to 228 between 1971 and 1981 and thereafter, recorded a decline to 189 by 1991. It is interesting to note that while the distribution of land is highly skewed in nature, it is relatively less skewed in the case of bovines, across the different size classes of operational holdings. In 1991, the landless, and the small and marginal holdings (94% of total holdings) accounted only for about 55% of the total area but about 85% of bovines; the semi-medium and medium holdings (5% of the total holdings) accounted for 38 % of the total area, but only about 15% of bovines; and the large holdings (less than 1% of the total holdings) accounted for 6 per cent of the total area but only 1 per cent of bovines. (see Table 5.2).

Table 5.1
Trends in the Distribution of Landholdings: Tamil Nadu, 1971-1991

Particulars	Year	Size classes of Landholdings						
		Landless	*Marginal*	*Small*	*Semi-medium*	*Medium*	*Large*	*All Sizes*
		0.00	0.00 - 1.00	1.01 – 2.00	2.01 - 4.00	4.01 - 10.00	> 10.02	
Number of Households (in '00)	1971	24451	20270	7258	4469	1643	196	58287
	1981	26228	31291	7668	3633	1472	120	70412
	1991	33062	44016	7975	3802	1148	171	90174
Total Area Operated (in '00 hect.)	1971	-	9821	10261	12287	9591	2820	44780
	1981	-	8669	10795	9781	8004	1890	39139
	1991	-	11824	11165	9974	5857	2328	41148
Average Size of Holding (in hect.)	1971	-	0.48	1.41	2.75	5.84	14.39	0.77
	1981	-	0.28	1.41	2.69	5.44	15.79	0.56
	1991	-	0.27	1.40	2.62	5.10	13.61	0.46

Source: GOI: (1982, 1988 and 1997d).

Table 5.2
Distribution of Bovines Across Size Classes of Landholdings in Tamil Nadu (1991)

Size class of Landholdings	*% Distribution of*		*Number of Bovines per*	
	Households	*Bovines*	*100 hect of Operated area*	*100 households*
Landless	36.66	0.50	-	1.16
Marginal	48.81	62.83	412.18	110.73
Small	8.84	21.69	150.71	211.00
Semi-medium	4.22	9.75	75.86	199.00
Medium	1.27	4.59	60.76	310.00
Large	0.19	0.65	21.52	293.00
All Sizes	100	100	188.53	86.03

Source: GoI: (1998a).

It is observed that the number of bovines per unit area (density) declines with the increase in size-class of holdings and the bovines per household also increase with the increase in size class of landholding classes. These relationships indicate that the resource base, i.e., land, largely determines the bovine holdings in a household. The argument that households with higher land base could maintain more bovine stock is supported by the distribution of the density of animals per holding. The number of bovines per household of the marginal holdings was only 1.96, and the corresponding figure for the large landholding class was 9.41. The number of bovines per unit of operated area, which declines with increase in the size class of landholdings, indicate that the pressure of bovines on land is more at the small and marginal holdings and that it declines with increase in the size class of landholdings. It is also observed that the dependency level of households on bovine holdings was much higher at the small and the marginal holdings and that it declines with the increase in size class of landholdings.

Over time, the shares of total bovines with the small and marginal holdings have increased and those of the medium and the large holdings have declined. The number of bovines per household and per acre were observed to have decreased in each size class of holdings, but the decline during the 'eighties was at a higher rate than during the 'seventies (see Table 5.3).

Table 5.3
Trends in Bovine Densities: Tamil Nadu, 1971-1991

Size class of Landholdings	*Bovines per 100 hect. of Op. Area*			*Bovines per 100 households*		
	1971	1981	1991	1971	1981	1991
Landless	-	-	-	24.81	4.89	1.16
Marginal	352.44	471.25	412.18	170.76	130.56	110.73
Small	212.73	188.24	150.71	300.75	265	211
Semi-medium	155.84	164.21	75.86	428.46	442.07	199
Medium	119.86	112.94	60.76	699.66	614.27	310
Large	90.31	79.67	21.52	1299.29	1258.18	293
All Sizes	213.71	227.56	188.53	164.18	126.49	86.03

Source: GOI: (1982, 1990 and 1997d).

The data based on the input survey (Agricultural Census) on the distribution of bovines across landholdings also did support these findings on the trends in the distribution of animals. It is observed that the proportions of total bovines with the small and the marginal holdings increased over time and those of the medium and large holdings declined (Table 5.4). During the year 1976-77, the marginal and small holding together accounted for 59 per cent of the total number of bovines, whereas, in 1986-87, the corresponding figure was 74 per cent.

Table 5.4
Trends in the Distribution of Bovine Population Based on Input Surveys: Tamil Nadu, 1976-77 to 1991-92

Size Class of holdings	*Distribution of Bovines (in %)*		
	1976-77	*1981-82*	*1986-87*
Below 1.00	33.47	43.74	51.35
1.00 - 1.99	25.88	24.88	22.25
2.00 - 3.99	24.39	24.88	15.94
4.00 - 9.99	13.70	9.81	8.49
10.00 & above	2.54	2.15	1.96
All size classes	100.00	100.00	100.00

Source: Input Survey, (various years).

As the ownership of animals is species-, and sex-based, which in turn is shaped by their use pattern and requirement, it is necessary to examine the compositional change in the distribution of bovines and the trends in the individual categories of bovine.

Changes in the Composition of Bovines

In order to understand the changes in the composition of bovines, the share of cattle to the total bovines, the cattle-buffalo ratio and the share of male stock to the total stock across size classes of land holdings, are examined and presented in Table 5.5.

Though cattle is the dominant species among the bovines, its proportion to the total bovine population has been declining over time and the proportion declines with increase in the size classes of land holdings. The significant reduction in the proportions observed in the semi-medium, medium and large size classes of land holdings may be attributed to the reduction in the work animal stock. This fact is reflected in the trends in the shares of adult bovines to total bovines and the adult males to the total stock, and the ratios of adult males to adult females.

Thus the available evidence[1] supports the argument that there has taken place a structural change in the distribution of bovines across size classes of land holdings in Tamil Nadu. Against this understanding we now examine the distribution of work and milch animals in detail.

Distribution of Work Animals in Tamil Nadu

The distribution of work animal population across size classes of land holdings as given by various NSS rounds is given in Table 5.6. It shows that the dependence on draught animal power is higher among the marginal and smallholdings than among the other size classes[2]. The density of work animals per 100 hectares of operated area shows a negative association with increase in the size class of landholdings. The reason for the observed high density at the marginal and the smallholding classes could be the indivisibility nature of draught animals. Moreover, along with increase in farm size, the requirement of draught animals need not necessarily increase in proportion

Table 5.5
Trends in the Composition of Bovines Across Landholding Classes: Tamil Nadu, 1971-91

Particulars	*Year*	*Size classes of Landholdings*						
		Landless	*Marginal*	*Small*	*Semi-medium*	*Medium*	*Large*	*All Sizes*
		0.00	*0.00 - 1.00*	*1.01 – 2.00*	*2.01 - 4.00*	*4.01 - 10.00*	*> 10.02*	
Species Ratio Cattle/Buffalo	1971	3.26	5.39	5.32	5.56	5.79	4.29	5.22
	1981	0.67	3.20	4.20	4.69	6.40	11.63	3.79
	1991	1.47	4.53	4.55	1.43	2.52	0.31	3.70
Adult Male Bovine/Adult Female Bovine	1971	0.53	2.03	1.54	0.60	1.11	1.19	1.37
	1981	0.09	0.74	0.86	1.00	0.96	1.43	0.83
	1991	0.47	0.63	1.05	0.65	0.46	0.37	0.70
Adult Male Cattle/Adult Female Cattle	1971	0.60	2.50	1.94	0.65	1.31	1.46	1.66
	1981	0.28	1.07	1.17	1.35	1.20	1.49	1.16
	1991	0.00	0.77	1.43	1.17	0.70	0.70	0.93
Adult Male Buffalo/Adult Female Buffalo	1971	0.25	0.55	0.37	0.42	0.34	0.37	0.43
	1981	0.00	0.07	0.07	0.12	0.08	1.14	0.08
	1991	0.00	0.13	0.05	0.18	0.10	0.28	0.12

Source: The same as for Table 5.3.

Table 5.6
Distribution of Work Animal Population Across Size Classes of Landholdings: Tamil Nadu, 1971-1991

Particulars	*Year*	*Size classes of Landholdings*						
		Landless	*Marginal*	*Small*	*Semi-medium*	*Medium*	*Large*	*All Sizes*
		0.00	*0.00 - 1.00*	*1.01 – 2.00*	*2.01 - 4.00*	*4.01 - 10.00*	*> 10.02*	
Distribution of WAP(%)	1971	2.64	39.09	24.31	21.11	10.67	2.18	100.00
	1981	0.26	43.14	22.08	20.65	11.40	2.46	100.00
	1991	0.09	56.95	29.21	10.16	3.18	0.41	100.00
WAP per 100 hect. ofoperated area	1971		167.66	99.80	72.37	46.87	32.60	94.07
	1981		138.28	56.83	58.67	39.59	36.20	71.00
	1991		97.31	52.86	20.58	10.98	3.60	49.11
WAP per 100 households	1971	4.54	81.23	141.09	198.97	273.59	468.99	72.27
	1981	0.28	38.31	80.00	157.94	215.33	571.71	39.46
	1991	0.06	26.14	74.00	54.00	56.00	49.00	22.41

Source: The same as for Table 5.3.

since the area commandable per work animal will be more at the larger holdings at which level the requirement of farm power could also be met from other sources, in addition to animal power.

These findings are further supported and strengthened by an independent survey on animal draught power status in Tamil Nadu conducted by the Tamil Nadu Veterinary and Animal Sciences University, under the ICAR-sponsored ad hoc scheme during the year 1987-88. The earlier findings such as the dominance of cattle among the total draught animals, the limited use of females (cows) for draught purposes, the positive association between the number of work animals per holding and the size class of land holdings and the negative association between the number of work animals per acre and the size class of land holdings as discussed earlier were supported by the survey results (Table 5.7). Interestingly, the survey has provided some additional information on the use pattern of draught animals, the value of draught animals and the hiring practices across size classes of holdings, aspects that are important for our analysis.

The average value per animal is low at the smallholdings and high at the large holdings, indicating that high valued animals are maintained by large holdings. As a large proportion of households did not posses any work animals, the question of how they could meet their draught requirements was answered by the hiring out and exchange practices, which played a major role in this regard. The practice of hiring out and exchange of animals was adopted by all categories of farmers but it was more prevalent among small farmers. According to the survey results, the proportion of farms involved in hiring out of work animals was the highest in small farms (79.69 %), followed by medium farms (46.0 %); the lowest proportion was observed in large farms (35.33%). Similarly, the proportion of pairs of draught animals used for exchange was the highest in small farms (42.47%) and the lowest in large farms (23.85%). Owing to the crucial and seasonal nature of draught power requirement and the indivisibility of draught animals, even in cases in which the

Table 5.7

Some Aspects of Draught Animals Across Size Class of Farms: Tamil Nadu, 1987-88

Particulars	*Category*	*Small*		*Medium*		*Large*	
		In Nos.	*In %*	*In Nos.*	*In %*	*In Nos.*	*In %*
Composition of draught Animals	Cattle	499	79.08	545	83.59	675	75.93
	Buffaloe	44	6.97	36	5.52	87	9.78
	Cow	88	13.95	71	10.89	127	14.28
	Total	631	100.00	652	100.00	889	100.00
No of Animals in pairs	Bovine	315.50		326.00		444.50	
Average number of pair of own draught animals	Per holding	1.05		1.09		1.48	
	per acre	0.33		0.16		0.10	
Area commanded by pair of animals (acre)		3.03		6.25		10.00	
Average Number of Draught Animals		2.10		2.19		2.94	
Average Age per Animal		8.97		8.98		8.80	
Average Value per Animal (in 0.00 Rs.)		1321.32		1467.33		1540.38	
Percentage of farms involved in hired-out			79.67		46.00		35.33
Percentage of pairs used for exchange			42.47		37.73		23.85
Animal use Pattern	Cultivation	132.11	36.51	189.76	58.95	255.99	77.95
	Hired out	201.23	55.62	103.27	32.08	57.28	17.44
	Transport	2.87	0.79	3.32	1.04	1.96	0.60
	Exchange	25.60	7.08	25.52	7.93	13.20	4.01
	Total	361.81	100.00	321.87	100.00	328.43	100.00
No. of Days worked (days of 6 hours per pair)		60.30		53.64		54.74	

Source: ICAR Survey (undated)

farm size is small and the area commanded by the animals is low, farmers are constrained to keep own animals. However, as the total demand/requirement for draught power for own cultivation is lower than the availability, at the level of the small farms, the surplus draught power hours are used for exchange or hiring.

An analysis of the animal use pattern during a whole year across size classes of farms discloses that the use of animal for own cultivation is very low for small farms and is positively related with the size class of farms. While the proportion of the hours used for cultivation to the total hours of work has been higher for large (78.0%) and medium (59.0%) holdings, it is very low in small farms (36.51%). Interestingly, the small farms hire out 56.62 per cent of the total number of work hours. The extent of hiring out of animals declines with increase in the size class of farms. This could be due to the fact that draught requirements for own use are higher on large farms. The work hours of animals used for own cultivation are lower among small farms; it is the hiring out practice that keeps these animals employed. In consequence, small farmers keep their work animals in employment more efficiently than medium and large farmers.

It is thus evident that the increase in the number of holdings, particularly marginal holdings, has necessitated an increase in work animal stock and that there has happened a significant reduction in the work animal stock per reporting household among the medium and large size class of landholdings. This statement is supported by evidence from the trends in tractorisation across size classes of land holdings (Table 5.8).

Tractorisation is seen to have taken place only in the medium and large land holding classes, but energisation of irrigation in almost all the categories of land holdings. The declining trend in the number of ploughs per operated area and per 100 households in each size class indicated decline in the use of the plough (the animal-driven cultivating equipment) and the growing importance of mechanical equipment.

Table 5.8
Trends in the Distribution of Tractors, Ploughs and Pumpsets: Tamil Nadu, 1971-1991

Particulars	*Year*	*Landless*	*Marginal*	*Small*	*Semi-medium*	*Medium*	*Large*	*All Sizes*
		Size classes of Landholdings						
		0.00	*0.00 - 1.00*	*1.01 – 2.00*	*2.01 - 4.00*	*4.01 - 10.00*	*> 10.02*	
Distribution of Tractors	1971	0.00	0.00	0.00	7.62	59.04	33.33	100.00
	1981	0.00	0.00	0.00	6.79	47.27	45.94	100.00
	1991	0.00	0.00	1.74	14.12	65.29	18.84	100.00
Distribution of Ploughs	1971	2.15	38.14	26.12	19.70	11.70	2.19	100.00
	1981	3.44	39.01	26.15	18.54	11.44	1.42	100.00
	1991	0.80	43.87	29.68	16.91	7.14	1.61	100.00
Distribution of Pumps	1971	0.98	16.69	24.48	29.28	22.62	5.95	100.00
	1981	1.01	28.22	27.78	25.21	14.97	2.81	100.00
	1991	1.03	33.28	31.40	19.84	12.21	2.25	100.00
Tractors per100 hect. of operated area	1971	-	0.00	0.00	0.02	0.17	0.32	0.06
	1981	-	0.00	0.00	0.03	0.25	1.05	0.11
	1991	-	0.00	0.04	0.39	3.06	2.22	0.67
Ploughs per 100 hect. of operated area	1971	-	168.24	110.25	69.45	52.84	33.62	96.73
	1981	-	167.13	89.97	70.39	53.08	27.92	94.89
	1991	-	94.41	67.65	43.14	31.00	17.59	61.84
Pumps per 100 hect. of operated area	1971	-	5.92	8.31	8.30	8.22	7.35	7.78
	1981	-	24.81	19.61	19.65	14.26	11.33	19.47
	1991	-	36.06	36.04	25.49	26.72	12.38	31.14

Contd...

		Size classes of Landholdings						
Particulars	*Year*	*Landless*	*Marginal*	*Small*	*Semi-medium*	*Medium*	*Large*	*All Sizes*
		0.00	*0.00 - 1.00*	*1.01 – 2.00*	*2.01 - 4.00*	*4.01 - 10.00*	*> 10.02*	
Tractors per 100 households	1971	0.00	0.00	0.00	0.05	0.97	4.59	0.05
	1981	0.00	0.00	0.00	0.08	1.39	16.57	0.06
	1991	0.00	0.00	0.06	1.02	15.62	30.26	0.30
Ploughs per 100 households	1971	3.81	81.52	155.87	190.96	308.46	483.66	74.32
	1981	4.86	46.30	126.65	189.50	288.70	440.94	52.74
	1991	0.61	25.36	94.71	113.16	158.16	239.47	28.22
Pumps per 100 households	1971	0.14	2.87	11.75	22.83	47.96	105.81	5.98
	1981	0.29	6.87	27.61	52.89	77.56	178.98	10.83
	1991	0.40	9.69	50.45	66.86	136.31	168.60	14.21

Source: The same as for Table 5.3.

The Input Surveys also provide information on the distribution of tractors and the ownership pattern (individually or jointly) of tractors across landholding classes (Table 5.9). The total number of tractors used for agricultural purposes have shown a steady and significant increase. The increasing trends in tractorisation are observed in all the size classes of landholdings. The distribution of tractors, which was highly skewed in favour of large farms during the mid-'sixties, had undergone significant change by the mid-'eighties. In 1976-77, the proportion of tractors owned by marginal farms was only 2.74 per cent; the corresponding figure was 36.89 per cent in 1986-87. During the early 'seventies, the proportion of tractors owned by semi-medium, medium and large size class of landholdings was about 75 per cent; the proportion declined, however, to about 50 per cent by the mid-'eighties indicating thereby that significant diffusion of tractorisation took place in the state during the 'eighties.

Table 5.9
Trends in the Distribution of Tractors and Ownership Pattern Across Size Classes of Landholdings: Tamil Nadu, 1976-77 to 1986-87

Size class of Holdings	*Number of Tractors*					
	Individually Owned		*Jointly Owned*		*Total*	
	1976-77	*1986-87*	*1976-77*	*1986-87*	*1976-77*	*1986-87*
Below 1.00	263	24669	0	880	263	25549
1.00 - 1.99	2045	8091	197	0	2242	8091
2.00 - 3.99	892	14168	307	370	1199	14538
4.00 - 9.99	3027	13295	822	436	3849	13731
10.00 & above	1273	6967	785	383	2058	7350
All size classes	7500	67190	2111	2069	9611	69259
	Number of Tractors 1000 Households					
	Individually Owned		*Jointly Owned*		*Total*	
	1976-77	*1986-87*	*1976-77*	*1986-87*	*1976-77*	*1986-87*
Below 1.00	0.07	5.05	0.00	0.18	0.07	5.23
1.00 - 1.99	1.82	6.78	0.18	0.00	1.99	6.78
2.00 - 3.99	1.31	22.79	0.45	0.60	1.76	23.39
4.00 - 9.99	9.94	51.54	2.70	1.69	12.64	53.23
10.00 & above	28.22	179.40	17.40	9.86	45.62	189.27
All size classes	1.23	9.60	0.35	0.30	1.58	9.9

Source: Input Survey, (various years).

This fact becomes further evident when we examine the trend in the number of tractors per 1000 households. The trend shows an upward swing in all the size classes of landholdings. An increasing preference for individual ownership of tractors is also evinced in all the size groups of land holdings. In fact, the joint ownership of tractors, which had been widely prevalent in the mid-'sixties, declined drastically by the mid-'eighties. Since tractors would be better utilised or are more needed in the larger landholdings, the number of tractors per household is positively associated with the size class of landholdings. This is a fact shown by the input surveys too.

In all the survey years, the number of tractors per household increases with the increase in the size groups of land holdings. The number of tractors owned per 1000 households was the lowest in the case of marginal farms (5.23) and the highest in very large farms (189.27). This evidence indicates the scale bias of tractorisation. In other words, though tractorisation is diffusing fast among all size groups of landholdings, its density with respect to households is far higher among large size groups than in small groups. The possession of tractors is undoubtedly biased in favour of large size groups of holdings.

As tractorisation is size-biased, one would expect that the effect of tractors on work animal holdings to be size-biased too and that the growth in tractors would have displaced the animal stock in the large size classes[3]. The argument that the dependence on work animals has declined drastically in the medium and large land holdings is clearly supported by the results of an independent survey conducted in paddy farms in selected districts of Tamil Nadu during 1993-94 (Table 5.10).

In both Tanjore and Periyar districts, the study observed that the use of animal power in large size paddy farms was nil and that it was very low in medium-size farms. While there existed a positive association between machine power and the size group of farms, a negative association was found between human and animal power and size class of farms. Both animal and human power are getting replaced by machine power in both the medium and the large farms. Thus, mechanization in agriculture has undoubtedly displaced the use of animal power and therefore the animal stock in medium and large size class of landholdings in Tamil Nadu.

Table 5.10
Extent of Mechanisation in Paddy Farms (Per Hectare) in Tanjore and Periyar Districts of Tamil Nadu, 1994-95

District	Source of Power	Unit	Size Class of Landholding			
			Small	*Medium*	*Large*	*All Classes*
Tanjore	Human	Man days	149	126	122	132.3
	Animal	Pair days	22	7	–	14.5
	Machine	Hours	8	19	24	20.9
Periyar	Human	Man days	159	130	128	139
	Animal	Pair days	24	7	–	15.5
	Machine	Hours	7.5	17	25	20.5

Source: Muruganathan (1996).

The fact of the decline in the use of work animals is highlighted also in the Farm Management Studies conducted in Coimbatore district of Tamil Nadu between the 'fifties and the 'seventies (Table 5.11). They indicated that the area commanded by a pair of bullocks had increased whereas the utilisation rates of bullocks had decreased during the period.

Table 5.11
Animal Use Pattern as per Farm Management Studies Conducted in Coimbatore District

Particuars	*Coimbatore*	
	1954-57	*1970-73*
Area commanded by a pair of bullocks	3.32	4.03
Average employment days per bullock pair per year	123.50	79.67
Percentage of employment in an year for a bullock pair	38.84	21.83
Utilisation of bullock labour per hectare (bullock pair days)	26.22	9.05

Source: Farm Management Studies, Coimbatore, Combined Reports for 1954-57 and 1970-73.

The shift in energy use pattern for various farm activities across size classes of landholdings is evident from the latest

59th round of NSS (see Table 5.12). The survey revealed the extent of energy use pattern across various size classes of landholdings shows its biased nature. The dependence on

Table 5.12
Percentage Distribution of Farmer Households by Primary Sources of Energy for Different Farm Activities across Size Classes of Landholdings in Tamil Nadu (2003)

		Primary Sources of Energy				
	Size Classes of landholdings (hectares)	*Electricity*	*Diesel/ Petrol / Kerosene*	*Animal Power*	*Others*	*Total*
Ploughing	<0.01	0	32.7	67.3		100
	0.01 - 0.40	3.4	59.1	37.5		100
	0.41 - 1.00	1.2	64.7	34.0	0.1	100
	1.01 - 2.00	1.4	71.3	27.3		100
	2.01 - 4.00	1.0	82.6	16.4		100
	4.01 - 10.00	1.6	89.6	8.7		100
	> 10	0	100	0		100
	All sizes	1.7	67.9	30.4		100
Irrigation	<0.01	100	0	0		100
	0.01 - 0.40	66.7	32.3	0.9		100
	0.41 - 1.00	65.6	34.4	0		100
	1.01 - 2.00	78.0	21.7	0.3		100
	2.01 - 4.00	86.6	12.8	0.6		100
	4.01 - 10.00	83.5	16.5	0		100
	> 10	100	0	0		100
	All sizes	72.4	27.3	0.3		100
Harvesting	<0.01	100	0	0		100
	0.01 - 0.40	31.0	66.1	2.8		100
	0.41 - 1.00	0	79.3	20.7		100
	1.01 - 2.00	.63	74.8	19.0		100
	2.01 - 4.00	.21	92.5	5.4		100
	4.01 - 10.00	0	100	0		100
	> 10	0	100	0		100
	All sizes	8.3	78.6	13.1		100
Threshing	<0.01	73.8	26.2	0		100
	0.01 - 0.40	14.8	59.6	25.6		100
	0.41 - 1.00	3.9	84.7	11.3		100
	1.01 - 2.00	4.2	83.8	12.0		100
	2.01 - 4.00	7.1	85.4	7.5		100
	4.01 - 10.00	6.5	92.5	0.9		100
	> 10	0	100	0		100
	All sizes	7.0	79.4	13.6		100

Source: GOI (2005b).

animal power is extremely low for operations such as ploughing and threshing. The use of animal power for irrigation has almost disappeared in all the size classes of holdings. However, the dependence on work animals for ploughing activities is relatively high among marginal and small landholding classes as there are constraints to using tractors and tillers in a very small area and holdings.

The dynamic changes that were taking place in the number of work animals, mechanisation of farm activities and distributional changes in bovines across size classes of landholdings are sharply brought out by two resurveys conducted in Tamil Nadu by Jeyaranjan (2004) and Retnam, Menon and Nair (2005) in their resurveys of villages in Tamil Nadu.

The resurvey of Iluppakkorai village in Thanjavur district of Tamil Nadu of the changes between the 1960s and the 1990's by Jeyaranjan (2004), has come up with the following observation:

> "In the present day land owners house is almost an empty cattle shed compared to the mid 1970s and early 1980s. Occasionally one finds one or two jersey cows for milk. Hey stalks are insignificantly small in size as compared to their mammoth proportions during the 1970s. The hybrid cows are stall-fed. Cattle as a draught power have declined very sharply. Almost the entire field preparation operations for all the crops are undertaken with tractors or power tillers. Further operations are carried out with human labour. Inaccessible and small plots are prepared with the traditional bullock drawn ploughs that are owned and hired out by a few labourer households. The importance of mechanised instruments has continued to grow. The tractor and power tiller owners have by now developed well established clientele network and the competition among them to hire out their services is very intense. Proliferation of tractors and tillers due to easier credit from nationalized banks had changed this market from a sellers market to a buyer market. Competition is accentuated further with the arrival of power tillers. Apart from the locally available power tillers, such machines also migrate like men during the season from across the

> Trichirappalli district. Bullock drawn ploughs and carts survived this onslaught, as they were to be deployed when machines were not available in time. Carts were used for transporting the banana yield to the market. They were also used to transport jaggery that was produced in the village to the market every day during the crushing season." (Jeyaranjan 2004).

The resurvey reports that machines have displaced animal power to a substantial extent in transportation. This is evident from the following extract:

> "Proliferation of mini lorries, mini vans and auto rickshaws have completely changed the logistics. A fleet of these vehicles wait in the nearby town. Merchants and middlemen encourage this mode of transport as they can redirect the load to another destination either within the district or outside without any additional handling charges. Due to these reasons, one hardly finds bullock pairs, ploughs and carts in the fileds and streets of the villages. The economy is driven more by hydro carbon energy than by animal energy." (idem)

Another process that has been entirely mechanized is irrigation. The study states thus:

> "There are around 80 electrical motors in the villages. Diesel driven engines substitute motors in irrigation. Free electricity is one important reason for such proliferation. Open wells have completely disappeared and so also the traditional techniques of well irrigation." (idem).

The study by Retnam, Menon and Nair (2004) also revealed the changing phenomenon of the cattle economy in Kadatty village. In Kadatty, the area under rice cultivation has been undergoing a rapid decline due to the shift in the cropping pattern towards coconut cultivation. The authors point out thus:

> "Prior to mechanization, labourers with bullocks got a considerable number of employment days as ploughmen. Owing to the existence of a favourable bullock labour market, tenant households hired out a higher number of male labour days than did the agricultural labour households during eighties. However, the number of days

> of employment obtained through ploughing which were around 50 to 60 earlier has become insignificant due to tractorisation during 2000.
>
> In 1980, the tenants were interested in maintaining bullocks because they brought in more days of employment; using of tractor for ploughing was not widespread then and all the available ploughing jobs were shared among themselves by tenants; In a situation in which employment was the main problem, tenants found it profitable to maintain bullocks and gain more days of employment. Gradual spread of mechanization in ploughing has resulted in a drastic decline in employment for bullock labour and ploughmen. Owing to non-profitability, tenants are not now interested in keeping bullocks. Of the 29 tenants in 1980, as many as 26 had bullocks, but by 2000, out of 40 tenants only 9 have bullocks. The decline in the requirement of draught power in agriculture has resulted in a sharp fall in the number of bullocks in the village between 1980 and 2000. The gradual shift in cropping pattern from rice to crops like coconut and banana appears also to have contributed to this process. However, the number of milch animals increased from 9 to 16. One of the important reasons cited for the increasing menace of cattle is the disappearance of grazing space in the recent past. Earlier the area lying on the southern side of the village served as a good grazing land. Over the years the landowners adjacent to the common land encroached upon it, and the farmers are now left without pastureland for their cattle". (Retnam *et al.* 2004).

Having examined the changes in the distribution of work animals in the context of the trends in mechanisation of agriculture we now turn to a discussion of changes in the distribution of milch animals.

Distribution of Milch Animal Population

As milch animal population has gained significance in the bovine complex, one would expect that the distribution of milch animals across land holding classes must also have changed accordingly. The direction and various other aspects of change in the distribution of milch animal population are discussed in the sections that follow:

The concentration of in-milk milch animal population in the marginal and smallholdings is reflected in the data on the distribution of milch animals (Table 5.13). In 1971, about 56 percent of the milch animals stock was distributed among marginal and smallholdings. The proportion increased to about 80 per cent by 1991. The fact of swelling of the milch animal population in small and marginal holdings is also reflected in the number of milch animals per 100 hectares of operated area and per 100 households.

The density of milch animals increases with increase in the size classes of landholdings, indicating that the size of land holding and milch animal holdings per household are positively related. That as farm size increases, fodder availability would also become higher, is a fact that facilitates the farmer to hold larger numbers of animals for milk production purposes.

The number of milch animals per gross cropped area (density) has shown a negative association with increase in the size class of landholdings. The reason for the high density at the marginal and smallholdings level could be the indivisibility nature of milch animals. Moreover, as dairying serves as a subsidiary occupation particularly to marginal and small farmers, the requirement of milch animals is higher among them than among larger holdings.

The foregoing findings on the distribution of milch animals are supported by Input surveys[4], the ICAR survey (Tamil Nadu) and the Techno-Economic Survey (Dharmapuri). The findings of the ICAR Survey on this subject are discussed below. The Techno-Economic Survey provides additional information of the distribution of milch animals among the landless farmers. As production of milk is considered an important commercial activity by rural agricultural labourers and other landless households, the landless households maintain a significant proportion of milch animals.

The ICAR survey conducted in Tamil Nadu indicated that small and medium farmers together accounted for ownership

Table 5.13
Trends in the Distribution of Milch Animal Population (In-milk): Tamil Nadu, 1971-1991

Particulars	Year	Size classes of Landholdings						
		Landless	*Marginal*	*Small*	*Semi-medium*	*Medium*	*Large*	*All Sizes*
		0.00	*0.00 - 1.00*	*1.01 – 2.00*	*2.01 - 4.00*	*4.01 - 10.00*	*> 10.02*	
Distribution of MAP (in-milk) (%)	1971	7.20	36.71	19.81	19.51	13.73	3.05	100.00
	1981	2.17	46.31	23.42	17.12	9.21	1.78	100.00
	1991	0.83	58.98	21.23	12.42	5.70	0.84	100.00
Cattle/Buffalo Ratio of MAP	1971	2.53	2.38	2.19	2.48	2.78	2.10	2.41
	1981	0.19	1.10	2.31	1.53	1.86	8.30	1.43
	1991	0.00	3.48	1.59	0.64	1.83	0.17	2.08
MAP per100 hect. of operated area	1971		57.77	29.84	24.54	22.12	16.72	34.52
	1981		75.21	30.54	24.64	16.21	13.23	35.97
	1991		82.42	31.43	20.58	16.07	5.95	40.16
MAP per 100 households	1971	4.55	27.99	42.18	67.47	129.14	240.58	26.52
	1981	1.16	20.84	43.00	66.33	88.16	209.00	20.00
	1991	0.42	22.14	44.00	54.00	82.00	81.00	18.33

Source: The same as for Table 5.3.

of the major proportion of milch animals; she-cattle dominate in the composition of milch animal holdings; the number of milch animals per household increase with rise in the levels of landholdings; and, the number of milch animals per acre decline with the rise in the levels of landholdings (Table 5.14). Though these findings clearly support the Input Survey results, they fail to provide any information about the distribution of milch animals among landless households.

However, a clue towards this information is available from a survey undertaken in the Dharmapuri district, Tamil Nadu during 1987-88. The survey reiterated the earlier findings of the NSS, ICAR and Input Surveys. In addition, it showed that landless households owned about 20 per cent of the milch animal stocks (Table 5.15). More over, the number of milch animals per household of both landless and marginal holdings was almost the same.

Table 5.14
Distribution of Milch Animals
Across Size Classes of Farmers: Tamil Nadu, 1989-90

Particulars	*Size class of Farmer*	*Species* *Cow*	*Buffalo*	*Bovine*
Number of Milch Animals	Small	209	104	313
	Medium	345	131	476
	Large	509	243	752
	All sizes	1063	478	1541
Distribution of Milch Animals	Small	19.66	21.76	20.31
	Medium	32.46	27.41	30.89
	Large	47.88	50.84	48.80
	All sizes	100.00	100.00	100.00
Composition of Milch Animals	Small	66.77	33.23	100.00
	Medium	72.48	27.52	100.00
	Large	67.69	32.31	100.00
	All sizes	68.98	31.02	100.00
Number of Milch Animals per Household	Small	0.70	0.35	1.05
	Medium	1.15	0.44	1.59
	Large	1.70	0.81	2.51
	All sizes	1.18	0.53	1.71
Number of Milch Animals per Acre	Small	0.22	0.11	0.33
	Medium	0.17	0.06	0.23
	Large	0.12	0.06	0.18
	All sizes	0.14	0.06	0.20

Source: ICAR Survey (undated).

Table 5.15
Distribution of Milch Animals
Across Size Classes of Farmers in Dharmapuri, Tamil Nadu, 1987-88

Particulars	*Size class of Farmer*	*Species*		
		Cow	*Buffalo*	*Bovine*
Number of Milch Animals	Landless	33	22	55
	Marginal	36	25	61
	Small	45	26	71
	Large	44	34	78
	All sizes	158	107	265
Distribution of Milch Animals	Landless	20.89	20.56	20.75
	Marginal	22.78	23.36	23.02
	Small	28.48	24.30	26.79
	Large	27.85	31.78	29.43
	All sizes	100.00	100.00	100.00
Composition of Milch Animals	Landless	60.00	40.00	100.00
	Marginal	59.02	40.98	100.00
	Small	63.38	36.62	100.00
	Large	56.41	43.59	100.00
	All sizes	59.62	40.38	100.00
Number of Milch Animals per Household	Landless	1.03	0.69	1.72
	Marginal	1.09	0.76	1.85
	Small	1.61	0.93	2.54
	Large	1.63	1.26	2.89
	All sizes	1.32	0.89	2.21

Source: Rajendran and Prabaharan (1989).

The distributional changes in the milch animal population may be attributed to the deliberate attempt of the Government through its various developmental policies, rural development programmes and several target-oriented schemes on the one hand, and changes in the milk economy such as growth in demand for milk, facilities for marketing and profitability in milk production, on the other.

Some supporting evidence of the contribution of the Integrated Rural Development Programme (IRDP) on the distribution of milch and draught animals is available. IRDP is one of the India Government's poverty alleviation programmes of rural development. Its object is to enable rural families identified as poor to cross the poverty line by providing them with productive assets and inputs. The assets are provided through financial assistance in the form of subsidy from the Government, and financial institutions advance term credit. The Programme is implemented in all the community blocks in the country. In Tamil Nadu financial assistance under IRDP has been extended to farmers for the purchase of milch and draught animals. Table 5.16 depicts the trends in the distribution of households according to forms of assistance received under IRDP in Tamil Nadu. The proportion of households, which received assistance to purchase of milch animals, is seen to have increased from 37 per cent to 41 per cent between 1987-88 and 1993-94 and further to 46 by 1999-2000. The share of households, which received assistance for purchase of draught animals, declined from 17 per cent to 7 per cent and further to 2 per cent during the same period. Thus, IRDP assistance is observed to have facilitated farmers to increase their milch animal stock. As IRDP focuses on small and marginal farmers, this finding provides an explanation on the observed changes in the distribution of milch animal population in Tamil Nadu.

Table 5.16
Distribution of Households by the Form of Assistance Received from IRDP in Tamil Nadu

Form of Assistance	*Distribution of Households (%)*		
	1987-88	*1993-94*	*1999-2000*
Milch Animal	37	41	46
Draught Animal	17	7	2
Sheep/Goat	12	23	20
Pumpset	4	3	1
Fish pond		0	0
Sewing Machine		2	1
Others	30	24	29
All	100	100	100

Source: GOI: (1993, 1997c and 2001c).

Conclusion

The trends observed in the work and milch animal population at the macro level were seen to be in conformity with the trends across size classes of land holdings also. The changes in the distribution of animals over time and the growing importance of milch animals, particularly among the marginal and small farmers, were significant. Not only did medium and large size landholdings reduce work animal stock significantly due to the process of mechanisation, marginal and smallholdings were also found to be reducing the size of their work animal holdings simultaneously increasing their milch stock. These changes could be a manifestation of the efforts being made by farmers for allocating their farm resources economically, in response to the growing importance of dairying in the state. However, it was observed that the dependence on work animals for draught power purposes among the marginal and small holdings would continue for some more time, till alternative sources of energies become viable, available, feasible and accessible to them. In sum, the changes in the distribution of bovine size and composition indicate the decline in the work animal population and the growing importance of milch animal population in the state.

The developments in the dairy sector and the factors shaping them are discussed in the next chapter.

Notes

1. The data available from the input surveys also indicate that the sex ratios have declined among marginal and small holdings implying a reduction of males or/and an increase of female stock. (See Appendix Table 5.10).
2. The changes in the distribution of work animals over time as provided by the Input Surveys suggest that the number of work animal population per reporting household increases with increase in the size class and that the size of land holding and draught animals per household are positively related. As farm size increases, draught requirements would be also go up making it necessary for farmers to hold to keep larger number of animals for work purposes. However, over time, there has happened a reduction in the working animal population particularly in the size groups of medium and large farmers (see Appendix Table 5.2).
3. In order to examine this aspect of the impact of tractorisation on work animal stock, an attempt is made to estimate the proportions

of animal and tractor power to total draught power across size classes of landholding for the Input Survey years. (See Appendix Table 5.3).

It could be seen that the proportion of tractor power has shown a steady increase in all the size classes and; of animal power, a steady decline. For instance, in the case of marginal holdings, the proportion of tractor power which had been only 1.3 per cent during the mid-'seventies rose up to 31.87 per cent by the mid-'eighties; similarly, in large holdinggs, the share increased from 64 to 81 per cent during the same period. These developments in the composition of farm power across size classes of landholdings indicate that the growth in tractorisation would have reduced the draught animal power requirement and thereby displaced the work animal stock in the medium and large holdings.

4. With reference to the distribution of milch animal population across size classes of land holdings and its changes over time, detail information is also available from the Input Surveys (see Appendix Table 5.4). They show that (a) the distributive proportion of households reporting females of both cattle and buffaloes to the total reporting households and the proportion of milch stock to the total milch stock across size classes of land holdings are the highest in the marginal and small holdings followed by semi-medium, medium and large size classes of holdings; (b) the proportion of households reporting adult females to the total households increases with size class levels indicating that dairying is a scale-biased activity; and, (c) the number of animals per reporting household and the total number of households increase with increase in the size class, an observation that supports our contention of scale bias and reveals that large farmers are able to maintain larger number of animals per household than small and marginal farmers are able to.

APPENDIX

Appendix Table 5.1
Trends in Bovine Sex Ratios Across Land holdings as per Input Surveys (1976-77 to 1986-87)

Trends in Sex Ratios of Bovines across Landholdings as per Input Surveys

Species	*Year*	*Size class of landholdings*					
		Below 1.00	*1.00 - 1.99*	*2.00 - 3.99*	*4.00 - 9.99*	*10.00 & above*	*All size classes*
Cattle	1976-77	1.51	1.60	1.45	1.30	1.03	1.45
	1986-87	1.37	1.54	1.53	1.36	1.14	1.42
Buffalo	1976-77	0.27	0.30	0.24	0.27	0.25	0.27
	1986-87	0.30	0.32	0.32	0.27	0.31	0.30
Bovine	1976-77	1.24	1.17	1.09	1.00	0.88	1.12
	1986-87	1.05	1.13	1.11	1.02	0.91	1.07

Source: Input Surveys, (various years).

Appendix Table 5.2
Trends in Distribution of Working Male Stock Across Size Classes of Landholdings

Particulars	*Size class of Holdings*	*Cattle*		*Buffalo*	
		1976-77	*1986-87*	*1976-77*	*1986-87*
Percentage of Households Reporting Male to the Total Households	Below 1.00	15.08	33.20	0.43	1.55
	1.00 - 1.99	37.31	55.54	2.03	2.88
	2.00 - 3.99	46.75	63.45	1.55	3.54
	4.00 - 9.99	48.84	72.96	2.10	2.90
	10.00 & above	41.79	77.89	0.37	4.64
	All size classes	24.60	41.41	0.93	2.02
Percentage Distribution of Working Male Stock	Below 1.00	35.03	51.38	31.71	46.01
	1.00 - 1.99	26.17	22.96	34.80	24.80
	2.00 - 3.99	23.94	15.95	17.36	21.39
	4.00 - 9.99	12.80	8.04	15.26	6.31
	10.00 & above	2.06	1.66	0.87	1.49
	All size classes	100.00	100.00	100.00	100.00
Number of Working Male Stockper Reporting Households	Below 1.00	2.06	2.04	1.68	1.30
	1.00 - 1.99	2.18	2.24	1.37	1.54
	2.00 - 3.99	2.62	2.61	1.48	2.08
	4.00 - 9.99	3.01	2.76	2.14	1.80
	10.00 & above	3.82	3.55	4.67	1.76
	All size classes	2.33	2.23	1.58	1.51

Source: Input Survey Tamil Nadu for the years 1976-77 and 1986-87.

Appendix Table 5.3
Trends in the Shares of Tractor and Animal Power to their Total Power Across

Trends in the Shares of Tractor and Animal Power to their Total Power Across Size Claases of Landholdings: Tamil Nadu, 1976-77 to 1986-87

Source of Power	*Year*	*Below 1.00*	*1.00 - 1.99*	*2.00 - 3.99*	*4.00 - 9.99*	*10.00 & above*	*All size classes*
		Share of Farm Power (in per cent)					
Animal	1976-77	98.7	87.09	91.91	65.69	36.13	85.63
Power	1986-87	68.13	75.21	54.18	38.29	19.38	60.63
Tractor	1976-77	1.3	12.91	8.09	34.31	63.87	14.37
Power	1986-87	31.87	24.79	45.82	61.71	80.62	39.37

Source: Input Survey (various years).

Appendix Table 5.4
Trends in Milch Animal Population Across Size Classes of Landholdings in Tamil Nadu

Particulars	*Size class of Holdings*	*Cattle 1976-77*	*Cattle 1986-87*	*Buffalo 1976-77*	*Buffalo 1986-87*
Distribution of	Below 1.00	37.86	59.11	28.89	53.73
Reporting	1.00 - 1.99	26.62	20.65	31.27	22.54
Households	2.00 - 3.99	23.08	12.98	24.84	15.45
(in %)	4.00 - 9.99	10.72	6.22	13.64	6.99
	10.00 & above	1.73	1.05	1.37	1.29
	All size classes	100.00	100.00	100.00	100.00
Distribution of	Below 1.00	34.10	53.36	28.37	49.12
Milch Animals	1.00 - 1.99	23.20	20.83	30.16	22.95
(in %)	2.00 - 3.99	24.74	14.85	24.62	17.35
	4.00 - 9.99	14.60	8.71	14.95	8.64
	10.00 & above	3.35	2.25	1.90	1.93
	All size classes	100	100	100	100
Number of Animals	Below 1.00	1.92	1.66	1.78	1.55
per Reporting	1.00 - 1.99	1.86	1.86	1.75	1.72
Households	2.00 - 3.99	2.28	2.11	1.80	1.90
(in Nos.)	4.00 - 9.99	2.90	2.58	1.99	2.09
	10.00 & above	4.14	3.93	2.54	2.53
	All size classes	2.13	1.84	1.82	1.69

Contd...

Particulars	Size class of Holdings	Cattle 1976-77	Cattle 1986-87	Buffalo 1976-77	Buffalo 1986-87
Number of Animals per Total Households (in Nos.)	Below 1.00	0.19	0.52	0.06	0.21
	1.00 - 1.99	0.46	0.83	0.24	0.40
	2.00 - 3.99	0.81	1.13	0.32	0.58
	4.00 - 9.99	1.07	1.60	0.43	0.70
	10.00 & above	1.66	2.73	0.37	1.04
	All size classes	0.37	0.68	0.14	0.30

Source: Input Surveys (various years).

6

MILK PRODUCTION IN TAMIL NADU: FACTORS AND SOURCES OF GROWTH

Introduction

Growth of milk production is shaped by socio-economic, technological and institutional factors, which act both on the demand and the supply sides. The demand-related economic factors which influence milk production include per capita income, population growth, urbanisation, price of milk and its substitutes, income/expenditure elasticity and consumption pattern. Technological and institutional factors are related more to the supply side than to the demand side. For instance, for augmenting milk production, farmers would take efforts to increase the productivity of milch animals, besides altering the composition of the milch animal stock. For increasing productivity technological improvement in breeding, feeding and management practices would be resorted to. Institutional factors such as in marketing (cooperatives), veterinary support (Animal Husbandry Department and AAVIN) and dairy schemes of the State may also be adopted. The dynamic linkages among these factors are depicted in the following flow chart.

Against this backdrop, this chapter is focused on an analysis of the trends, sources of growth, and factors of growth of milk production in Tamil Nadu.

Trends and Sources of Growth in Milk Production

Trends

Estimates of milk production based on sample surveys conducted by different agencies are available for a number of years; these surveys have used diverse methods of data collection that are not strictly comparable[1]. According to the IARS estimate[2], the total milk production in Tamil Nadu during 1965-66 was about 8.7 lakh tonnes. The estimated milk production as per the Integrated Sample Surveys[3] was about 17 lakh tonnes in 1977-78. Thus, within a period of about 13 years, the production of milk had reportedly, almost doubled, the annual average growth rate being 7.18 per cent (See Appendix Table 6.1). During the subsequent two decades beginning from 1977-78, milk production steadily increased except in a few years.

The estimated production of milk during 2000-01 was 4899.17 Metric Tonnes (M.T), which comprise of 63 per cent of cow milk and 37 per cent of buffalo milk. In general, an uneven growth path and a shift in the composition of milk production are observed during the period. The rate of growth of milk production had been higher to the mid-'eighties than that since then. The share of cow and buffalo milk had remained at around 53 per cent and 47 per cent respectively up to the mid-'eighties, and thereafter, the relative shares changed and remained at 63 per cent and 37 per cent respectively in 2000-01.

The milk yield levels basically measure the productivity levels of milch animals[4]. The National Sample Surveys reveal that the yield levels of buffaloes are higher than those of cows; and that of both the species are higher in urban areas than in rural areas not only in Tamil Nadu but also in all-India[5]. According to the IARS survey, in the mid-'sixties, the average milk yield per day per cow in- milk was about 1.220 kg and that of the milch she-buffalo 1.960 kg. By the mid-'seventies, the yield rates of both the cow and the she- buffaloes increased to 1.888 kg and 2.534 kg respectively. The period between 1977-78 and 2000-01, witnessed a further growth to 3.977 kg and

Chart-1

Factors Shaping Sources of Growth in Milk Production

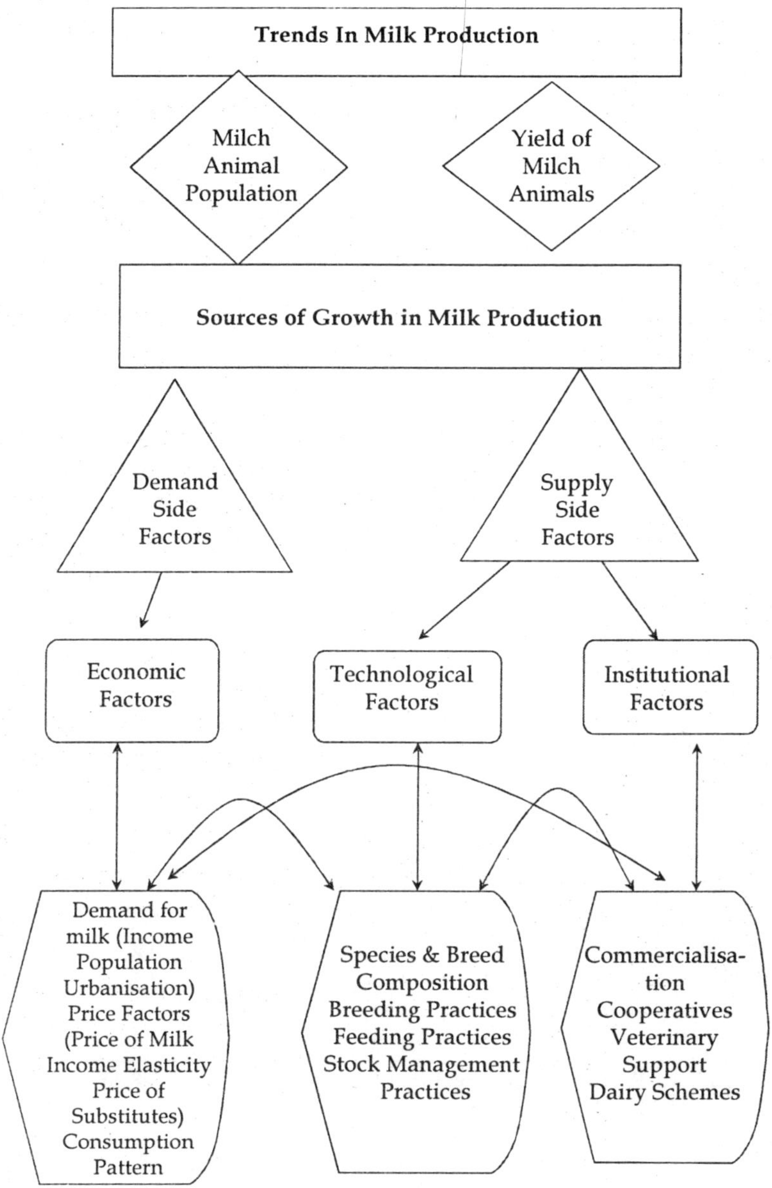

4.059 kg respectively (Table 6.1 and Figure 1). The productivity of milch cows has been increasing at a much higher rate than that of milch buffaloes.

Table 6.1
Trend in Milk Yield per day
Animal in-Milk/ Milch Animals in Tamil Nadu

	Milk yield per day (in kgs.)				*Yield Ratio (Cow/buffalo)*	
	per animal in-milk		*per milch animal*			
Year	*Cow*	*She-buffalo*	*Cow*	*She-buffalo*	*In-milk*	*Milch*
1965-66	1.220	1.960	0.510	1.010	0.62	0.50
1977-78	1.888	2.534	0.729	1.221	0.75	0.60
1978-79	1.841	2.586	0.656	1.125	0.71	0.58
1979-80	2.011	2.850	1.050	1.702	0.71	0.62
1980-81	1.932	2.931	0.965	1.619	0.66	0.60
1981-82	2.018	2.814	0.710	1.360	0.72	0.52
1982-83	2.122	2.942	0.890	1.440	0.72	0.62
1983-84	2.625	3.116	1.011	1.491	0.84	0.68
1984-85	2.675	3.278	1.352	2.199	0.82	0.61
1985-86	2.524	3.464	1.532	2.180	0.73	0.70
1986-87	3.019	3.543	1.712	2.132	0.85	0.80
1987-88	2.927	3.315	1.502	1.966	0.88	0.76
1988-89	2.801	3.376	1.521	2.157	0.83	0.71
1989-90	2.924	3.227	1.664	1.946	0.91	0.86
1990-91	2.855	3.223	1.654	2.009	0.89	0.82
1991-92	2.761	3.298	1.783	1.967	0.84	0.91
1992-93	2.927	3.314	1.865	1.719	0.88	1.08
1993-94	2.953	3.441	1.930	1.866	0.86	1.03
1994-95	3.162	3.506	2.042	2.412	0.90	0.85
1995-96	3.336	3.537	2.025	2.227	0.94	0.91
1996-97	3.464	3.583	2.112	2.237	0.97	0.94
1997-98	3.534	3.682	2.187	2.299	0.96	0.95
1998-99	3.658	3.802	2.320	2.398	0.96	0.97
1999-2000	3.817	3.914	2.531	2.450	0.98	1.03
2000-01	3.977	4.059	2.921	2.588	0.98	1.14

Source: (i) Report on the Integrated Sample Survey, 1977-78 to 2000-01, (various years). (ii) Singh *et.al,* (Undated).

Though official estimates show the trends in milk production and the composition and productivity of milch

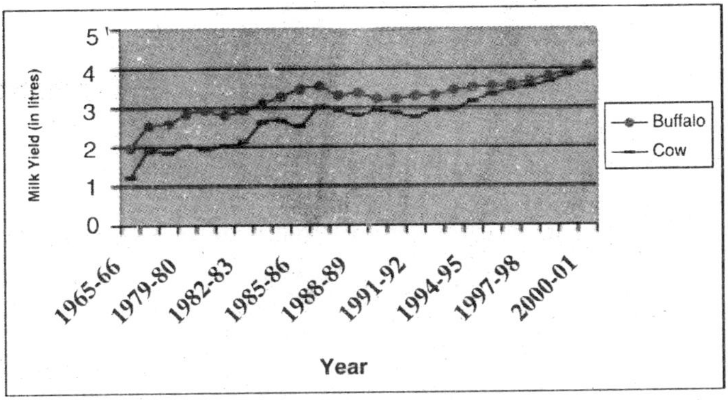

Figure 1: **Trends in Milk Yield Levels**

animals, they are inadequate for in-depth analysis. A significant difference is observed between the estimated milch animal stock based on the survey results and the census data. During 1966 and 1982, the estimates of milch animal population obtained from the Sample Surveys are found to be lower than those reported in the Livestock Census; in 1989, 1994 and 1997, the former estimates are higher than the latter, though the difference between the two sources was small (4 per cent) during 1977.

According to the 1982 Livestock census, the total milch animal population (in-milk + dry) in the state was about 4.55 million, but the estimate of the Integrated Sample Survey was only 3.66 million, recording a difference of about 20 per cent between the two. According to the 1989 Livestock census, the total milch animal population both in-milk and dry together in the state was about 4.3 million, but the Integrated Sample Survey estimated it at 5.3 million, recording a difference of 10.20 lakh or about 24 per cent of the Census data. For other years also, similar discrepancy is observed (Table 6.2). More over, while the Census showed an increase during 1982 over 1977, the Sample Survey showed a decline. As such, the sample survey provides under-estimates of the size of the milch animals herd in certain years and over-estimates in certain other years. Moreover, the difference between the Census and the Sample estimates varies significantly from time to time. In order to obtain comparable estimates of milk production, it becomes imperative therefore to re-estimate the total milk production in the State.

Table 6.2
Comparison of Number of Milch Animal Population (in-milk+dry) in Tamil Nadu as per Livestock Census and Integrated Sample Surveys

Source of Data	*Species*	*Milch Animal Population (in '000)*					
		1966	*1977*	*1982*	*1989*	*1994*	*1997*
Census Data (C)	Cattle	2462	2628	3026	2809	2882	3171
	Buffalo	1105	1395	1526	1469	1333	1248
	Total	3567	4023	4552	4279	4215	4419
Survey Data (S)	Cattle	2020	2837	2431	3453	2966	3047
	Buffalo	870	1350	1230	1846	1709	1941
	Total	2890	4187	3661	529	4674	4988
Difference	Cattle	442	-209	595	-644	-83	124
(D)={(C)-(S)}	Buffalo	235	45	296	-376	-376	-693
	Total	677	-164	891	-1020	-459	-569
% Difference	Cattle	17.94	-7.97	19.67	-22.91	-2.90	3.92
{(D)/(C)}*100							
	Buffalo	21.28	3.25	19.39	-25.60	-28.17	-55.54
	Total	18.98	-4.08	19.57	-23.83	-10.89	-12.87

Source: (i) Livestock Census, Tamil Nadu, 1966, 1977, 1982, 1989, 1994 and 1997.
(ii) Report on Integrated Sample Survey,, 1977-78, 1982-83, 1989-90, 1994-95 &1997-98.
(iii) Singh D. *et.al*, (Undated).

We have used for the purpose data of the number of milch animals that are in-milk obtained from livestock Census reports and of the average yield per animals in milk reported in the sample surveys and, re-estimated[6] the total milk production in the state for the Census years. The revised estimates of milk production thus obtained are given in Table 6.3. Significant difference is observed in the trends in milk production obtained from the sample survey estimates and the estimates derived here; the latter estimates are considered relatively comparable.

Table 6.3
Revised Estimates of Milk Production in Tamil Nadu: Trends and Composition

	Milk Production (in '000 tonnes)			*Composition of Milk Production(%)*		
Year	*Cattle*	*Buffalo*	*Total*	*Cattle*	*Buffalo*	*Total*
1956	259.92	291.30	551.22	47.15	52.85	100.00
1961	386.93	380.22	767.15	50.44	49.56	100.00
	(9.77)	(6.10)	(7.83)			
1966	531.94	491.93	1023.87	51.95	48.05	100.00
	(7.50)	(5.88)	(6.69)			
1974	820.92	690.72	1511.64	54.31	45.69	100.00
	(6.79)	(5.05)	(5.96)			
1977	937.08	786.88	1723.96	54.36	45.64	100.00
	(4.72)	(4.64)	(4.68)			
1982	1301.07	1046.34	2347.41	55.43	44.57	100.00
	(7.77)	(6.59)	(7.23)			
1989	1759.32	1191.11	2950.43	59.63	40.37	100.00
	(5.03)	(1.98)	(3.67)			
1994	2199.28	1193.42	3392.70	64.82	35.18	100.00
	(5.00)	(0.04)	(3.00)			
1997	2868.38	1220.43	4088.81	70.15	29.85	100.00
	(10.14)	(0.75)	(6.84)			

Note: Figures in brackets indicate annual average growth rates.
Source: Computed data based on Livestock Censuses and ISS reports.

It may be observed that the total milk production in the state had increased from 551 Metric Tonnes (MT) in 1956 to 1023 MT in 1966. It increased further to 2347 MT by 1982 and to 4088 MT by 1997. Thus, the production of milk recorded a seven-fold increase within a period of four decades. It is also seen that the rates of growth of milk production had been higher upto the early 'eighties after which year they slowed down upto the early 'nineties. Though milk production had shown a steady increasing trend from the early 'eighties upto the late 'nineties, the growth rate fell initially and rose up later. It may be noted that the growth rate of buffalo milk output was lower than that of cow milk in all the periods.

A structural change in the composition of milk production has taken place in the state. In the mid-'sixties, the shares of cow and buffalo milk to the total milk production were almost equal. The production of cow milk was estimated to be 531

MT in 1966, which accounted for 51.95 per cent of the total milk production; the buffalo milk production was 491 MT, during that year accounting for 48.05 per cent of the total milk production. Over time, this composition changed significantly in favour of cow milk. By the early 'eighties, the share of cow milk rose to 55 per cent; it increased further to 70 per cent by 1997. The corresponding changes in the percentage share of buffalo milk were to 45 per cent by 1982 and to 30 per cent by 1997.

The composition of the milch animal population also underwent significant change. In the mid-Sixties, the share of milch buffaloes in the total stock of milch animals was only about 25 per cent, but they contributed about 50 per cent of the total milk production. By the 'nineties, the share of milch buffalo stock increased to 28 per cent, but the share of buffalo milk declined to 30 per cent. A major factor that could be attributed to the observed structural change in the composition of milk-producing stock is the breeding policy in the state, which is biased towards improving the quality of milch cows.

The foregoing discussion shows that the milk sector of the state has been highly dynamic in recent decades. Milk production has shown a steady increase while the species composition of the milch stock has been shifting towards the cow. The growth of milk production was achieved through the expansion of milch animal population and by improving the productivity of milch animals. In order to explore the relative contribution of these factors and the changes in them over time, we examine the sources of growth and their contributions in the sections which follow.

Sources

The sources of growth in milk production may be analysed in two ways: (a) by components and (b) by factors. By components we mean the cow milk and the buffalo milk, which together constitute the total milk production in the state. By factors we refer to the milch animal stock and the productivity of milch animals, which determine total milk production in the state. While the former is additive and absolute, the latter is multiplicative and relative. We examine below the sources of growth in milk production and the changes in their contribution over time from both the components and the factors point of view. The analysis of the sources of growth is confined to the period 1956 to 1997. To capture the changes in the contributions by its components or factors, the period is sub-divided into three sub-periods: Period-I refers to 1956-66, Period-II refers to 1966-82, and Period-III refers to 1982-97.

Component Approach

Changes in total milk production caused by changes in cow milk production and buffalo milk production estimated for the sub-periods and for the entire period 1956-1997 are given in Table 6.4. The estimates of the relative contributions by components are positive in all the sub-periods as well as for the entire period. About three-fourths of the increase in total milk production was accounted for by cow milk and the remaining one-fourth by buffalo milk during sub-periods II and III, namely between 1966 and 1997. The relative contributions changed significantly from one sub-period to another. During sub periods I and II, the share of cow milk to the increase in total milk production was around 56 per cent; the corresponding share rose to 90 per cent by sub-period-III (1982-97). Obviously, the relative contribution of buffalo milk has shown a steady decline. Cow milk has therefore been the major decisive component in the rise in milk production in Tamil Nadu.

Table 6.4
Contributions by Components to the Increase in Milk Production in Tamil Nadu

Period	*Increase in Total Milk Production Contributed by*		
	Year	*Cow Milk*	*Buffalo Milk*
I	1956 to 1966	57.55	42.45
II	1966 to 1982	58.11	41.89
III	1982 to 1997	90.00	10.00
Entire	1956 to 1997	73.74	26.26

Note: Figures are in percentages.

Factor Approach

The growth in milk production must have been due either to increase in the milch animal population or by increase in their productivity or to changes in both. In order to find out the relative contributions of these factors, an attempt is made to decompose the contribution of these factors, using the additive decomposition model[7] used by Nair (1985) Dhas (1986 & 2001) and Brithal (1999). The growth of milk production is decomposed into population effect and productivity effect. The analysis pertains to the three sub-periods1956 to 1966, 1966 to 1982 and 1982 to 1997 and to the entire period (1956 to 1997). Also, the exercise is carried out separately for cow and buffalo milk and for total bovine milk production. The results of the decomposition exercise are given in Table 6.5.

The dominant factor contributing to the growth in milk production is the productivity (yield) of the milch animals. About 47 per cent of the growth in bovine milk production between 1956 and 1997 was contributed by the yield effect, 13 per cent by population effect and the remaining 39 per cent due to interaction effects. The dominance of the yield effect is true in the growth of both cow milk and buffalo milk.

Table 6.5
Relative Contributions (%) of Different Factors in the Growth of Milk Production

Output	*Source of Contribution*	*Period-I*	*Period-II*	*Period-III*	*Entire Period*
		1956-1966	*1966-1982*	*1982-1997*	*1956-1997*
Bovine Milk Production	Population Effect	11.25	31.73	24.26	12.84
	Yield Effect	80.95	48.41	64.19	47.77
	Interaction Effect	7.81	19.86	11.55	39.38
Cow Milk Production	Population Effect	2.71	28.09	26.88	9.11
	Yield Effect	94.61	51.13	55.24	47.48
	Interaction Effect	2.68	20.77	17.88	43.41
Buffalo Milk Production	Population Effect	34.70	37.00	-40.89	19.95
	Yield Effect	52.71	48.41	151.17	48.93
	Interaction Effect	12.60	19.86	-10.28	31.13

The analysis of the relative contributions by sub-periods gives interesting insights. In the case of bovine milk, the predominance of the yield effect is observed in all the sub-periods. The contribution of the population effect declined from 32 per cent to 24 per cent between the periods II and III. In the case of cow milk, yield was the major contributing factor in all the sub-periods indicating thereby that the rate of growth of the milch cattle population remained lower than that of the yield. In the case of buffalo milk, the population effect during the sub-period III was negative which was more than compensated by the very high and positive yield effect. It is thus proved again that both the population and the productivity factors have contributed for the growth in the production of milk in the state. We now turn to a discussion of these factors.

Factors Influencing Milk Production and Productivity of Milch Animals

Technological Factors

Technology has an important role in determining the pace and pattern of milk production and the performance of the dairy economy. In order to raise the productivity of milch animals[8], technological changes were recommended both in breeding and feeding practices. Accordingly, high-yielding bovines were introduced and the existing stocks were improved by cross-breeding using the artificial insemination technology. Along with efforts for improvements in the breed quality, attempts were also made in bringing about technological changes in feeding practices with a view to realizing to the maximum extent possible the production potentiality of the animals.

Breeding Technology

The productivity of milch animals is highly influenced by their breed character. Hence, efforts were initiated to popularise high-yielding (cross-bred cows and murrah-graded buffaloes) animals. Cross-breeding of cattle and upgrading of buffaloes were the main thrusts of the breeding technology used for raising milk production. The rationale for this strategy was that the new breeds are more productive and their unit cost of milk production is lower than of the local non-descript breeds. The yield rate of the exotic and crossbred cows was found to be almost double the amount of the milk yield of the non-descript cows (Table 6.6). Official agencies and individual researchers advocated cross-breeding in cows and upgrading of buffaloes for increasing the milk production.

Table 6.6
Trends in Average Milk Yield Per Day by Breed Type of Cows in Tamil Nadu

	Milk Yield Per day (in kgs.)				*Ratio*	
	Non-Descript		*Exotic & Crossbred*		*(Non Descript/ Crossbred)*	
Year	*In milk*	*In Milch*	*In milk*	*In Milch*	*In milk*	*In Milch*
1990-91	2.389	1.371	4.857	3.208	0.49	0.43
1991-92	2.259	0.902	4.497	2.932	0.50	0.31
1992-93	2.338	0.960	4.817	3.130	0.49	0.31
1993-94	2.362	0.978	4.865	3.076	0.49	0.32
1994-95	2.420	1.480	5.253	3.945	0.46	0.38
1995-96	2.492	1.436	5.369	3.748	0.46	0.38
1996-97	2.393	1.348	5.551	4.038	0.43	0.33
1997-98	2.399	1.182	5.724	3.501	0.42	0.34
1998-99	2.477	1.453	5.896	3.749	0.42	0.39
1999-2000	2.576	1.583	6.000	3.955	0.43	0.40
2000-01	2.698	1.704	6.002	4.255	0.45	0.40

Source: Integrated Sample Survey Reports, Tamil Nadu, (various years).

Though cross breeding of the indigenous breeds of cows with exotic breeds and of local buffaloes with murrah buffaloes could be effected both by natural service and artificial insemination[9], the latter approach was emphasised in all the dairy development projects in Tamil Nadu. The artificial insemination (AI) programme was vigorously persuaded from the Fifth Plan period onwards. This strategy aimed at improving the genetic quality of the milch animals at large and orienting the developmental programmes increasingly towards dairying.

Owing to the advantages of artificial insemination, efforts were initiated to adopt this technique for genetic improvement and breed development of mich animals. Increasing the coverage of animals by artificial insemination and improving the efficiency of artificial insemination were the two major aspects on which due attention was given.

The importance of the spread and development of artificial insemination in Tamil Nadu could be understood from the data available from the National Sample survey of the 30th round (1975-76). The diffusion of artificial insemination[10] in Tamil Nadu was relatively higher than in all-India during the mid-'seventies[11]. As implementation of artificial insemination was mooted as a major plank of the breed improvement efforts during the subsequent periods also, one would expect a drastic improvement in the breeding practices over time. Though NSS does not provide any further details on this direction, there are other sources of information, which suggest further improvements. Particularly, the Integrated Sample Surveys,[12] independent studies based on field surveys[13] and the activities of Dairy Cooperatives[14] help us understand the trends in the development of breeding technology[15] in Tamil Nadu.

The AI facilities were extended to farmers by the Animal Husbandry Department through their veterinary institutions and by the Milk Producer's Cooperative Societies. A major share (about 75 per cent) of the AIs was carried out by the Department of Animal Husbandry (Appendix Table 6.3).

In the early 'eighties, only about 10 per cent of AIs were done through milk cooperatives; the percentage increased to 20 by the end of the 'eighties and to 25 by the mid 'nineties. In terms of the absolute number of AIs performed, a steady increase is observed during the eighties and the nineties. The number of AIs done in 1981-82 was 14.7 lakh; the number increased to 32.4 lakh by 1989-90 and further to 35.8 lakh in 1997-98. However, in terms of the growth rates, there took place a sharp decline from 10 per cent to 1 per cent between the 'eighties and the 'nineties. Thus, there was a boom in the spread of artificial inseminations in the 'eighties and the growth in the number of AIs slowed down in the 'nineties.

The number of calves born as a ratio of the number of artificial inseminations performed referred to as the 'success rate' was estimated to be around 25 per cent in the 'nineties. This indicates that the breeding technology has been relatively inefficient, reckoned in terms of the conception rate. Data available with the cooperatives also corroborate this.

The cooperatives provide information on the number of artificial inseminations (AIs) done in the state and the number of female calves born (FCB) in each year for the period 1982-83 to 1997-98. Both AIs and FCB registered significant rise during the period (Table 6.7).

Table 6.7
Trends in Artificial Inseminations (AIs) Done by Cooperatives and Female Calves Born in (FCB) Tamil Nadu

Year	*AIs Done in ' 000*	*Female Caves Born (FCB)*	*FCB/AIs (in %)*	*AIs/FC*
1982-83	170	15935	9.37	10.67
1985-86	379	41754	11.02	9.08
1988-89	550	68398	12.44	8.04
1991-92	698	80151	11.48	8.71
1994-95	885	111235	12.57	7.96
1997-98	899	95344	10.61	9.43

Source: Compiled from records of the TCMPF, Chennai.

The growth in the number of AIs done and the number of female calves born slowed down during the 'nineties, compared to those of the 'eighties. The number of AIs done in 1982-83, which stood at 1.7 lakh increased to 6.61 lakh by 1988-89, thus recording an annual growth rate of 48 per cent. In 1997-98, the number of AIs done was 8.99 lakh, and the annual growth rate during the period 1989-90 to 1997-98, was only about 4.5 per cent. The trends in the number of AIs performed and in the number of female calves born were in conformity. The performance of artificial inseminations is revealed from the conception rate of female calves due to AIs (which is measured by FCB divided by AIs done) and the ratio of the number of AIs performed per FCB. The conception rate of females born by AI ranged between 9 per cent to 12.5 per cent and the number of AIs per birth of females between 8 and 10.5. There is thus scope for improving the performance of the AIs in the state. In the 'nineties, the AI performance level slightly declined from that of the earlier period; this observation calls for a close look both at the policy and the implementation levels[16].

The net effect of the developments in the breeding technology is reflected in the significant change in the breed composition of the milch animal population (particularly, among the cattle stock) in the state. In absolute numbers, the total cross-bred milch cattle in the state increased from 3.25 lakh to 14.17 lakh, whereas the stock of indigenous cattle declined from 26.26 lakh to 19.25 lakh between 1982 and 1997 (Table 6.8). The increase in the stock of cross-bred animals in the total stock of milch cattle is reflected in its share to the total cattle. The share of cross-bred cattle to the total milch cattle was only 9.31 per cent by 1982, which increased to 14.95 per cent by 1989 and further to 28.48 per cent by 1997, indicating the shift in the breed composition in favour of cross-bred cattle stock. During these years, the share of indigenous breeds to the total number of milch cattle declined from 75.27 per cent to 70.87 per cent and further to 56.75 per cent, indicating a steady fall in the relative importance of indigenous breeds among the milch cattle.

In the case of milch buffalo population, a marginal change in the breed composition is observed in the state. In absolute numbers, the graded buffalo population increased from 2.31 lakh to 2.72 lakh between 1982 and 1997; and the local buffalo population declined from 14.60 lakh to 10.65 lakh during this period. The share of graded buffalo population slightly increased from 13.42 per cent to 19.99 per cent, while the share of local buffalo declined from 84.86 per cent to 78.31 per cent during the years between 1982 and 1997. Though the changes in the breed composition have been marginal, it is important to note that the shift has been in favour of graded buffalo population.

Along with changes in the breeding practices, structural changes in feeding practices particularly in the feeding of milch animals also took place. Only if both go together, would the fruits of genetic improvement become available. We examine below the changes in the feeding practices in general and feeding of milch animals in particular in the state.

Table 6.8
Trends in Breed Composition of Milch Animal Stock by Species in Tamil Nadu (1982-97)

Species	*Breed*	*Milch Animal Population (in '000)*				*Share to the Species Total*			
		1982	*1989*	*1994*	*1997*	*1982*	*1989*	*1994*	*1997*
Cattle	Exotic	33	9	16	16	0.95	0.30	0.52	0.46
	Native Pure	505	437	487	486	14.47	13.88	15.29	14.31
	Cross-bred	325	471	777	142	9.31	14.95	24.39	28.48
	Local	2626	2231	1906	1925	75.27	70.87	59.80	56.75
	Total	3488	3148	3187	3187	100	100	100	100
Buffalo	Murrah	30	36	28	28	1.2	2.22	1.93	1.70
	Graded	231	250	232	232	13.42	15.44	15.97	19.99
	Local	1460	1332	1193	1193	84.86	82.34	82.10	78.31
	Total	1720	1617	1454	1454	100	100	100	100

Source: Livestock Census-Tamil Nadu for the years 1982, 1989, 1994 and 1997.

Feeding Technology

The technology adopted in feeding could be understood by examining the feeding practices followed and the composition of feed inputs fed to the animals. The importance of feeding the animals systematically had been realised right from the beginning of this century. Efforts were made to quantify the nutrient requirement of animals of various types and categories, to assess the nutrients of feeds and fodders, to recommend 'feeding standards' for animals of different categories and to suggest optimum balanced rations (Arora 1978). A review of the studies on these aspects reveals the following:

1. Feeding practices are of three types: grazing, stall-feeding and a combination of both. Feeding practices vary according to seasons, regions, and the breed and type of animals maintained. When dairying develops with high-yielding animals, feeding practices also shift from grazing first to grazing and stall-feeding and later to stall-feeding alone. Such shifts in feeding practices are also conditioned by population growth and its pressure on land and changes in land use and cropping patterns and agrarian relations.
2. Feed cost is the major item of cost of milk production and the prices of feeds and fodders are closely associated with their nutrient contents.
3. The nutrient requirements of animals vary significantly across sex, age, breed, species and their functional category.
4. The nutritional requirement of milch animals is influenced by their body weight (maintenance and growth), reproduction status and lactation levels.
5. The nutrition values of feeds and fodder vary significantly across dry, green and concentrate feedstuffs.
6. While 'Feeding Standards' can be suggested, it is difficult to recommend a balanced ration (optimal

combination of inputs which provides the required nutrients at low cost) particularly for the unorganised dairy sector, as the nutrient values and prices of feed inputs vary significantly across regions, seasons and individuals.

7. Concentrate feeds and mixtures that are generally of high value in terms of their nutrient content are fed so as to augment milk yield. There exists a positive association between quantity of concentrates fed and average milk yield. Hence, the quantity of concentrate feed inputs fed is considered an important quantitative indicator of feeding improvement.

Therefore there is a need to examine changes in the feeding practices followed and in the quantities and qualities of feed and fodder inputs fed to the animals over time. Though information on these aspects is available from the NSS reports and Integrated Sample Surveys, problems of comparison, compilation and interpretation[17] remain.

The feeding practices by type of milch animals and by seasons are revealed from the IARS results (see Appendix Table 6.4). The majority of animals used to be fed by grazing and stall-feeding and among the different categories of animals, animals in-milk were given top preference for stall-feeding, followed by animals not-in-milk. A major share of young stock is fed by grazing. The practice of stall-feeding is more prevalent among buffaloes, than among cattle. The feeding practices adopted were significantly influenced by seasons[18]. As the survey does not provide any information about the share of animals under the stall-feeding practice exclusively, it may be argued that such a practice (stall-feeding only) was not significant during the mid-'sixties in the state.

The Integrated Sample Surveys (ISS) provide information on the percentage distribution of animals under the three types of feeding separately for milch cows and buffaloes from 1977-78 onwards. In the mid-'sixties, stall-feeding alone was nil, about 77 per cent of milch cattle and 84 per cent of milch buffaloes being fed by grazing and stall-feeding (Table 6.9). By the late-'seventies, the level of dependence on grazing declined to 9.70

per cent among cattle and 7.50 per cent among buffaloes. The practice of exclusive stall-feeding existed among 10 per cent of cows and 5 per cent of buffaloes; the share of animals that were both grazed and stall-fed also increased. During the early 'nineties, the share of animals exclusively under stall-feeding increased significantly along with a fall in the share of animals under the category grazed and stall-fed, while an increase was noticed in the share of animals under grazed alone. During 2000-01, the feeding practices changed further, and that too significantly. There was only about 2 per cent of milch animals exclusively under grazing and 8 per cent of animals exclusively under stall-feeding, about 90 per cent of animals coming under grazing and stall-feeding. The shifts in the feeding practices are a reflection of the changes in both the demand and the supply situations. As the quality of the milch animal stock has been improving in the state due to intensive breeding efforts, the resultant high-yielding varieties of milch animals required closer attention on feeding. Therefore, the practice of stall-feeding was in rising demand. On the other side, due to population pressure and its impact on the land use pattern, the extent of land available for grazing has been progressively declining in the state. Moreover, due to over-grazing and other reasons, the quality of the remaining grazing lands would have also declined. These aspects would have led to reduction in the dependence on grazing and to a progressive shift in the feeding practices from grazing to stall-feeding.

Table 6.9
Distribution of Milch Animals by Feeding Practices in Tamil Nadu

Year	*Percentage of Milch Animals*					
	Cattle			*Buffalo*		
	Grazed	*Stall-fed*	*Both*	*Grazed*	*Stall-fed*	*Both*
1965-66	22.59	0.00	77.41	16.09	0.00	83.91
1977-78	9.70	9.70	80.60	7.50	5.40	87.10
1980-81	9.05	8.77	82.18	0.33	7.40	92.27
1990-91	3.70	14.50	81.80	3.80	9.10	87.10
2000-01	1.75	7.64	90.61	0.79	3.66	95.55

Source: Singh *et. al.*, (undated), and Integrated Sample Survey Reports, 1977-78, 1980-81, 1990-91 and 2000-01.

When the practice of stall-feeding gained importance as a dairy management practice for improving milk yield levels and increasing total milk production, changes in the feed composition must have also taken place. To verify such changes we may compare the situations between the mid-sixties and the late seventies, based on the data provided by the IARS and Integrated Sample Surveys. The data pertain to (a) distribution of milch animals by the composition of feeds and fodders fed to them; and (b) the average quantity of feeds and fodders fed per animal by species and feeding type.

The milch animals, which were exclusively stall-fed or were both stall-fed and grazed, are provided, different combinations of feed inputs. Though the feed inputs are of several varieties, forms, and nutrient content, they may be broadly divided into two categories: roughages[19] and concentrates[20]. Milch animals are fed with green fodder, dry fodder and concentrates, but their inter se proportions vary significantly. Such variations are due to the breed and type of milch animal, milk yield, the price of feeds, the season of the year and the availability of feeds and fodder. The various compositions of feeding may be grouped into six categories as shown here under:

(a) Green fodder only

(b) Dry fodder only

(c) Green fodder + Dry fodder

(d) Green fodder + Concentrates

(e) Dry fodder + Concentrates

(d) Green fodder + Dry fodder + Concentrates

As far as an animal is concerned, whatever may be the composition of the feeds, it requires not only certain minimum level of nutrients like Total Digestible Nutrients (TDN), Digestible Crude Protien (DCP), Calcium and Phospherus, but also, dry matter to fill the belly capacity. These nutrients and dry matter content are available at various levels[21] across the feed items and they vary significantly between the broad groups specified.

The quantity of concentrates fed is an important indicator of the improvements in the feeding practice. The 30th round of the National Sample Survey provided a detailed account of concentrate usage in Tamil Nadu during 1975-76. The average milk yield was found to increase with quantity of concentrates used, in both the rural and the urban areas in the case of both cattle and buffaloes (Appendix Table 6. 5). The share of animals in-milk not fed with concentrates was 39.44 per cent in cattle and 19 per cent in buffaloes, in rural areas. The corresponding figures for urban areas were 28.26 per cent and 18.40 per cent respectively. Of the animals fed with concentrates, the majority were fed with less than 1 kg per day. The proportion of animals fed with concentrates declined with increase in the levels of concentrates used.

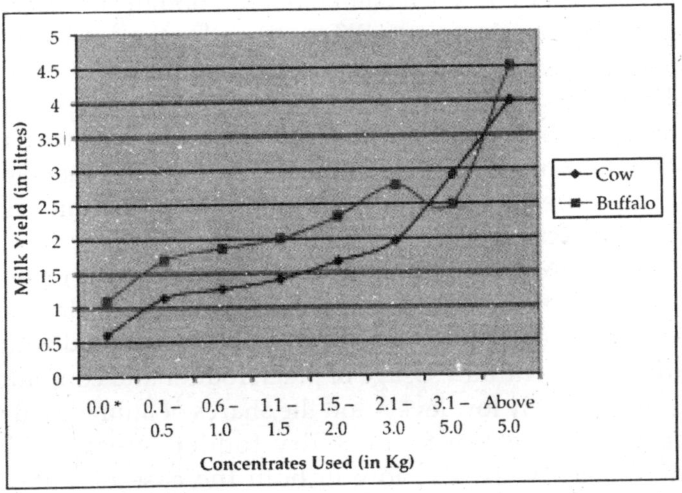

Figure 2: **Relationship Between Concentrates Used and Milk Yield (Rural Tamil Nadu)**

The relationship between the quantity of concentrates used and the milk yield is reinforced by the NSS results for the year 1975-76 which give the distribution of animals in-milk and quantity of milk yield per animal in-milk classified by species and concentrates used, in Tamil Nadu (See Appendix Table 6.6).

It is seen that with increase in the levels of milk yield, the concentrates used also increased, both in the rural and the urban areas and that too in both cattle and buffaloes.

Farmers were thus seen to be conscious of and rational in the use of concentrates. The animals of nil or low milk yield level are fed with small quantities of concentrates. As most of the milch animals (above 90 per cent) yielded less than 2 litres of milk per day, the concentrates used had to be restricted. Though we do not have similar information to extend our argument for more recent years, we would expect that a major development in the use of concentrates would have happened in the context of the increase in the proportion of high-yielding varieties of milch animals and the increase in their milk yield levels in recent years.

For ideal feeding of milch animals a combination of dry + green + concentrates is recommended. Though such scientific feeding standards are available, the adoption of them gets momentum only if dairying is given due importance by farmers and milk production becomes commercialised. Keeping these aspects in mind we take up a discussion of the changes in the distribution of animals by feed composition and the average quantity of feeds fed during the period from the mid-'sixties to the late 'seventies.

During the mid-'sixties, about 43 per cent of the cattle and 36 per cent of the buffaloes used to be fed with dry fodder alone. Almost an equal share of animals was also fed with dry fodder + concentrates. Usage of green fodder and concentrates was at extremely low levels and the shares of animals fed with green fodder, green fodder+ dry fodder, green fodder + concentrates were also low in both the case of cattle and buffaloes (Table 6.10). Only about 8 per cent and 12 per cent of cattle and buffaloes respectively were fed with green + dry+concentrates. However, the situation changed drastically in a decade. In 1977-78, about 33 per cent of cows and 40 per cent of buffaloes were fed with green+dry+concentrates. The share of animals fed with dry fodder alone declined to 10 per cent and 7 per cent respectively among cattle and buffaloes.

Table 6.10
Trends in the Distribution of Milch Animals by the Composition of Feeds and Fodders Fed by Species in Tamil Nadu (1965-66 & 1977-78)

	Cattle	*Buffalo*		
	1965-66	*1977-78*	*1965-66*	*1977-78*
Gren fodder	2.22	6.71	2.07	2.15
Dry fodder	43.38	9.95	36.14	7.28
Green+Dry fodders	5.20	11.91	6.32	7.95
Green fodder+Concentrates	4.59	9.80	5.69	5.28
Dry fodder+Concentrates	36.52	28.58	37.63	36.88
Green+Dry fodders+Concentrates	8.08	33.05	12.16	40.46
Total	100.00	100.00	100.00	100.00

Source: Singh *et.al.* (undated) and ISS (1977-78).

Along with the changes in the distribution of animals by feed composition, the average quantity of feeds fed per animal also changed. There was a marked increase in the average quantity of feeds and fodders fed per animal per day in almost all the categories of feeding composition (Table 6.11). The marginal decline in the quantity of concentrates fed in the categories dry+concentrates and green + dry + concentrates in cattle might have been compensated by the increase in the supply of fodders. It appears that deliberate efforts were made in adjusting the quantity of feeds and fodder towards a rational feeding practice which would improve the productivity (or milk yield) levels of the milch animals in the state, between the mid-'sixties and the late-'seventies.

The trends in the per-head availability of feeds and fodder over time are shown in Table 6.12. Though no data are available for the entire period, information exists for the mid-'sixties, late-'seventies and the 'nineties, on a comparable basis.

There has been a steady increase in the per head availability of green fodder and concentrates and a marginal decline in the availability of dry fodder during the 'nineties. The management of feeding has of course improved and developed and explains the improvements in the milk yield and the milk production levels.

Table 6.11
Changes in the Average Quantity of Feeds and Fodders Fed Per Animal by Species and Feeding Type in Tamil Nadu (1965-66 & 1977-78)

		Quantity of Feeds & Fodders (in 0.00 kgs)			
		Cattle		*Buffalo*	
Feeding Type	*Feed Type*	*1965-66*	*1977-78*	*1965-66*	*1977-78*
Green Fodder Only	Green	21.01	16.54	18.43	0.00
Dry Fodder Only	Dry	9.17	19.16	8.33	0.00
Green & Dry Fodder	Green	8.58	13.63	10.87	5.59
	Dry	8.68	13.61	8.69	5.91
Green & Concentrates	Green	25.23	14.26	25.78	5.83
	Concentrates	2.10	3.02	1.93	0.64
Dry & Concentrates	Dry	10.64	12.63	10.30	13.45
	Concentrates	2.26	1.37	1.92	2.09
Green, Dry & Concentrates	Green	10.91	12.70	12.14	6.49
	Dry	7.80	12.22	7.74	9.49
	Concentrates	2.02	1.61	2.11	2.33

Source: The same as for Table 10.

Table 6.12
Trends in Per Head Availability of Feeds and Fodder in Tamil Nadu (1965-66 to 2000-01)

Year	*Per head Feed Availability (in 0.00 kgs)*					
	Cattle			*Buffalo*		
	Green	*Dry*	*Concentrates*	*Green*	*Dry*	*Concentrates*
1965-66	2.95	8.95	1.08	4.01	8.38	1.09
1977-78	8.33	11.17	1.21	5.62	12.47	1.11
1978-79	2.71	10.89	1.79	3.11	10.07	1.93
1990-91	5.23	5.33	1.68	4.39	6.14	2.23
1991-92	5.80	5.10	2.70	5.00	4.30	2.40
1992-93	6.20	6.10	2.70	6.10	6.40	2.40
1993-94	7.10	6.90	2.80	7.40	7.60	2.40
1994-95	7.70	6.10	2.80	7.30	7.50	3.00
1995-96	7.80	6.40	3.00	7.50	7.60	3.30
1996-97	7.40	6.50	3.00	7.30	7.40	3.10
1997-98	6.80	6.50	3.20	7.60	7.70	3.10
1998-99	7.20	6.80	3.60	8.00	7.90	3.50
1999-2000	7.30	7.10	3.70	8.10	8.00	3.60
2000-01	5.73	6.90	2.90	4.83	6.23	2.53

Source: The same as for Table 6.1.

The production of milk will be an attractive proposition to the farmers if the parity between the prices paid on inputs and the prices received on the sale of milk and milk products remains favourable to them. A large number of studies conducted in various parts of the country (Panse *et al.* 1963, Puri and Singh 1964, Acharya *et al.* 1973, Reddy and Mathur 1980 & 1981, Ramasamy *et al.* 1981, Patel *et al.* 1982, Rekib *et al.* 1987, Vashist and Katiha 1988, Rajendran and Prabharan 1993, Raj and Gupta 1994, Sharma and Singh 1994a, b&c, Shah and Sharma 1994, Sangu 1995, Ttipathi 1995, Badal and Dhaka 1998, Rao *et al.* 2004) reveal that a major share of the cost of milk production was accounted for by feed cost. Also, since feed constitutes the main purchased input in milk production, comparison of feed prices and milk prices would give a fair idea of the changes in price parity. While comparing milk prices with feed prices it is important to make a distinction between concentrates and other feeds. Since milch animals are highly responsive to concentrate inputs, changes in the relative prices of milk and concentrate feeds will have a better effect on the productivity of milch animals.

Data on the wholesale price index of milk, concentrates and dry fodder during the past three decades are given in Table 6.13. The price of milk has been moving at a higher rate than the price of feeds such as paddy straw and rice bran during the period under reference. However, the price of milk and ground nut oil cake were increasing almost at a same rate during the initial years and thereafter the latter increased more rapidly than the former. In fact, milk price had been increasing more rapidly than that of the oil cake up to the mid-'seventies.

Table 6.13
Trends in Whole Sale Prices of Milk, Dry Fodder and Concentrates in Tamil Nadu (1965-2000)

	Index Number (1965=100) of Whole Sale Prices			
		Dry fodder	*Concentrates*	
Year	*Milk*	*Paddy Straw*	*Rice bran*	*Groundnut oil cake*
1965	100.00	100.00	100.00	100.00
1970	147.98	104.00	112.72	129.36
1975	209.26	150.58	223.78	198.32
1980	280.27	195.15	263.16	294.91
1985	426.01	369.86	309.79	444.73
1990	538.12	394.18	506.33	683.44
1995	622.00	558.39	586.28	773.53
2000	1017.82	545.79	852.76	1104.28

Source: Annual Statistical Abstract of Tamil Nadu, (various years).

During the period up to the mid-'seventies, when it was highly favourable to milk producers, the farmers must have fed their animals with larger quantities of dry fodder and concentrate feeds. And during adverse periods, farmers would have reduced their dependence on costly concentrates like oil cakes and depended on less costlier items such as rice bran and other fodder crops.

Given the fact that animals are highly responsive to feed input[22] in general, and concentrate inputs in particular, the use of concentrates would have contributed to a significant increase in the productivity of milch animals. Though the profitability of feed use in milk production would have declined in the post-1975 period, farmers would have reduced the use of feeds only if the marginal revenue from feeds was less than their marginal cost. The increase in the productivity of milch animals in the post-'seventies period indicates that the marginal revenue from feed input was higher than the marginal cost. We also have some evidence to show that farmers were feeding their animals in-milk much better in the late-'seventies than in the mid-'sixties. It was observed earlier that in both the species, the consumption of concentrate feed had increased at a higher rate than that of dry fodder. Besides, the percentage of animals fed with concentrates increased between the 'sixties and the 'nineties. Such an increase in the proportion of animals fed with concentrates was also due to the increase in the rate of commercialization of milk production.

It may be also seen that there was heavy dependence on purchased items of feeds and fodder in Tamil Nadu, than in the rest of India. For concentrate feed items such as oil cakes, grains and oil seeds, the dairy enterprises were almost exclusively dependent on the market; the demand for items such as bran and husk, was met to about one-third of the total from the market and the balance from home production; for items such as fodder, grass and straw, 70 to 80 per cent dependence was on home production (in rural areas) and the rest on the market. The existence of dairy enterprises with heavy dependence on purchased inputs itself implies that milk production is a highly commercialised activity in Tamil Nadu.

The 30th Round of the National Sample Survey (GOI 1984) provides details about the proportion of animals fed with concentrates, the quantities of concentrates fed and the link between concentrates fed and the productivity of milch animals. In Tamil Nadu, 64 per cent of the animals were fed with concentrate feeds[23] (which accounts for the bulk of the expenses on purchased inputs) whereas for the country as a whole the corresponding figure was only 30 per cent. Also, the use of concentrate feeds per animal in-milk was higher in the state.

The higher use of concentrate feed in situations, in which the commercialisation of the milk economy is high, reflects the attempts made by milk producers to increase productivity of their milch animals[24] and to obtain the maximum advantage from the marketing of milk. This tendency is consistent with the findings from a large number of response function studies. They show that the yield of animals tends to increase significantly with increase in the level of concentrate feeding. The data on the level of milk yield and the use of concentrate feeds for cows and she-buffaloes in-milk for rural and urban areas of Tamil Nadu, supplied by the 30th Round of National Sample Survey (GOI 1984), which was analysed earlier, also showed a similar relationship[25].

In addition to improvements in breeding and feeding practices, there is a need to adopt efficient dairy herd management practices for maintaining the quality of stock and augmenting milk yields, and economic utilisation of scare resources. Some such practices are the maintenance of high milk-yielding animals belonging to lower parity orders.

Dairy Herd Management Practices

The distribution of milch animals based on milk yield levels[26] is one of the important indicators of herd management practices. According to the 30th round of the National Sample Survey (GOI. :1984) conducted in 1975-76, the share of animals yielding no milk to the total milch animal stock was higher in rural areas than in urban areas and it was higher among cattle than among buffaloes[27] (Table 6.14). In the case of rural Tamil Nadu, more than 55 per cent of milch cattle and 33 per cent of milch buffaloes yielded less than 1 litre of milk. For the urban region, the corresponding figures were about 23 per cent and 18 per cent respectively. The shares of animals yielding more than 3 to 4 litres and above 4 litres were very low and remained at around 5 per cent. A comparison of Tamil Nadu with all-India shows that the qualitative performance of the milch animal stock in the state in terms of its yielding capacity was very poor[2].

Table 6. 14
Distribution of Milch Animals Across Size Group of Milk Yield by Regions and Species in Tamil Nadu and All India (1975-76)

Size Group of Milk Yield (in litres)	*Tamil Nadu*				*All India*			
	Rural		*Urban*		*Rural*		*Urban*	
	Cattle	*Buffalo*	*Cattle*	*Buffalo*	*Cattle*	*Buffalo*	*Cattle*	*Buffalo*
0	13.97	3.24	1.88	0.40	16.42	1.39	4.76	0.72
0.01-0.50	26.44	13.12	8.93	5.81	31.69	11.03	18.06	5.26
0.51-1.00	29.33	20.75	17.80	12.48	24.97	17.78	21.65	10.64
1.01-2.00	21.49	31.26	31.53	26.30	16.62	26.58	25.23	21.24
2.01-3.00	6.20	18.17	18.00	28.38	5.39	14.41	12.74	16.06
3.01-4.00	1.22	10.76	11.13	15.62	2.87	13.12	8.25	15.53
4.01-5.00	0.64	2.02	3.88	6.41	1.01	6.10	3.98	9.70
5.01-7.00	0.64	0.57	5.11	3.59	0.77	6.61	3.65	12.94
7 +	0.07	0.11	1.74	1.01	0.26	2.98	1.68	7.91
All Classes	100.00	100.00	100.00	100.00	100.00	100.00	100.00	100.00

Source: GOI (1984).

The changes in the distribution of milch stock by milk yield levels become clear when the data from IARS and ISS sources are analysed. In the mid-'sixties, 86 and 74 per cent of the milch cows and buffaloes respectively were yielding less than 2 kgs of milk each, and only 2 and 4 per cent were yielding 4 kgs and above each, respectively (see Appendix Table 6.7). This pattern of distribution of milch cows and buffaloes across milk yield levels has shown a steady and significant change over the period since then. In the late 'seventies and thereafter, the share of milch animals yielding low levels of milk declined significantly and that of high-yielding stock increased remarkably. In 1977-78, 52.60 per cent of cows and 29.70 per cent of buffaloes yielded less than 2 kgs of milk each, and 21.90 per cent of cows and 20.40 per cent of buffaloes yielded more than 4 kgs of milk each. The existence of a lower proportion of buffaloes yielding low levels of milk yield than of cows reflects the importance of buffaloes as a dairy species during this period. From the mid-'eighties, the proportion of animals yielding more than 4 kgs of milk each sharply increased and the proportion of animals yielding less than 2 kgs of milk each sharply declined. In 2000-01, there were only 2.70 per cent of cows and 0.19 per cent of buffaloes yielding less than 2 kgs of milk each; and 61.88 per cent of cows and 59.25 per cent of buffaloes yielding more than 4 kgs of milk each. Thus, a significant shift came about in the distribution of animals, a shift from low to high milk yield levels.

The changes that took place in the distribution of milch cows were due partly to the changes in the breed composition of cows[29] (Appendix Table 6.8 provides details on the proportion of cows by yield levels, separately for indigenous, exotic and crossbred cows for the period between 1991-92 and 2000-01). While a large number of indigenous cows are found distributed among the lower levels of milk yield, a major proportion of exotic and crossbreds come at the higher yield levels. It is interesting to observe that the share of exotic and crossbred cows yielding less than 1 kg of milk each was almost nil in all the years. Moreover, among both indigenous and exotic and crossbred cows, the share of animals with yield of more than 4 kgs each was increasing steadily, indicating a positive impact in the distribution of milch cows due to changes in the milk economy.

With regard to the existence of milch animals yielding 'no milk', we have some information from the IARS survey conducted during 1965-66 and the National Sample Survey conducted during 1975-76. Though these sources are not strictly comparable in terms of the methodology adopted in the collection of data, some broad inferences are possible. For both cattle and buffaloes, the share of milch animals reporting 'no yield' declined significantly during the decade from the mid-'sixties to the mid-'seventies[30]. Obviously the share of animals yielding no milk in the state would have declined further by the end of the century.

With the change in the distribution of animlas across different milk yield levels, changes in the distribution of animals across lactation order and by age are also observed. The age of an animal and the lactation parity are important physical characteristics of the milch animal stock that have significant bearing on productivity levels of animals and thus on milk production. In several studies[31], these two variables, age and lactation parity number, are used interchangeably to understand their effect on milk production. The 30th round of the National Sample Survey (GOI: 1984) clearly revealed the association between lactation parity and milk yield[32]. As the milk yield level increases with the lactation parity upto a certain level and remains steady thereafter, the distribution of the milch animals pattern is also influenced accordingly. Moreover, as the lactation parity and the age of animals are positively correlated, the distribution of milch animals by age group shows a similar pattern as is evident in the age-group-wise distribution of female animal stock by species and regions in Tamil Nadu (see Appendix Table 6. 9). It may be seen that about 90 per cent of the female animals of both the species were within the age group of less than 9 years. In fact, the share of animals starts declining from the age of above 7 years onwards and the decline becomes sharp and significant from the age of 10 years and above.

The distribution of milch animals by lactation parity or age is thus seen to have significant implications for milk production. Against this backdrop, we examine the trends in the distribution of milch animals by lactation parity in Tamil Nadu, using the data available from the Integrated Sample Surveys for the period 1977-78 to 2000-01 (Appendix Table 6.10).

It was noted that in both the species, cattle and buffaloes, a major proportion of milch animals is of the second lactation parity and about 80 to 90 per cent of milch animals are of the first four lactation parities. Certain marginal changes in the distribution of animals by lactation order have taken place over time. The share of animals of the first lactation parity marginally declined. The share of animals of the second and third lactation parities marginally increased. But the share of animals of the fourth lactation parity remained almost unchanged. And the share of animals in the above fifth lactations parities declined steadily. These changes in the distribution pattern indicate the deliberate efforts being made by the animal rearers for eliminating the animals of the higher parities of lactation, and increasing the milch stock of the second to the fourth location parities, which are the very high productive lactation parities[33]. The observed order of change in the distribution of milch animals by lactation parity is found to be the same across all breed types of cows (see Appendix Table 6.11).

The changes in the milch animal population and its composition, and the technological developments in dairying could be attributed partially also to changes in the livestock development and veterinary supports programmes in the state, as is explained in the ensuing section.

Institutional Factors

Government policies and programmes of animal husbandry are focussed basically on developing the quality and the number of animals, since it is realised that given the low productivity and the scarcity of land, it is difficult to sustain a huge cattle population. The question of availability of land received great attention of the policy makers. In addition to extension services, provision of veterinary and health facilities and breeding services has been the major strategy adopted to achieve the goals. The developments of the market as an institution and of commercialisation of dairying also have played decisive roles in shaping the milk economy.

Veterinary Support

While the beginning of veterinary services in India dates back to 1868, an organised attempt was made in the then Madras State only during the year 1891 with the formal inauguration of the Civil Veterinary Department. The name of the department was changed in 1948 to the Department of Animal Husbandry (Pattabiraman 1958). The department was concerned about the problems connected with livestock, in health and in disease. Development activities such as prevention of disease, treatment of animals and other extension work were carried out through veterinary hospitals, veterinary dispensaries, veteri-nary hospitals-cum-key village centres, veterinary dispensaries-cum-key village centres and clinical laboratories. Of all the measures implemented by this department towards the improvement of cattle, the Key Village Scheme and the Intensive Cattle Development Project have been the most important.

The Key Village Scheme was started in 1952-53, during the First Five Year Plan period. This scheme gave attention to all aspects of improvement including feeding, management, disease control and marketing of livestock. Initially, 15 key village blocks were covered by the scheme. During the Second Five Year Plan period, 23 key village blocks and under the Third Plan period, 18 key village blocks were established. During the year 1966-67, there were 75 key village blocks and 650 key village sub-centres in the state. One of the important aspects of this scheme is the compulsorily castration of all the scrub bulls in the area and permission of only pedigree bulls to propagate by natural service or artificial insemination.

During the beginning of the Fourth Plan (1964-65), it was realised that the overall availability of milk was far lower than the minimum quantity re-quired, in the context of increasing human population. A crash programme of the development of cattle, known as Intensive Cattle Development Project (ICDP), was therefore introduced. This project emphasised a package of practices for cattle development, which included genetic improvement through breeding, artificial insemination and cross-breeding, increased feeds and fodder production, disease control and maintenance of health of the animals, improved management practices and dairy extension work. The project included installation of feed plants to provide mixed rations of high quality. Assistance was also given to the formation of milk producers associations and milk marketing agencies. Initially, the project was started in the districts of Madras, Coimbatore and Madurai and latter extended to Tirunelveli, Tanjore and Pudukottai.

During 1970-71, the Operation Flood project, the largest dairy development programme of India since independence, was introduced in the State. This project aimed at increasing milk production quickly by laying special emphasis on cross-breeding of indigenous breeds of cattle with bulls and also with semen collected from exotic breeds of dairy cattle, and mobilizing milk from rural producers through co-operatives and distributing it in the urban centres (GOTN 1972). Initially, the project was introduced in 9 milk-shed areas viz, Chingelput, South Arcot, North Arcot, Salem, Dharmapuri, Trichy, Coimbatore, Madurai and Nilgris. The specific programmes under this projects were (i) Milk Produc-tion Enhancement Programme (ii) Input Provision (iii) Artificial Insemina-tion Service (iv) Animal Health Service (v) Feeds and Fodder Programme and (vi) Farmers' Organisations. Cross-breeding of the indigenous breeds with artificial insemination was emphasised in this project and pursued vigorously.

The preceding review of programmes and policies during the plan era indicates that the livestock strategies of the period emphasised improvement of the quality of the animals through artificial insemination and the developmental programmes have been increasingly dairy oriented. The emphasis on the quality of animals is reflected also in the increase in the number of veterinary institutions, animals treated and castrations done in the state (Appendix Table 6.12). In 1956-57, the number of veterinary institutions in the state was 107, which had treated 2.30 lakh bovines and performed 0.7 lakh castrations. By 1961-62, the number of institutions increased to 224 and the number of bovines treated and on which castrations were done to 6.71 lakh and 1.85 lakh respectively. By 1985-86, the number of veterinary institutions increased to 772, which together treated 56.69 lakh bovines and castrated 2.22 lakh bovines. In 1997-98, there were 955 veterinary institutions, which treated 85.97 lakh and castrated 6.87 lakh bovines.

Thus, there was an increase of 8 times in the case of veterinary institutions and 36 times in the case of animals treated with in a period of four decades (between 1956-57 and 1997-98). The number of animals treated grew at a much more rapid rate indicating that veterinary institutions covered a large stock of the animal population. The functional efficiency of the veterinary institutions, which is quantified as the number of bovines treated per institute, showed a steady and significant increase (from 2151 during 1956-57 to 9002 by 1997-98) recording a 318 per cent increase. This experience indicates that when facility is expanded, the number of animals covered per institute also increases thus benefiting an increasing number of animals.

The increase in the standard of veterinary health facility available in the state becomes evident also from the growth in the number of veteri-nary institutions expressed in relation to the increase in the bovine population for the census years (Appendix Table 6.13). During the year 1956, the number of milch animals per veterinary institution was 34675; the corresponding figure for 1997 was a mere 4777. This showed that the number of veterinary institu-tions was increasing faster than milch bovine population.

The accessibility and quality of veterinary services in the state is evident from the Situation Assessment Survey of Farmers carried out by the NSSO as part of the 58th and 59th rounds (GOI 2003b and 2005a). The results of the survey indicated that the spread of veterinary institutions among villages in Tamil Nadu is relatively wide and that their accessibility[34] for the farmers has increased to a fair extent. With regard to the usage and the quality of the services[5] it is reported that while in all-India 30 per cent of households used veterinary services, the corresponding figure for Tamil Nadu was 45 per cent. About 96 per cent of the users reported that the services were adequate and about 99 per cent of the users were satisfied with the quality of veterinary services in the state.

Commercialisation and Milk Marketing

The development of commercialisation of dairying has been one of the major institutional factors responsible for the growth of milk production. According to the 30th Round of the National Sample Survey (1975-76) the estimated milch animal population in Tamil Nadu was 2.56 million of which 1.16 million were in-milk. The animals in-milk were owned by about 13.5 per cent of the rural households. It may be noted that the proportion of households owning milch animals was lower in Tamil Nadu than in all-India (Table 6.15). Since the proportion of households having animals in-milk was very low in the state, the rest of the households depended on the market to meet their requirements. It is evident that the extent of commercialization of the milk economy was higher in Tamil Nadu than in all-India. In Tamil Nadu, 40 per cent of the total milk requirement is met by purchase from the market whereas, the corresponding figure is reported to be around 20 per cent only at the all-India level.

The extent of dependence on purchased milk and its variations across rural and urban regions and by monthly per capita expenditure classes were also observed in the same source of data. The dependence on purchased milk was higher in urban areas than in rural areas (Appendix Table 6.14). While the share of purchased milk to the total quantity of milk consumed was about 40 per cent in rural areas, the corresponding figures was about 85 per cent in urban areas, in terms of both quantity and value.

According to the All-India Rural Debt and Investment Survey (1961-62), the proportion of households producing milk in the state was about 14.5 per cent. Of the estimated number

Table 6.15

Selected Indicators of Commercialisation of the milk Economy in Rural Areas (1975-76)

Indicators		*Tamil Nadu*	*All-India*
Estimated number of households (in millions)		6.42	84.57
Estimated number of milch animals (in millions)		2.56	55.51
Estimated number of animals in milk (in millions)		1.16	29.47
Number of households possessing animals in milk (in millions)		0.87	13.48
Number of households reporting sale of milk (in millions)		0.39	10.64
Households reporting sale of milk & milk products (in millions)		0.39	4.61
Percentage of households possessing animals in milk		13.55	15.94
Percentage of households reporting consumption of milk		31.46	52.88
Consumption of home produced milk (in litres)		0.64	2.33
Consumption of purchased milk (in litres)		0.41	0.47
Percentage of animals fed with concentrate feeds		64.00	30.00
Average input of concentrates fed per animal (in kg)	cow	0.60	0.30
	she-buffalo	0.90	0.80

Source: Government of India (1978).

of producer households, 28.4 per cent reported sale of milk. The proportion of households producing milk in the state had risen to about 18.5 and the proportion of producer households selling milk stood at about 44 per cent in the mid-seventies. Though the two sets of figures are not strictly comparable, the magnitude of the values is a clear indication of the fact that commercialization of the milk economy increased rapidly between the early sixties and the mid-seventies.

When commercialization of milk production develops, it would attract more commercial rearers towards dairying. It is seen that the proportion of households reporting possession of no milch animals declined from 86 per cent to78 per cent during the period between 1975-76 and 1993-94. The proportion of households possessing cows only had increased from 9 to 14 per cent while the corresponding proportion in the case of buffaloes marginally declined from 6 to 3 per cent during this period (Table 6.16). These trends indicate that dairying has steadily been gaining importance in the household economy.

Table 6.16
Percentage of Households Reporting Possession of Milch Animals in Tamil Nadu (Rural)

Category	*Percentage of Households*	
	1975-76	*1993-94*
Cows only	8.80	14.00
Buffaloes only	5.63	3.30
Cows & Buffaloes	N.A	1.50
None	86.44	78.50

Note: Total includes the not recorded cases too.
Source: Government of India (1978) and (1998b).

Another important aspect of commercialization of milk production is the performance of dairy enterprises. By dairy enterprises we refer to households, which have taken up dairying as a commercial activity and which maintain more than a certain number of milch animals. The 30th round of the National Sample Survey provide some information about dairy enterprise households. The dairy enterprises possessing 5 or more adult[36] bovines (cows and she-buffaloes together), as defined by the survey, were not many either in the rural or in the urban areas by the mid-seventies (Table 6.17). The estimated number of dairy enterprises was 73119, accounting for 1.14 per cent of the total number of estimated households. In the urban areas, only 0.38 per cent households come under the category of dairy enterprise households.

However, it is found that the proportion of households having dairy as a main occupation in Tamil Nadu was lower than at the all-India level in both the rural and the urban areas. The status of Tamil Nadu is lower than that of all-India also in the case of access to resources for these enterprises. The proportion of rural households reporting land for grazing was only 2 per cent in Tamil Nadu, while the corresponding figure was 27 per cent for all-India. Similarly, the share of rural households reporting availability of land for fodder was estimated to be 5 per cent in Tamil Nadu as against 19 per cent in all-India.

The survey revealed that the major proportion (more than 60 per cent) of dairy enterprise holdings possessed 5-9 female animals and about 25 per cent of the holdings possessed 10-14 female bovines in both the rural and the urban areas. With regard to the sources of milk available in the households, the enterprise households depended on purchased milk, but the level of their dependence was very low. More than 98 per cent of the total milk was produced within the households and only about 1-2 per cent of the milk was purchased in both the rural and the urban areas. In this context, it is worth examining the contribution of dairy cooperatives in Tamil Nadu.

Dairy Cooperatives

The cooperative (AAVIN) set up has established 5 milk products factories, 43 chilling centres, and a good marketing network (The salient features about the activities of AAVIN, Tamil Nadu are given in Appendix Table 6.15). With the rapid increase in the number of dairy cooperatives, consequent on the launching of the Operation Flood Project in the state, the share of the organised sector in the milk market increased rapidly in recent years. During 1982-83, the total number of

Table 6.17

Some Features of Dairy Enterprise Households in Tamil Nadu and All-India (1975-76)

Particulars		*Tamil Nadu*		*India*	
		Rural	*Urban*	*Rural*	*Urban*
Estimated Number of Households (00)		64193	28744	846359	228949
Number of Dairy Enterprise households		73119	10901	1541822	92051
Percentage of enterprise households		1.14	0.38	1.82	0.40
Percentage of households having dairy as main occupation		4.76	32.32	8.16	48.11
Percentage of Enterprise households reporting	land for grazing	2.71	0.42	27.23	0.17
	Land for fodder etc	4.76	0.83	19.39	1.86
	land & shed structure	99.21	98.08	97.45	93.2
	transport equipments	5.19	8.64	13.95	28.94
Percentage distributionof Enterprise holdings by number of female bovines	5-9	62.38	65.20	57.94	61.04
	10-14	25.48	24.46	29.67	25.07
	15-19	7.08	4.81	7.36	7.68
	20 & above	5.06	5.54	5.03	6.20
	Total	100.00	100.00	100.00	100.00
Number of animals per enterprise	5-9	6.98	7.18	6.83	7.13
	10-14	11.42	11.45	11.56	11.62
	15-19	16.32	16.46	16.66	16.50
	20 & above	25.32	28.49	26.93	28.44
	Total	9.70	10.20	9.58	10.29

Contd...

Particulars		Tamil Nadu		India	
		Rural	Urban	Rural	Urban
Sources of milk	Produced	98.38	98.15	98.13	97.57
	Purchased	1.62	1.85	1.87	2.43
	Total	100.00	100.00	100.00	100.00
Use pattern of milk	Sold	42.28	83.45	29.74	84.97
	Used for milk products	4.26	0.95	18.08	2.16
	Consumed at home	53.46	15.60	52.18	12.87
	Total	100.00	100.00	100.00	100.00
Percentage share of Purchased value to the Total value of consumption	Fodder	24.12	58.64	12.47	72.68
	green grass	27.08	87.56	13.28	68.65
	Straw	13.55	69.46	13.26	78.57
	oil cake	95.41	99.05	96.05	98.55
	Grains	90.43	99.77	34.48	89.87
	Bran	74.56	96.38	67.02	98.13
	Husk	77.70	92.55	15.27	92.34
	oil seeds	90.46	100.00	92.89	96.51

Source: GOI (1979)

dairy cooperatives in the state was 3061, which increased to 6110 by 1987-88, and further to 7485 by 1995-96. Along with this, the total procurement as well as the total sale of milk by the cooperative sector have been showing an increasing trend. Further, there has also been a rapid increase in the number of farmers who have been brought into the cooperative sector and in the services extended by the cooperatives (Table 6.18).

Table 6. 18
Selected Indicators of Growth and Performance of Dairy Cooperatives in Tamil Nadu

Year	*Dairy Coop Societies (functional)*	*Farmers enrolement (in '000)*	*Animals covered (in '000)*	*Cattle feed Sold (in MT)*	*Cases Treated (in '000)*	*Procurement of milk per day (in'000 lit.)*	*Milk Sale per day (in'000 litres)*
1982-83	3061	476	492	5176	304	478	552
1985-86	5425	798	775	13710	480	824	799
1990-91	7257	1858	1360	37947	480	1164	1137
1995-96	7485	2114	1397	26174	733	1455	1455
1999-2000	7361	2212	1326	14946	809	1219	1474

Source: Annual Reports of AAVIN (various years) and Tamil Nadu: An Economic Appraisal (various years).

Though the organised dairy cooperative sector showed significant growth in Tamil Nadu during the 'eighties and the 'nineties, its contribution to marketing is still low and the proportion has remained unchanged in recent years (Table 6.19).

It may be seen that the share of total procurement to total milk production was only 4.29 per cent in 1977-78; the proportion increased to 7.43 per cent by 1982-83 and further to 15.82 per cent by 1989-90. The share of milk procured has increased to 35 per cent by 20001-02. Hence, it could be argued that the institutional factor i.e, the growth in the number of milk cooperatives, must have facilitated developments in the commercialization of dairying. In recent years, several private organised dairies have come up and taken the task of milk marketing in urban centres. Needless to say, they did accentuate the process of commercialisation of milk in Tamil Nadu.

Table 6.19
Trends in Share of Procurement to the Total Milk Production in Tamil Nadu

Year	*Total Milk Procurement in '000 litres*	*% share of Procurement to the Total Milk Production*
1977-78	740.39	4.29
1982-83	1744.70	7.43
1989-90	4668.35	15.82
1994-95	5259.65	15.50
1999-2000	6077.25	36.40
2000-01	6205.00	34.70
2001-02	6387.50	35.07

Source: The same as for Table 6.18.

We have discussed the changes in the technological and institutional factors, which affect the supply of milk. There are factors acting from the demand side too influencing the trends in milk production, which we shall discuss in the next section.

Demand-Related Factors

The demand for milk is influenced by factors such as size and composition of human population[37], urbanization, per capita income[38], price of milk, the relative prices of its close substitutes[39], availability of milk and the consumption pattern of milk[40]. Efforts were made during the 'seventies to estimate the demand for milk under certain assumptions (Nair 1978, Dhas:1986): the demand estimates had limited reliability due to the following reasons: (a) The figures of state income are usually under-estimates and it is difficult to determine accurately the order of underestimation involved; (b) in demand estimates, it is assumed in general that the distribution of income remains unchanged. But in reality[41] such an assumption is not valid; (c) the effect of price changes on the demand for milk is usually left out as it is observed to be difficult to take account of this factor; (d) in general, the consumption of milk is more widespread and higher in urban areas than in rural areas. Because of the urban-rural differences in milk consumption, to obtain finer estimates of the demand for milk, it is necessary to have separate estimates for each sector. As no reliable estimates are available separately for rural and urban incomes, it is not possible to make such an attempt; (e) the expenditure (or the income) elasticity changes over time and therefore, demand estimates have to incorporate such changes; and, (f) the expenditure elasticities and the consumption patterns of milk vary across age, sex, occupation and income groups.

Though the purpose of our analysis is not to estimate the exact demand for milk, we are interested to understand the possible directional change in the supply-requirement gap[42] for milk in Tamil Nadu in relation to the growth in milk production, based on revised estimates. Accordingly, the requirement estimates[43] are compared with the milk production estimates for the Livestock Census years (Table 6.20).

Table 6.20
Trends in Requirement and Availability Gap of Milk in Tamil Nadu

Years	*Estimated Requirement of milk (in '000 Tonnes)*	*Estimated Production / Supply of Milk (in '000 Tonnes)*	*Requirement-Supply Gap (in '000 Tonnes)*	*Percentage of Shortfall (in %)*
1956	2551.68	551.22	-2000.46	78.40
1961	2705.06	767.15	-1937.91	71.64
1966	2991.51	1023.87	-1967.64	65.77
1974	3472.26	1511.64	-1960.62	56.47
1977	3644.36	1723.96	-1920.40	52.70
1982	4000.08	2347.41	-1652.67	41.32
1989	4358.86	2950.43	-1408.43	32.31
1994	4630.53	3392.70	-1237.83	26.73
1997	4780.28	4088.81	- 691.47	14.47

Source: Own Estimates.

The estimated requirement[44] for milk was 2.6 million tonnes in 1956 and 4 million tonnes in 1982. The requirement increased further to 4.8 million tonnes by 1997. The estimate of the production of milk in these years were 0.55 million tonnes, 2.35 million tonnes and 4.1 million tonnes respectively. It could be seen that the requirement-supply gap had been narrowing steadily over the entire period. While the shortfall of supply was estimated at 78 per cent during the 'sixties, it declined to 41 per cent by the early 'eighties and further to 14 per cent by the late 'nineties. Thus, during the past four decades the production of milk has been almost catching up with the growth in requirements.

The dynamism in milk production was induced by the behaviour of the major factors influencing demand such as human population, urbanisation, per capita income, expenditure elasticities, and price behaviour of milk and its close substitutes.

The size[45] and composition[46] of human population have significant bearing on the demand for milk. In Tamil Nadu, the total human population that had been 29.97 million in 1951, increased to 62.11 million by 2001, recording a 107 per cent increase and 2.14 per cent growth rate during the period. The growth rate of human population was the highest during the 'sixties; thereafter it declined steadily (Table 6.21). The growth rate of the urban human population was higher than that of the rural population during all the decades since 1951 indicating that the composition of human population is changing in favour of the urban population. The proportion of the urban population to the total population which had been about 24 per cent in 1951, increased steadily to 44 per cent by 2001. Tamil Nadu is one among the states of India, which recorded the highest level of urbanisation (Rajalakshimi 2001, GOTN 2003, GOI 2005c). Thus, the growth in the human population and the trends in the rural-urban composition of the human population give some explanation for the growing demand for milk in Tamil Nadu.

If the growth in human population and urbanisation has taken place in association with corresponding increase in income levels, its effect on the demand for milk would have been very high (The trends in the state income[47] and the per capita income during the period from 1970-71 to 2000-01 are given in Appendix Table 6.16). It is seen that in current prices, the Net State Income as well as the Per Capita Income showed a steady growth in Tamil Nadu during this period. In real terms, however, marginal fluctuations are observed during 1974-75, 1982-83 and 1986-87, despite a steady upward overall trend; see Table 6.22.

Table 6.21
Trends in Human Population and Rural-Urban Composition in Tamil Nadu (1951-2001)

Year	*Human Population (in million)*			*Percentage Share*			*Growth rate*		
	Rural	*Urban*	*Total*	*Rural*	*Urban*	*Total*	*Rural*	*Urban*	*Total*
1951	22.66	7.31	29.97	75.61	24.39	100.00	-	-	-
1961	24.70	8.99	33.69	73.31	26.69	100.00	0.90	2.30	1.24
1971	28.73	12.46	41.19	69.74	30.26	100.00	1.64	3.86	2.23
1981	32.46	15.95	48.41	67.05	32.95	100.00	1.30	2.80	1.75
1991	36.78	19.08	55.86	65.85	34.15	100.00	1.33	1.96	1.54
2001	34.87	27.24	62.11	56.14	43.86	100.00	-0.52	4.28	1.12

Source: Census in Tamil Nadu, (various years).

Table 6.22
Annual Growth Rates of State and Per Capita Income in Tamil Nadu

Period	*Annual Average Growth Rate (in per cent)*			
	State Income		*Per Capita Income*	
	Current Prices	*Constant Prices (1970-71)*	*Current Prices*	*Constant Prices (1970-71)*
1970-71 to 1995-76	11.44	2.60	8.61	0.55
1975-76 to 1980-81	18.73	2.50	16.05	0.95
1980-81 to 1985-86	17.91	6.02	14.98	4.01
1985-86 to 1990-91	20.45	6.46	18.04	4.88
1990-91 to 1995-96	23.16	6.52	21.03	5.21
1995-96 to 2000-01	12.62	6.65	12.32	5.56

Source: Computed from Tamil Nadu–An Economic Appraisal, (various years).

The state income in real terms was growing at the rate of about 2.5 per cent during the 'seventies, increased to 6 per cent by the early 'eighties and further to about 6.5 per cent thereafter. The per capita income was increasing at a rate less than one per cent during the 'seventies, recorded a growth rate of 4 per cent by the early 'eighties and about 5 per cent from mid-'eighties onwards. Thus, a progressive growth in the state and per capita income is observed.

Based on these trends it is presumed that the combined effect of population growth and income increase is likely to have been positive on the growth in demand for milk in the state. However, it is germane in this context to examine the trends in income elasticities[48] of the demand for milk. As expenditure elasticities[49] can be treated on par with income elasticities, we analyse the movement of expenditure elasticities of milk and milk products in Tamil Nadu both in the rural and the urban areas. It is seen that the expenditure elasticities in all the years, in both the rural and the urban areas, have remained positive and above one (except for the urban areas for the year 1999-2000). In other words, for every one per cent increase in per capita expenditure, there has been more than one per cent increase in the expenditure on milk and milk products (Table 6.23). Milk and milk products are considered luxury goods as their consumption increased with increase in income or expenditure. The concerned expenditure elasticity was 1.351 in rural areas and 1.669 in urban areas, by the mid-'sixties. The elasticity values had reached their highest levels (1.943 for rural and 2.029 for urban) by 1983. Thereafter, they showed a steady decline and reached a level of 1.641 for rural and 0.942 for urban areas in 1999-2000. The trends in the expenditure elasticities thus indicate that the importance of milk and milk products as luxury goods had been increasing both in rural and urban areas up to the early eighties and that thereafter, they were becoming more of the nature of necessary goods.

Table 6.23
Trends in Expenditure Elasticities for Milk and Milk Products in Tamil Nadu

		Expenditure Elasticities	
Year	*Round*	*Rural*	*Urban*
1964-65	19th	1.351	1.669
1972-73	27th	1.885	1.553
1977-78	32nd	1.808	1.660
1983	38th	1.943	2.029
1986-87	42nd	1.905	1.599
1993-94	50th	1.704	1.212
1999-2000	55th	1.641	0.942

Source: Computed from GOI (various years): *Results of Consumption. Expenditure*, NSS 17th, 19th, 27th, 32nd, 38th, 42nd, 50th and 55th rounds.

Thus, the trends in expenditure elasticities also indicate that milk and milk products have become products of widespread consumption under the influence of rising incomes. However, it is appropriate in this context also to examine the movement of prices and their effect [50]on the consumption of milk.

Price of Milk and Its Substitutes

Though the use pattern of milk stands separately from those of other consumption items, in terms of nutrient content and allocation of expenditure over various food items, expenditure on milk is comparable to expenditure on products such as meat, fish and egg. Keeping this aspect in mind, the wholesale prices[51] of milk, *ghee*, fish and egg, and the retail prices of milk, meat, fish and egg for the period 1965-2000 are analysed for understanding the changes in milk price in relation to the prices of its close protein substitutes (Appendix Table 6.17).

The wholesale prices of milk and egg were seen to be increasing at much slower rates than of the prices of fish. The changes in the wholesale prices were almost of the same order for milk, egg and fish upto the early 'eighties, and thereafter, the price of fish started increasing at a higher rate than of milk and egg. A similar pattern of change in the retail prices is also observed.

A slow increase in the price of milk would positively contribute to more widespread use of milk and milk products and the increase in the demand for milk. The price movements were favourable to increase in the quantity of milk consumption and also to the spread of milk consumption across various categories of the population and regions. This aspect is discussed elsewhere under changes in the consumption pattern of milk in Tamil Nadu. As changes in the price of milk are found to be relatively slow compared to those for fish and meat, it is reasonable to argue that the importance of milk in the consumption basket would have increased due to its affordability and availability. Thus, the trends in the prices of milk and its close substitutes indicate that prices played a positive role in increasing the demand for milk in the state.

Thus, changes in the demand determinants of milk such as human population, state and per capita incomes, income/ expenditure elasticities and the price of milk and its close substitutes, clearly support the argument that the demand for milk in the state has been increasing steadily over time and that it facilitated the process of commercialisation of milk production.

As far as the use pattern of milk is concerned, a wide difference is observed between the rural and the urban areas. In the case of rural areas, a major proportion (about 53 per cent) of milk was consumed at home; about 42 per cent in Tamil Nadu (and 30 per cent in all-India) of the total production is sold in the market. The dairy enterprises in the rural areas were more market- oriented[52] due partly to the demand for milk that exists in the urban areas and to the other market linkages.

The developments on the commercial side of dairying would get a fillip if the milk marketing system also improves. According to the 30th Round of the National Sample Survey, Cooperatives supplied 11.2 per cent and 6.6 per cent respectively of the urban consumption of cow and buffalo milk during 1975-76. The urban producer households supplied about 42 and 47 per cent respectively of the urban households with cow and buffalo milk. The second largest supplier of milk to urban households was the private trader (Table 6.24). In the rural sector, bulk of the non-producer households (about 78 per cent) obtained milk directly from the producer households.

Table 6.24
Percentage of Urban Households Reporting Consumption of Cow and Buffalo Milk by Source-wise Supply in Tamil Nadu (1975-76)

	Percentage of Urban Households Reporting Consumption of	
Source of Supply	*Cow milk*	*Buffalo milk*
Government	2.16	4.70
Cooperatives	1.24	6.66
Urban milk producers	41.67	47.16
Rural milk producers	3.26	4.83
Traders	39.02	36.04
Others	2.67	0.60
Total	100.00	100.00

Source: GOI: (1978).

The distribution pattern of milk would have undergone changes in recent years due to developments in the organised milk marketing system in the state. In association with these developments, the consumption pattern of milk has also been undergoing significant change in the state. There exists a close linkage between commercialisation of milk production and the consumption pattern of milk. While the latter could activate the process of commercialisation, it could also result from the former. Whatsoever it may be, both jointly influence the demand for milk in the state. We now turn to examine the changes in the milk consumption pattern.

Consumption Pattern of Milk

Milk, meat, egg and fish are the main sources of animal protein in the Indian diet. According to one estimate about two-thirds of the per capita animal protein intake in India is derived from milk[53]. Though there exists considerable inter-regional variations in the composition of animal protein intake and its unit cost, milk forms the single largest source of animal protein in all the regions. Though about 69 per cent of the population in rural areas and 65 per cent in urban areas are non-vegetarians non-vegetarian items except milk are consumed only at frequent intervals by both the rural and the urban households[54]. On the other hand, both vegetarians and non-vegetarians consume milk on a regular basis. In other words, irrespective of whether a person is a vegetarian or a non-vegetarian, milk forms an important item in his/her dietary requirement. Since the supply of fish has been on the decline in recent years and the scope for expanding the production of meat is limited, milk is likely to continue to remain the most important source of animal protein in the Indian diet.

Earlier studies (Vaidyanathan 1983, Nair 1987, Singh RKP *et al.* 1996, Birthal 1996) on the consumption of milk and milk products have drawn the following inferences: (a) milk is the principal source of animal protein in the Indian diet and given the limited scope for increasing the production of other sources of animal protein, its importance will continue to remain undiminished; (b) the pace of the spread of milk consumption is very low in the lower expenditure/income groups and it tends to rise significantly with rise in income levels. The spread of consumption is higher in the urban areas than in the rural areas. It is also higher in regions where the resource endowment for milk production is better; (c) the levels of milk consumption are higher in the urban areas than in the rural areas. However, in the higher expenditure groups, urban consumption is lower than rural consumption; (d) the commercialisation of milk production offers scope for better distribution of milk among lower income groups. (e) the consumption pattern of milk is resource-based, class-(expenditure/income) biased and region-specific; and, (f) the availability of milk and milk products has a major influence on their consumption.

Against such a background, changes in the consumption pattern of milk in Tamil Nadu, the linkages between consumption of milk and other close protein substitutes and the changes on these over time may be examined. On aspects on which time-series data are not available, the discussion is restricted to specific periods and comparison with all-India is attempted. The changes in the milk consumption pattern and the levels of consumption have been analysed from quantity[55], expenditure [56]and nutrition angles[57].

In Tamil Nadu, 31.46 per cent of the households in the rural areas and 60.69 per cent in urban areas reported consumption of milk during the mid-'seventies. By 1993-94, this scenario improved significantly and 52.3 per cent of households in rural areas and 68 per cent of households in urban areas reported consumption of milk. Subsequently, by 1999-2000, the share of households reporting consumption of milk increased further to 60.10 per cent and 79.70 per cent respectively in the rural and the urban areas of Tamil Nadu (Table 6.25). These figures indicate that the spread of milk consumption both in the rural and the urban areas of Tamil Nadu steadily increased significantly during the past three decades. Moreover, the decline in the differentials between the rural and the urban levels of consumption declined significantly during the period.

Table 6.25
Trends in the Percentage of Households Reporting Consumption of Milk: Tamil Nadu, 1975-76 to 1999-2000

	Percentage of Households Reporting Milk Consumption			
Region	*1975-76*	*1987-88*	*1993-94*	*1999-2000*
Rural	31.46	43.00	52.30	60.10
Urban	60.69	70.70	68.00	79.70

Source: Government of India: (1978, 1991, 1997b and 2001a).

With the rise and the spread of milk consumption, the quantity of milk consumed increased across all areas, both rural and urban (Table 6.26). In the rural areas, the per capita monthly milk consumption during early 'sixties was 0.76 litres; the corresponding figures were 1.05 litres during the mid-'seventies, 2.12 litres in 1993-94 and 2.39 litres in 1999-2000. Similarly, in the urban areas, the per capita milk consumption increased from 2.03 litres during the early 'sixties to 2.25 litres during the mid-'seventies to 3.80 litres in 1993-94 and to 4.77 litres in 1999-2000. Thus, a steady increase in the per capita consumption of milk over time in both rural and urban Tamil Nadu is observed. The increase in milk consumption has been sharper in the more recent period between 1975-76 and 1999-2000, than between 1961-62 and 1975-76, both in the rural and the urban areas. The ratio of the per capita milk consumption between rural and urban areas indicates that the rural-urban disparity has been narrowing down during the entire period from 1960-2000.

Table 6.26
Trends in Per Capita Milk Consumption by Regions in Tamil Nadu

	Per Capita Milk Consumption (in litres)				
Region	*1961-62*	*1975-76*	*1987-88*	*1993-94*	*1999-2000*
Rural	0.76	1.05 (2.73)	1.56 (4.05)	2.12 (7.18)	2.39 (2.51)
Urban	2.03	2.25 (0.77)	3.30 (3.89)	3.80 (3.03)	4.77 (5.10)
Rural / Urban Ratio	0.37	0.47	0.47	0.56	0.50

Note: Figures in brackets are annual percentage growth over the previous period.
Source: Government of India: (1969, 1978, 1991, 1997b and 2001a).

The trends in the consumption expenditure and in the relative importance of various items to total consumer expenditure, by regions in Tamil Nadu between 1972-73 and 1999-2000 are given in Appendix Table 6.18. While it may be seen that the absolute value of per capita expenditure on various items showed a steady increase during the reference period, the relative importance of these items showed differential trends. The per capita expenditure on milk and milk products was Rs. 1.14 in 1972-73, and Rs. 25.22 in 1999-2000 in the rural areas. The corresponding values of expenditure in urban areas were Rs. 3.39 and Rs. 57.95 respectively.

Both in the rural and the urban areas, the relative share of expenditure on food to the total consumer expenditure declined in the state. However, a divergence in the trends among food items is observed. The proportion of expenditure on cereals and its substitutes (which constitutes the major source of calorie and protein) showed a sharp decline in both rural and urban sectors. The proportions on sugar, salt and species also declined steadily. On the other hand, a slight improvement is observed in the proportion on pulses and pulse products, milk and milk products, edible oils, meat, fish and egg, vegetables, fruits and nuts, and beverages and refreshments. This above trend in the consumption pattern is reflected both in the rural and the urban areas. The relative share of expenditure on milk and milk products in total expenditure showed a steady increase from 3.02 per cent to 4.91 per cent in rural areas and a marginal decline from 6.28 to 5.96 in urban areas between the period 1972-73 and 1999-2000. The steady increase in the share of expenditure on milk and milk products to the total food expenditure observed in both the rural and the urban areas reinforces the fact that milk and milk products gained significant importance in the consumption basket of the people in Tamil Nadu.

These trends are clearly evident also from the index numbers of per capita expenditures on major items (Table 6.27). In both the rural and the urban areas, the expenditure on non-food items increased at a much higher rate than expenditure on food items. Among the food items, expenditure on cereal and cereal substitutes recorded a growth rate lower than that on other food items in both the areas. The growth order of expenditure on milk and milk products was the highest in rural areas and the second highest in urban areas. The index numbers of expenditures on milk and milk products during 1999-2000 were 2212 and 1709 respectively in the rural and the urban areas.

Table 6.27
Index Numbers of the Monthly Per Capita Expenditure of Major Items and the Percentage Change in the Expenditure between Different Rounds in Tamil Nadu by Regions

Region	*Items of Expenditure*	*Index Numbers (Base: 1972-73 =100)*						*Percentage Change Over the Earlier Round*				
		27th	*32nd*	*38th*	*42nd*	*50th*	*55th*	*27th-32nd*	*32nd-38th*	*38th-42nd*	*42nd-50th*	*50th-55th*
		1972-73	*1977-78*	*1982-83*	*1986-87*	*1993-94*	*1999-2000*	*1972-73 to 1977-78*	*1977-78 to 1982-83*	*1982-83 to 1986-87*	*1986-87to 1993-94*	*1993-94 to 1999-2K*
Rural	*Cereals &Cereal Substitutes*	100	146.40	250.92	276.70	466.71	596.94	46.40	71.39	10.27	68.67	27.91
	Pulses &Pulse Products	100	157.86	273.57	435.00	832.86	1620.00	57.86	73.30	59.01	91.46	94.51
	Milk &Milk Products	100	170.18	327.19	510.53	1160.53	2212.28	70.18	92.27	56.03	127.3	90.63
	Meat, Egg &Fish	100	160.14	293.71	405.59	883.92	1714.69	60.14	83.41	38.10	117.9	93.99
	Total Food	100	153.32	269.01	364.26	679.77	1112.38	53.32	75.46	35.41	86.62	63.64
	Total Non-Food	100	205.68	371.21	524.91	1033.33	2018.56	105.68	80.48	41.40	96.86	95.34
	Total Expenditure	100	167.98	297.69	409.26	778.83	1363.55	67.98	77.21	37.48	90.30	75.08
Urban	Cereals & Cereal Substitutes	100	150.42	273.91	302.12	512.34	746.83	50.42	82.09	10.30	69.58	45.77
	Pulses & Pulse Products	100	158.38	263.96	457.87	762.44	1533.50	58.38	66.67	73.46	66.52	101.13
	Milk & Milk Products	100	151.62	291.45	450.15	808.26	1709.40	51.62	92.22	54.45	79.55	111.50
	Meat, Egg & Fish	100	153.96	290.59	461.39	913.37	1707.40	53.96	88.75	58.77	97.96	86.94
	Total Food	100	151.31	276.51	393.99	691.51	1280.50	51.31	82.74	42.49	75.51	85.17
	Total Non-Food	100	173.98	350.54	579.24	1025.04	2696.90	73.98	101.48	65.24	76.96	163.10
	Total Expenditure	100	159.46	303.11	460.55	811.35	1798.70	59.46	90.09	51.94	76.17	121.69

Source: GOI (various years):*Results of Consumption Expenditure*, 27th, 32nd, 38th, 42nd, 50th and 55th rounds.

The trends in the per capita intake of nutrients showed differential patterns across various types of nutrients and regions (Table 6.28). Both in the rural and the urban areas, the per capita intake of energy does not show any steady trend. In fact, it has fluctuated. But, in the intake of protein and fat, definite trends are observed. In the rural areas, the per capita intake of protein declined marginally from 49.20 gm in 1972-73 to 44.90 gm in 1999-2000, whereas, in the urban areas, it increased steadily from 44.60 gm in to 51.70 gm during the same period. On the contrary, the per capita fat intake increased steadily both in the rural and the urban areas during the period.

Table 6.28
Trends in Per Capita Per Diem Intake of Energy, Protein and Fat in Tamil Nadu by Regions Based on Various Rounds of NSS

			Per Capita Per Diem Intake of				
			Energy	*Protein*	*fat*		
Region	*NSS Round*	*Year*	*k cal*	*gm.*	*gm*	*Monthly Per Capita Expenditure (0.00 Rs.)*	*Percentage of Food Expenditure to the Total Expenditure*
Rural	27th	1972-73	1955	49.20	18.40	37.70	71.99
	38th	1983	1861	47.00	22.00	112.23	65.05
	50th	1993-94	1884	46.80	24.70	293.62	62.83
	55th	1999-2000	1826	44.90	29.50	514.06	58.73
Urban	27th	1972-73	1841	44.60	23.60	54.02	64.07
	38th	1983	2140	45.00	29.00	163.74	58.45
	50th	1993-94	1922	48.70	33.90	438.29	54.61
	55th	1999-2000	2030	51.70	43.20	971.64	45.61

Source: GOI: (1983, 1989a, 1997a, 2001d).

While the share of food expenditure in total expenditure declined steadily over time, the intake of protein and fat was increasing. These trends indicate that the composition of food intake changed towards items that yielded more of protein and fat. This is clearly evident from the analysis of the trends in the relative contributions of the various items of nutrient intake over time. In general, various food items contribute calorie and protein intakes whereas, animal products such as ghee, butter and meat, and edible oils basically constitute items of fat intake. The trends in the proportion of calorie obtained from food groups in total calorie intake by region are given in Table 6.29. The relative contribution of cereal and cereal substitutes that were the dominant contributors to the calorie intake is found to have been declining over time. The proportion of the contribution from milk and milk products, meat, egg and fish, and edible oil and oil seeds; increased in both the rural and the urban areas. Similarly, the trends in the relative contributions of various items to the protein intake also indicate the growing importance of milk and milk products in the consumption pattern in both the areas (Table 6.30).

Table 6.29
Trends in Percentages of Calorie from Food Groups by Regions in Tamil Nadu

		Percentage of Calorie from Food Group					
		I	*II*	*III*	*IV*	*V*	
Region	*Year*	*Cereals, Roots & Tubers, Sugar & Honey, & Cereal Substitutes*	*Pulses & Nuts*	*Milk & Milk Products, Meat, Egg & Fish*	*Edible Oil & Oil Seeds*	*Fruits & Vegetables Spices & Prepared Foods*	*Total*
Rural	1971-72	81.31	6.97	3.22	3.70	4.80	100.00
	1983	80.38	4.40	3.17	3.93	8.12	100.00
	1993-94	76.07	5.70	4.76	5.13	8.34	100.00
	1999-2000	72.65	7.49	5.74	7.08	7.04	100.00
Urban	1971-72	59.36	6.75	5.97	5.42	9.71	100.00
	1983	66.19	4.52	5.04	5.43	25.65	100.00
	1993-94	60.14	6.88	7.96	6.79	12.18	100.00
	1999-2000	61.39	8.03	9.66	9.05	11.88	100.00

Source: The same as for Table 6.28.

Table 6.30
Trends in Percentage of Total Intake of
Protein From Different Food Groups by Regions in Tamil Nadu

Food Groups	*Percentage of Total Intake of Protein*					
	Rural			*Urban*		
	1983	*1993-94*	*1999-2000*	*1983*	*1993-94*	*1999-2000*
Cereals	70.66	64.21	60.36	59.63	53.84	48.97
Pulses	10.91	11.11	13.92	13.72	13.36	14.95
Milk & Milk Products	3.60	6.12	7.39	8.36	10.56	12.99
Meat, Fish & Egg	6.20	5.81	7.37	6.31	6.83	8.84

Source: GOI: (1989a, 1997a, 2001d).

Conclusion

To sum up: our analysis in this chapter examined the trends in milk production, its sources of growth and the factors that are shaping its demand and supply. Though there has taken place a steady increase in the production of milk, a declining trend in the growth rates of milk production has been in evidence from the early 'eighties. As far as the productivity trends are concerned, it was seen that the productivity levels of cows have been increasing at a much faster rate than that of buffaloes from the early 'eighties. Consequent on the trends in productivity levels, the composition of milk production has been changing towards cow milk, indicating a structural change in the production of milk. The dynamic change in the dairy economy of Tamil Nadu seen as the growth in milk production is contributed both by increasing milch animal population and productivity of milch animals.

The changes in the relative contributions of the components/factors to the growth in milk production have been due partly to certain structural changes in the characteristics of the milch animal stock and partly to their management practices. The observed changes in the breeding and feeding technologies and the dairy head management practices have positively contributed to improvements in the productivity of milk animals and thereby increase in milk production in the state. There has taken place a boom in the spread of artificial insemination in the 'eighties; but, the growth in the number of AIs performed has slowed down during the 'nineties. The performance of AIs, revealed from the conception rate and the ratio of the number of Ais performed per calves born, indicated a similar pattern of declining performance in recent years. However, the net effect of the breeding technology on milch animal population is an increase in the share of crossbred cows to the total milch animal population.

Feeding technology and practices have also improved in the state. The proportion of milch animals that are kept under grazing has declined drastically and the major proportion has shifted to the category of both grazed and stall-fed'. Moreover, a marked increase has happened in the average quantity of feeds and fodder fed per animal per day in almost all the categories of feeding, namely grazing, stall-feeding, and both. The percentage share of animals fed with green fodder + concentrates and green fodder + dry fodder + concentrates has also increased, indicating improvements in feeding practices. It is observed that there has taken place a steady increase in the per head availability of green fodder during the 'nineties. Thus, the available evidence indicates that the feeding management would have contributed to the growth in milk yield and milk production to a large extent.

The trends in the wholesale prices of milk, dry fodder and concentrates indicated that the price of milk has been moving at a higher rate than the prices of paddy straw and rice bran. However, the price of ground nut oil cake has been increasing more rapidly than milk price from the post 1975 period. It is argued that the profitability of feed use in milk production would have declined if oil cakes were used as concentrate feeds during this period of hike in prices. However, farmers would not have reduced the use of concentrates if the marginal revenue were greater than marginal cost and if the rate of commercialisation increased. As there is evidence of higher use of purchased feeds and increase in commercialisation of milk, our argument is that better feeding practices with concentrates would have continued steadily so as to achieve the productivity potentials of the milch animals and maximise the returns from dairying.

The technological developments in breeding and the adoption of efficient herd management practices have also played an important role in augmenting milk yield levels and milk production. The share of high-yielding varieties of animals to the total milch animal population was on the increase in the state. Moreover, the share of animals reporting 'no yield' has declined and the animals at the higher lactation parity and age-groups have also declined, indicating the deliberate efforts made by the animal rearers in eliminating the animals of low productivity. In support to this development, veterinary support facilities available in the state are remarkably progressing, indicated by the increase in the number of veterinary institutions and bovines treated per institute.

In addition, there were indications that commercialisation of the milk economy increased rapidly in the state. Production of milk for market and treatment of dairy activity as a commercial enterprise were actuated by the involvement of dairy cooperatives in milk marketing. The cooperative sector has been expanding steadily and there has also been a rapid increase in the number of farmers brought into the cooperative sector. Though the contribution of the cooperative sector to the total milk marketing is still low and has remained unchanged in recent years, several private organised dairies have taken up milk marketing in urban areas. Thus, the process of commercialisation and development of milk production was contributed both by the private and the cooperative sectors.

An analysis of factors affecting milk production and productivity of milch animals looked at from demand side was also attempted. It was estimated that though the demand for milk has been increasing steadily, the supply of milk has been also catching up. Growth in the human population, urbanisation and per capita income has supported the growing demand for milk in the state. The trends in the expenditure elasticities indicated that milk and milk products have become products of widespread consumption and that the importance of milk in the human diet is growing in both the rural and the urban areas. The trends in the prices of milk and its close substitutes indicate that the price factor has played a positive role in increasing the demand for milk in the state. The slow increase in the price of milk has contributed to the widespread use of milk and milk products across various categories of the population and the regions.

It was observed that the percentage of households reporting consumption of milk and per capita milk consumption have been increasing steadily. In fact, the rural-urban disparity in milk consumption has been narrowing down. The trends in the relative share of expenditure on milk and milk products to total expenditure and the relative contribution of various items into protein intake indicated the growing importance of milk and milk products in the daily consumption of households.

Thus, the fact of the growth in milk production and productivity of milch animals is established unequivocally; the roles played by the supply and the demand side factors have also been highlighted.

Notes

1. The Institute of Agricultural Research and Statistics (IARS) conducted a sample in 1965-66 to collect data on yield rates of milch animals and on other bovine practices in Tamil Nadu (Singh et.al. undated). Data for the mid-'seventies are available from the 30th Round of the National Sample Survey (1975-76). Both in terms of the sampling frame and the mode of data collection, the NSS results are not comparable with those of the IARS survey. Another source of data on milk production is the Integrated Sample conducted by the State Animal Husbandry Department which forms part of a larger effort by the Ministry of Agriculture of the Government of India to build up reliable milk production estimates for the country. The estimates obtained from these surveys are fairly comparable with those of the IARS Survey. The Integrated Sample Survey began in Tamil Nadu during 1977-78 and has been continuing since then. Estimates of milk production and yield of milch animals are available from the Animal Husbandry Department for the years 1977-78 to 2000-01.

2. This survey had coverage of 324 villages and 7,776 households in rural areas, and it provides data on milk production relating to 4,898 cows and 2,607 she-buffaloes in- milk selected through a stratified multi-stage sampling method. The state was divided into a certain number of basic strata, each stratum being roughly equivalent to a district in size. A cluster of two adjoining villages in each stratum was the unit at the primary stage of sampling. The second stage of sampling was a cluster of two households and the third stage sample unit was the animals in- milk in these households. Data on milk production were collected by the actual weighing method. The entire survey period of a year was divided into three seasons and data were collected for each season separately.
3. The design employed in these surveys was stratified random sampling. Each animal husbandry district in the state formed a stratum. In the rural areas the unit at the primary stage of sampling was a group of villages. A cluster of two adjacent households having livestock formed the second stage unit. The animals in-milk in the selected households constituted the third stage unit for recording yield. In the urban areas, a town formed the first stage of sampling unit from which a block was selected for the selection of households and animals. The data were collected from the selected households through periodical visits of trained enumerators.
4. The milk yield data are available from NSS, IARS and the Integrated Sample Surveys. In addition, several independent surveys conducted as part of micro level studies also provide valid information on the productivity levels of milch animals. The IARS survey provides data for the year 1965-66 and the Integrated Sample Surveys provide data from the year 1977-78 onwards; and, these two sources are fairly comparable.
5. The National Sample Survey provides yield information only for the year 1975-76. It may be noted that the yield of both the species of the state was lower than that of all-India.

Quantity of Milk Yield (0.00 litre)
Per Animals in-milk by Species, Region (1975-76)

Place	*Average Quantity of Milk Yield (in 0.00 litres)*			
	Rural		*Urban*	
	Cattle	*Buffalo*	*Cattle*	*Buffalo*
Tamil Nadu	1.02	1.80	2.27	2.60
All India	1.05	2.61	1.98	3.60

Source: GOI (1984).

6. To estimate milk production, we used the following formula:

   $$Mo = Mp \times Yp \times 365$$

   where,

   Mo = Annual Milk Production

   Mp = Number of Milch Animal Population that are in-milk

   Yp = Average daily yield per animal in-milk

7. The decomposition model used for this purpose is similar to the model employed for decomposing growth in crop output into area and productivity effects (Minhas and Vaidyanathan: 1965).

8. The productivity of milch animals is highly influenced by the breed character of the stock and the quantum and quality of feed inputs given. By improving the breed character, the genetic quality of bovines could be levelled up, and by improving the feeding and the feeding practices the potential milk yield could be achieved.

9. Artificial insemination is a method of deposition of semen in the female reproductive tract by artificial means. This method was popularised for certain comparative advantages over natural services (mating directly). On the one hand, through natural services, a bull can hardly impregnate about 80-100 females in a year. Moreover, at times, natural mating causes hazards by spreading coital diseases among the animals in the area and the continuous use of one bull in an area results in lower performance of the progenies due to in-breeding depression. On the other hand, artificial insemination helps in better utilisation of pedigreed bulls, wider coverage by one bull, control of coital diseases, minimisation of the cost of rearing bulls and avoidance of in-breeding.

10. In fact, Tamil Nadu occupied the second top position next to Kerala in the diffusion of AI in rural areas among cattle stock; the third position among buffaloes; the fifth position among cattle in urban areas; and the third position among buffaloes in urban areas, during the mid-'seventies.

11. The comparative performance of Tamil Nadu and All India situation could be seen from the following table.

Distribution of Milch Animals by Species over Artificial Insemination, 1975-76

Place	*Percentage of Milch Animals*			
	Rural		*Urban*	
	Cow	*Buffalo*	*Cow*	*Buffalo*
Tamil Nadu	4.63	6.54	15.84	11.50
All India	2.36	1.73	9.58	4.12

Source: GOI: (1984).

12. The Integrated Sample Surveys provide information on the distribution of animals by breeding practices for the period from 1977-78 to 1983-84. According to this source, about 56 per cent of cows and 58 per cent of buffaloes were dependent on natural services in 1977-78 and the share increased to 77 per cent and 81 per cent respectively by 1981-82 (See Appendix Table 5. 2). From 1981-82 onwards, a decrease in the share of animals that are under natural service and an increase in the share of animals under artificial insemination could be observed in both cows and buffaloes.
13. For instance, a comparison of the studies conducted at Dharmapuri district, Tamil Nadu by Gopalaswamy and Radhakrishnan (1979) and by Rajendran and Prabaharan (1989) indicates that the diffusion of artificial insemination has increased significantly between the late seventies and late eighties. Thus, breeding practices in the state underwent a structural change.

Trends in Breeding Practices in Dharmapuri District, Tamil Nadu

Type of Practice	*1977-78*	*1987-88*
Natural Service	97.00	14.17
Artificial Insemination	3.00	85.83
Total	100.00	100.00

Source: 1. Gopalaswamy and Radhakrishnan (1979) and
2. Rajendran and Prabaharan (1989).

14. Dairy cooperatives provide not only marketing support to its members, but also it provides AI services, veterinary supports, input supply, fodder seed supply and other extension services.
15. The development of breeding technology in Tamil Nadu is shown by the trends in the number of artificial inseminations done in the state.

16. In this context, it became worthwhile to examine the relative merits of liquid and frozen semen breeding technologies. While it had been observed and argued that efficiency of liquid semen technology was better than that of the frozen semen technology, in terms of success rate, it was encouraged and vigorously implemented.
17. The 30th round of the NSS provides details about the quantity of concentrates fed to milch animals and the relation of this practice to milk yield. The IARS survey provides information on various aspects such as percentage of animals under different feeding practices and average consumption of feeds and fodder per day per animal by seasons, types of animals (in-milk, dry and young stock), and species and by composition of feed inputs. The Integrated Sample Surveys provide data about the percentages of milch animals by feeding practices and quantity of feeds and fodders fed per animal per day from the year 1977-78 onwards. The ISS results are compiled and published in different ways, a practice which creates problems in analysing long term trends in feeding practices. Keeping this aspect in mind, the data are analysed with caution.
18. During the summer seasons, grazing was low and therefore, grazing-cum-stall-feeding practice was being followed among both cattle and buffaloes. The practice of grazing was relatively higher during the rainy season, followed by the winter season.
19. Roughages are bulky feeds containing high proportion of fibre content and low proportion of total indigestible nutrients. Roughages are of two types: green fodder and dry fodder. Green fodder includes various types of grass, cholam fodder, sugarcane tops, lucerne and other items of cereals and plants that are fed in green to the animals. Dry fodder includes straws and hays such as paddy straw, cholam straw and similar other straw items and grasses that are over ripe and fed in dry form either directly or after processing.
20. Concentrates are low in fibre content and high in total digestible nutrients. Concentrates are fed to animals either as a single item of food or in combination with other feeds or as a feed mixture.
21. Theoretically speaking, the required nutrients and dry matter could be obtained either dry in from or as green fodders or concentrates. But, in practiee, such a situation of alternatives does not exist because the dry matter and the nutrient content vary

significantly across these items and the belly capacity of the animals and the price factors act as constraints. Feeding with large quantities of green or dry fodder is not possible as the belly capacity of an animal is fixed; similarly, large quantities of concentrates would be unviable due to the price factor and excessive wastage of certain nutrients.

22. See Ramasamy *et al.* (1981), Reddy and Mathur (1981), Mellor and Ponteves (1964), Dhondyal and Singh (1965), Jacob *et al.* (1971), Singh and Jha (1975), Gangadharan (1980), Kumar and Singh (1980) and Rao (1985).
23. In the survey, oilcake, crushed pulse, gram, grains, bran, husk, oil seeds and gur are categorised under concentrates.
24. In a survey conducted at Coimbatore District of Tamil Nadu, it was observed that animals at high levels of milk yield are fed with more concentrate feeds (Albert Christopher Dhas, 1984).
25. The analysis indicates that there exists a positive association between commercialisation of the milk economy, use of concentrate feeds and productivity of milch animals. Therefore, it is possible to expect that the commercialisation of milk economy to be one of the factors that contributed to the increase in the productivity of milch animals in the state.
26. Naturally, one would expect the concentration of milch animals at the higher levels of milk yield when dairying is treated as a commercial activity and the distribution of milch animals is expected to shift towards higher levels of milk yield where dairying is gaining importance and commercialisation of milk production intensifies in any region/state. Concurrently, there would be a reduction in the number of unproductive cows.
27. This is true for both Tamil Nadu and all-India. Similar discrepancy between rural and urban areas and between cattle and buffaloes could be observed in the distribution of milch animals by yield levels.
28. If improvements are effected through genetic and management practices, they would lead to developments in dairying and milk production and a change in the distribution of milch animals in favour of higher milk yield levels.
29. Exotic and cross-breds are proved to be high-yielding in nature and economical; a shift towards such high yielding breeds would certainly alter the distribution of animals.

30. The share of milch cows yielding no milk during the mid-sixties was 20.30 per cent, the corresponding figures was 13.97 per cent for the mid-'seventies. Similarly, the share of milch buffaloes reporting no yield declined from 9.40 per cent to 1.39 per cent during this period.

Trends in Share of Milch Animals Reporting 'No Yield' in Tamil Nadu

Species	*IARS Result (1965-66)*	*NSS Result (1975-76)*
Cattle	20.30	13.97
Buffalo	9.40	1.39

Source: Singh (Undated) GOI (1984).

31. For details, refer Apte (1982) NABARD (1987).
32. The distribution of milch animals by order of lactation is given below:

Average Milk Yield by Order of Lactation by Species and by States (1975-76)

Species	*State*	*Milk Yield by Order of Lactation*									
		I	*II*	*III*	*IV*	*V*	*VI*	*VII*	*VIII*	*IX & above*	*Total*
Cattle	Tamil Nadu	1.02	1.02	1.03	1.00	1.33	1.69	1.69	0.99	0.00	1.03
	All India	1.00	1.02	1.13	1.11	1.14	1.10	1.16	1.20	1.10	1.05
Buffalo	Tamil Nadu	1.74	1.74	1.88	1.85	1.73	2.35	2.15	2.91	4.00	1.80
	All India	2.39	2.65	2.75	2.73	2.65	2.49	2.66	2.49	2.50	2.61

Source: GOI:1984

33. The increase in the proportion of the stock of the second lactation parity without an increase in the stock of the first lactation parity could be possible by purchase/import of animals.
34. The results of the NSS 59th rounds is presented below:

Distribution of Farmer Households by Distance from Veterinary Services in Tamil Nadu and All-India (2003)

Region	*With in Village*	*Outside Village*						
		<2 km	*2-3 km*	*3-10 km*	*10-20 km*	*>20 km*	*n.r*	*Total*
Tamil Nadu	37.3	12.8	30.6	14.4	4.2	0.7	-	100
All India	23.5	10.2	28.8	23.2	10.7	3.3	0.4	100

Note: The data relates to kharif season.
Source: GOI (2005a).

35 . Percentage of Farmer Households Reporting Use of Veterinary Services and their Adequacy and Quality in Tamil Nadu and All-India (2003).

Region	*Percentage of farmer households using veterinary services*	*Percentage of user farmer households receiving adequate veterinary services*	*Percentage of user farmers households reporting quality of veterinary services as*		
			Good	*Satisfactory*	*Poor*
Tamil Nadu	44.8	95.8	74.5	24.5	1.0
All India	30.3	87.0	55.7	38.7	5.6

Note: The data relates to kharif season.
Source: GOI: (2005b).

36. Adults were defined as females over 3 years of age and also those up to the age of 3 years but calved at-least once or in-calf on the date of listing.

37. The size of the population, which represents the consumers/ market in total, is expected to have a positive association with the demand for milk. As the pattern and the levels of milk consumption vary across age, sex, religion, region and socio-economic and employment groups, the composition of the population in terms of such groups and its change over time have significant influence on the demand for milk.

38. The effect of income on the demand for milk is positive as has been highlighted in several earlier studies (Gandhi and Mani 1995, Sharma and Kuber Ram 1991, Birthal:1996).

39. Raj (1969) had identified edible oils and meat, fish and egg as close substitutes for milk fat and milk protein respectively. The analysis by Nair and Vaidyanathan 1978 and Vaidyanathan 1982 did not conclusively show that these commodities are close substitutes for milk. Vaidyanathan 1982 cited certain factors, which limit substitutability of these items for milk.

40. The disparity between regions and socio-economic groups, and among different family compositions in respect of consumption of milk was studied by Jatrana and Sangwan 1996, Thirunavukarasu *et al.* 1992, Lata and Kuber 1986, Singh *et al.* 1996 Prabaharan and Sivaselvam 1986, Rajendran and Prabaharan

1993, 1989, Maninder Kaur 1989, Sharma and Kuber Ram 1991 Keshari and Malik 1998, and Kumar *et al.* 1995.

41. Suryanarayana (1980) observed that the inequality in the distribution of consumer expenditure widened in the state during the period 1961-73.

42. As per the official estimates, the per capita availability of milk during 2000-01 was 219 gms, which indicated a shortfall of 2 per cent against the requirement of 220 gms (recommended by the ICMR and National Institute of Nutrition). Over time, the gap between the availability and requirement has been narrowing down.

Trends in Per Capita Availability and Requirement of Milk in Tamil Nadu (Official Estimates)

Year	*Per Capita Milk Availability (gms)*	*Shortfall over ICMR recommendation*
1993-94	173	27.17
1995-96	185	18.92
2000-01	216	1.85

Note: The per capita requirement of milk per day as per ICMR recommendation is 220 grams.

Source: Tamil Nadu: An Economic Appraisal (various years).

43. The requirement of milk is estimated by multiplying the population and the per capita requirement.

44. The requirement levels do not indicate the actual demand. The demand for milk is determined by several factors such as population growth, price of milk and its close substitutes and increase in income.

45. The effect of human population on demand for milk is direct in nature. Higher the human population, higher would be the demand for milk and vice versa.

46. As far as the composition of human population is concerned, there are various dimensions such as sex, age, occupation, religion, caste, socio-economic status and regional composition each of which has a differential impact on the demand for milk. Among them, the rural-urban composition of human population is an important dimension. As the level of urban consumption of milk are higher than those of rural

consumption and as milk is considered to be more of a necessary product in urban areas unlike in rural areas, the demand for milk will be higher in urban areas than to rural area. Hence, the growth of urban population does influence the demand for milk positively.

47. The state domestic income that measures the volume of all goods and services produced within the state during a year facilitates the overall assessment of the growth of the state. The per capita income is also used as a measure of the level of development of a state. As the estimates of the state income and per capita income are influenced by the price factor, these estimates are deflated with the price index with the base of the 1970-71 price level.

48. Though the value of the income elasticity of demand for milk that shows the percentage change in the existing demand for milk due to one per cent change in the income is observed to be greater than one, the trends in the value of income elasticity have different implications. Unfortunately, we have no data available to estimate the income elasticities on demand for milk. Instead, we have information on the total expenditure and expenditure on milk and milk products across various expenditure groups over time, which facilitate estimation of the expenditure elasticities on milk and milk products.

49. In order to estimate the expenditure elasticities, we require information on the expenditure on milk and milk products and on the total consumption expenditure. The required information is available in the various rounds of Consumer Expenditure Surveys conducted by NSS that provides data across expenditure groups. Using these data, the expenditure elasticities are estimated for the years 1964-65, 1972-73, 1977-78, 1983, 1986-87, 1993-94 and 1999-2000. Expenditure elasticities are estimated separately for rural and urban areas using the following lograthimatic functional form.

$$\log Y = a + b \log X \text{ where}$$

Y = per capita consumer expenditure on milk and milk products, X = Per capita total consumer expenditure and b = parameter value = expenditure elasticity

50. Milk and milk products cannot be treated as an exceptional item that it does not affect by price. When price increases it would have a depressing effect on the milk consumption

and thereby the total demand for milk. However, if the increase in the price of milk is lower than that of the other animal protein substitutes such as meat, fish and egg, one would expect that the demand for milk would increase further and the effect of the increase in milk price would be negative. This aspect of price effect on demand for milk was examined by analysing the trends in price of milk and other related products.

51. The wholesale prices and retail prices published in the Agricultural Prices in India by the Ministry of Agriculture, Government of India has been compiled for our analysis. Though the data are provided annually by these sources, for our understanding, they are compiled quinquennially from 1965 onwards.

52. This aspect of market orientation is likely to have changed drastically in recent years as the growth in the dairy cooperatives was significant from the late seventies and the period therafter, once the Operation Flood Projects was implemented in Tamil Nadu.

53. For a detailed discussion of this, see K.N. Nair 1987.

54. Vaidyanathan 1983.

55. In order to derive insights into the changes in milk consumption from quantity point of view, we have used the data on the per capita consumption of milk and milk products (in value terms) from the various rounds of the National Sample Survey.

56. The changes in the consumption expenditure on milk and milk products are examined in comparison with the other items of consumption as provided by the NSS, in order to get insights from expenditure point of view.

57. The changes in the relative contribution of milk and milk products to the total intake of calorie and protein are analysed, from the nutrition point of view.

APPENDIX

Appendix Table 6.1
Trends in Milk Production and Its Composition as per the Official Estimates

	Total Milk Production (in 000 tonnes)				*Composition of milk (%)*		
Year	*Cow*	*Buffalo*	*Total*	*Annual Percentage Growth*	*Cow*	*Buffalo*	*Total*
1965-66	458.00	411.00	869.00		52.70	47.30	100
1977-78	894.35	785.58	1679.93	7.18	53.24	46.76	100
1978-79	929.31	797.27	1726.58	2.78	53.82	46.18	100
1979-80	996.33	863.74	1860.07	7.73	53.56	46.44	100
1980-81	906.06	831.88	1737.93	-6.57	52.13	47.87	100
1981-82	1010.77	874.68	1885.45	8.49	53.61	46.39	100
1982-83	978.73	809.69	1788.42	-5.15	54.73	45.27	100
1983-84	1506.87	1054.71	2561.58	43.23	58.83	41.17	100
1984-85	1662.09	1184.04	2846.13	11.11	58.40	41.60	100
1985-86	1818.80	1299.55	3118.35	9.56	58.33	41.67	100
1986-87	1963.03	1331.54	3294.57	5.65	59.58	40.42	100
1987-88	1849.00	1260.14	3109.15	-5.63	59.47	40.53	100
1988-89	1879.62	1358.14	3237.76	4.14	58.05	41.95	100
1989-90	2065.01	1344.95	3409.97	5.32	60.56	39.44	100
1990-91	2021.60	1353.06	3374.66	-1.04	59.91	40.09	100
1991-92	1982.58	1374.24	3356.82	-0.53	59.06	40.94	100
1992-93	2081.33	1386.83	3468.15	3.32	60.01	39.99	100
1993-94	2102.28	1422.07	3524.34	1.62	59.65	40.35	100
1994-95	2210.20	1483.59	3693.78	4.81	59.84	40.16	100
1995-96	2273.47	1517.36	3790.83	2.63	59.97	40.03	100
1996-97	2370.18	1606.33	3976.51	4.90	59.60	40.40	100
1997-98	2431.81	1628.77	4060.58	2.10	59.90	40.10	100
1998-99	2578.27	1694.57	4272.84	5.20	60.30	39.70	100
1999-2000	2828.29	1745.54	4573.83	7.00	61.80	38.20	100
2000-01	3094.75	1804.42	4899.17	7.10	63.10	36.90	100

Source: (i) Integrated Sample Survey Reports, 1977-78 to 2000-01, (various years).
(ii) Singh *et. al*, (Undated).

Appendix Table 6.2
Trends in Shares of Milch Animals by Breeding Practices in Tamil Nadu: 1977-78 to 1982-83

(in percentage)

Year	*Milch Animals by Breeding Practices*					
	Cattle			*Buffalo*		
	Natural	*Artificial*	*Total*	*Natural*	*Artificial*	*Total*
1977-78	56.25	43.75	100.00	58.03	41.97	100.00
1978-79	74.40	25.60	100.00	74.70	25.30	100.00
1979-80	75.65	24.35	100.00	72.64	27.36	100.00
1980-81	64.72	35.28	100.00	63.47	36.53	100.00
1981-82	76.90	23.10	100.00	80.90	19.10	100.00
1982-83	63.70	36.30	100.00	62.10	37.90	100.00
1983-84	56.50	43.50	100.00	53.10	46.90	100.00

Source: Integrated Sample Surveys, Tamil Nadu, (various years).

Appendix Table 6.3
Trends in Number of Artificial Inseminations Done in Tamil Nadu

	Number of AIs (in lakh) done by			*Share (%)of AIs done by*		
Year	*DAH-VI*	*TCMPF*	*Total*	*DAH-VI*	*TCMPF*	*Total*
1981-82	12.98	1.68	14.66	88.54	11.46	100.00
1989-90	25.77	6.61	32.38	79.59	20.41	100.00
1990-91	26.88	6.75	33.63	79.93	20.07	100.00
1991-92	22.74	6.98	29.72	76.51	23.49	100.00
1992-93	25.69	7.63	33.32	77.10	22.90	100.00
1993-94	16.33	8.49	24.82	65.79	34.21	100.00
1994-95	25.56	8.85	34.41	74.28	25.72	100.00
1995-96	25.72	9.15	34.87	73.76	26.24	100.00
1996-97	25.25	8.71	33.96	74.35	25.65	100.00
1997-98	26.82	8.99	35.81	74.90	25.10	100.00

Note: DAH-VI refers to Department of Animal Husbandry Veterinary Institution and TMMPF refers to Tamil Nadu Cooperative Milk Producer's Fedetation Ltd.

Source: Tamil Nadu Economic Appraisal (various years)

Appendix Table 6.4
Distribution of Animals According to Feeding Practices by Species, Seasons and Status of Animals in Tamil Nadu, (1965-66)

Season	Status of Animal	Percentage Distribution of Animals					
		Cattle			Buffalo		
		Grazed	Grazed+ Stallfed	Total	Grazed	Grazed+ Stallfed	Total
Rainy	InMilk	21.40	78.60	100.00	14.70	85.30	100.00
	Dry	33.90	66.10	100.00	34.60	65.40	100.00
	Young stock (1-3)	53.20	46.80	100.00	41.00	59.00	100.00
	Young stock (<1)	79.00	21.00	100.00	68.30	31.70	100.00
Winter	InMilk	17.00	83.00	100.00	17.80	82.20	100.00
	Dry	44.80	55.20	100.00	38.20	61.80	100.00
	Young stock (1-3)	50.50	49.50	100.00	38.90	61.10	100.00
	Young stock (<1)	68.80	31.20	100.00	58.00	42.00	100.00
Summer	InMilk	18.00	82.00	100.00	6.60	93.40	100.00
	Dry	23.80	76.20	100.00	18.80	81.20	100.00
	Young stock (1-3)	41.40	58.60	100.00	30.40	69.60	100.00
	Young stock (<1)	61.20	38.80	100.00	34.70	65.30	100.00
OverAll	InMilk	18.80	81.20	100.00	12.52	87.48	100.00
	Dry	32.17	67.83	100.00	28.24	71.76	100.00
	Young stock (1-3)	46.98	53.02	100.00	34.54	65.46	100.00
	Young stock (<1)	66.54	33.46	100.00	47.00	53.00	100.00

Source: Singh D., *et. al* (undated).

Appendix Table 6. 5
Percentage Distribution of Animals in Milk and Quantity of Milk Yield Per Animal In-Milk by Species and Concentrates Used in Tamil Nadu, (1975-76)

	Rural				*Urban*			
	Cattle		*Buffalo*		*Cattle*		*Buffalo*	
Amount of Concentrates Used	*% share of animals in-milk*	*Average milk yield (0.00 litre)*	*% share of animals in-milk*	*Average milk yield (0.00 litre)*	*% share of animals in-milk*	*Average milk yield (0.00 litre)*	*% share of animals in-milk*	*Average milk yield (0.00 litre)*
0.0 *	39.44	0.61	19.18	1.10	28.26	1.49	14.80	1.87
0.1 – 0.5	29.32	1.14	28.10	1.70	24.80	1.92	20.91	1.84
0.6 – 1.0	16.94	1.27	26.78	1.86	17.54	2.55	28.00	2.48
1.1 – 1.5	5.89	1.41	8.81	2.00	8.65	2.44	12.79	3.07
1.5 – 2.0	5.90	1.67	11.39	2.32	11.22	3.37	10.24	2.97
2.1 – 3.0	1.81	1.96	3.49	2.77	5.21	3.20	7.62	3.74
3.1 – 5.0	0.63	2.92	2.14	2.49	3.87	2.71	4.42	4.42
Above 5.0	0.07	4.00	0.11	4.50	0.45	6.38	1.22	4.74
All classes	100.00	1.03	100.00	1.60	100.00	2.27	100.00	2.59

Source: GOI (1984).

Appendix Table 6.6
Percentage Distribution of Animals In-Milk and Quantity of Milk Yield Per Animal in-Milk Classified by Species and Concentrates Used in Tamil Nadu, (1975-76)

		Cattle			*Buffalo*		
			Average Quantity of			*Average Quantity of*	
Region	*Size Group of Milk Yield (litre)*	*% shareof animals in-milk*	*milk yield (litre)*	*Concentrates Used*	*% shareof animals in-milk*	*milk yield (litre)*	*Concentrates Used*
Rural	0.0 0*	13.97	0.00	0.20	3.24	0.00	0.30
	0.01 - 0.50	26.44	0.40	0.30	13.12	0.45	0.40
	0.51 - 1.00	29.33	0.91	0.60	20.75	0.93	0.70
	1.01 - 2.00	21.49	1.66	0.80	31.26	1.69	0.90
	2.01 - 3.00	6.20	2.65	0.90	18.17	2.66	1.30
	3.01 - 4.00	1.22	3.65	1.40	10.76	3.66	1.30
	4.01 - 5.00	0.64	4.69	2.10	2.02	4.61	1.70
	5.01 - 7.00	0.64	6.69	2.10	0.57	6.49	1.50
	above 7.00	0.07	16.00	1.00	0.11	9.60	0.50
	All classes	100.00	1.02	0.60	100.00	1.80	0.90
Urban	0.0 0*	1.88	0.00	0.30	0.40	0.00	0.00
	0.01 - 0.50	8.93	0.42	0.40	5.81	0.41	0.50
	0.51 - 1.00	17.80	0.93	0.80	12.48	0.94	0.70
	1.01 - 2.00	31.53	1.74	0.90	26.30	1.86	1.00
	2.01 - 3.00	18.00	2.66	1.20	28.38	2.71	1.20
	3.01 - 4.00	11.13	3.66	1.40	15.62	3.65	1.50
	4.01 - 5.00	3.88	4.76	1.50	6.41	4.80	1.90
	5.01 - 7.00	5.11	6.02	2.20	3.59	6.21	2.60
	above 7.00	1.74	10.65	2.60	1.01	8.87	4.80
	All classes	100.00	2.27	1.00	100.00	2.60	1.20

Source: GOI. (1984).

Appendix Table 6.7
Percentage Distribution of
Milch Animals by Levels of Milk Yield in Tamil Nadu

		Percentage Distribution of Animals According to					
		Milk Yield Levels (in kgs.)					
Species	*Year*	*< 0.9*	*1-1.9*	*2-2.9*	*3-3.9*	*4+*	*Total*
Cow	1965-66	64.20	21.80	7.60	4.40	2.00	100.00
	1977-78	18.40	34.20	15.10	10.40	21.90	100.00
	1980-81	9.20	38.50	28.50	15.10	8.70	100.00
	1985-86	12.68	21.21	21.63	16.62	27.86	100.00
	1990-91	1.73	4.81	34.61	28.89	29.96	100.00
	1995-96	0.68	5.00	25.03	17.42	48.88	100.00
	1996-97	0.52	5.24	20.00	17.16	57.08	100.00
	1997-98	0.65	11.48	17.05	18.12	52.71	100.00
	1998-99	1.80	6.00	17.32	14.23	60.66	100.00
	1999-2000	1.78	6.66	17.43	14.93	59.20	100.00
	2000-01	2.70	9.02	13.98	12.43	61.88	100.00
Buffalo	1965-66	46.00	28.20	12.80	8.70	4.30	100.00
	1977-78	46.00	28.20	27.90	22.00	20.40	100.00
	1980-81	6.50	23.20	33.70	18.70	23.50	100.00
	1985-86	4.60	19.50	28.69	24.28	28.13	100.00
	1990-91	5.20	13.70	26.82	43.52	23.34	100.00
	1995-96	1.46	4.86	20.53	26.92	46.87	100.00
	1996-97	0.62	2.23	13.71	37.93	45.51	100.00
	1997-98	0.31	2.89	17.29	26.98	52.53	100.00
	1998-99	1.24	0.64	7.81	36.54	53.77	100.00
	1999-2000	0.95	1.03	7.53	36.91	53.58	100.00
	2000-01	0.19	3.32	18.54	18.69	59.25	100.00

Source: Singh *et al.* (undated) and Integrated Sample Surveys, Tamil Nadu, (various years).

Appendix Table 6.8
Percentage Distribution of Cows by Levels of Milk Yield and Breeds in Tamil Nadu

		Distribution of Animals according to Levels of Milk Yield						
Breed	*Year*	*< 0.9*	*1-1.9*	*2-2.9*	*3-3.9*	*4-4.9*	*5+*	*Total*
Indigenous	1991-92	2.40	28.50	62.60	6.30	0.20	-	100.00
Cow	1992-93	2.60	31.10	45.10	20.70	0.50	-	100.00
	1993-94	4.00	27.90	41.90	17.70	6.60	1.90	100.00
	1994-95	3.60	27.00	44.20	16.90	7.10	1.20	100.00
	1995-96	4.65	15.06	47.65	24.95	4.80	2.89	100.00
	1996-97	1.09	12.47	47.36	24.09	13.33	1.66	100.00
	1997-98	1.55	27.94	36.09	24.93	8.47	1.03	100.00
	1998-99	5.10	16.82	45.04	25.72	6.84	0.48	100.00
	1999-2000	4.92	18.07	44.65	25.01	7.34	0.00	100.00
	2000-01	9.41	24.30	26.68	17.66	16.28	4.36	100.00
Exotic and	1991-92	-	-	4.10	27.80	64.20	3.90	100.00
Cross-bred	1992-93	-	15.00	34.60	39.50	9.50	1.40	100.00
Cows	1993-94	-	.70	2.40	8.10	20.50	68.30	100.00
	1994-95	-	0.80	2.90	8.20	20.60	67.50	100.00
	1995-96	0.31	1.57	11.22	12.98	17.66	56.26	100.00
	1996-97	0.20	1.23	4.82	13.82	24.36	56.08	100.00
	1997-98	0.06	0.69	4.57	13.66	21.06	59.95	100.00
	1998-99	0.00	0.12	2.28	8.00	18.05	71.56	100.00
	1999-2000	0.00	0.22	2.05	9.24	19.33	69.16	100.00
	2000-01	0.28	2.76	7.07	7.82	14.14	67.94	100.00

Source: Integrated Sample Survey–Tamil Nadu, (various years).

Appendix Table 6.9
Distribution of Female Animal Stock Across Age Groups by Species, Regions in Tamil Nadu and All-India (1975-76)

Age Group (Completed Years)	*Percentage Distribution of Female Animals*							
	Tamil Nadu				*All India*			
	Rural		*Urban*		*Rural*		*Urban*	
	Cattle	*Buffalo*	*Cattle*	*Buffalo*	*Cattle*	*Buffalo*	*Cattle*	*Buffalo*
0	10.59	13.71	17.07	14.80	11.38	12.36	15.08	14.43
1	9.18	9.41	9.35	6.57	9.83	8.95	10.29	6.92
2	10.45	10.63	8.68	5.14	11.53	11.55	10.09	6.73
3-4	18.19	18.81	17.22	11.10	15.04	13.46	14.75	9.48
5-6	21.82	18.55	18.38	20.76	17.84	15.28	17.11	15.52
7-9	18.96	18.66	19.82	26.84	21.28	22.64	20.13	27.72
10-12	8.77	8.89	7.34	11.76	9.96	11.88	9.40	14.51
13-15	1.78	1.01	2.03	2.76	2.48	3.00	2.28	3.65
16-18	0.11	0.17	0.07	0.28	0.49	0.64	0.53	0.76
19+	0.08	0.03	0.02	0.00	0.12	0.17	0.18	0.19
Not recorded	0.08	0.12	0.00	0.00	0.04	0.07	0.16	0.08
All ages	100.00	100.00	100.00	100.00	100.00	100.00	100.00	100.00

Source: Government of India: (1984)

Appendix Table 6.10
Percentage Distribution of
Milch Animals by the Order of Lactation in Tamil Nadu

		Percentage distribution of milch animals by Order of Lactation						
Species	*Year*	*1*	*2*	*3*	*4*	*5*	*6+*	*Total*
Cattle	1977-78	42.88	34.44	17.08	3.95	1.13	0.52	100.00
	1980-81	13.83	20.65	26.47	15.15	10.23	13.67	100.00
	1985-86	19.40	26.46	23.16	14.69	5.99	10.30	100.00
	1990-91	30.20	38.60	26.70	4.00	0.50	0.00	100.00
	1995-96	16.50	35.27	29.33	14.56	3.77	0.57	100.00
	1996-97	21.31	35.22	24.19	11.82	5.51	2.15	100.00
	1997-98	25.80	41.31	23.33	7.29	2.21	0.07	100.00
	1998-99	20.75	40.33	28.50	8.81	1.57	0.24	100.00
	1999-2000	22.27	39.22	30.17	6.40	1.83	0.31	100.00
	2000-01	12.70	40.31	28.67	11.58	3.05	3.69	100.00
Buffalo	1977-78	40.58	30.80	20.41	6.57	1.30	0.34	100.00
	1980-81	14.90	23.20	28.30	14.60	9.10	9.90	100.00
	1985-86	18.65	30.66	24.70	10.24	6.13	9.62	100.00
	1990-91	30.10	38.90	25.50	4.70	0.80	0.00	100.00
	1995-96	9.92	32.23	29.56	19.21	8.29	0.79	100.00
	1996-97	16.42	35.06	28.37	14.83	5.33	0.00	100.00
	1997-98	13.23	42.94	33.41	9.19	1.24	0.00	100.00
	1998-99	14.14	36.24	40.27	9.23	0.94	0.18	100.00
	1999-2000	16.01	36.38	42.91	3.17	1.16	0.37	100.00
	2000-01	8.70	31.17	35.87	14.04	5.38	4.85	100.00

Source: Integrated Sample Surveys, Tamil Nadu, (various years).

Appendix Table 6.11
Percentage Distribution of Cows
by the Order of Lactation by Breeds in Tamil Nadu

		Distribution of Cows according to Order of Lactation by Breed					
BBreed Type	*YYear*	*1*	*2*	*3*	*4*	*5+*	*Total*
IndigenousCows	1991-92	30.30	36.30	23.30	7.50	2.60	100.00
	1992-93	8.60	31.30	32.40	21.10	6.60	100.00
	1993-94	8.20	24.10	31.10	26.90	9.70	100.00
	1994-95	5.00	25.10	36.40	22.60	10.90	100.00
	1995-96	13.60	34.20	31.81	15.95	4.44	100.00
	1996-97	18.71	36.85	25.14	11.63	7.67	100.00
	1997-98	21.00	47.11	26.18	5.29	0.42	100.00
	1998-99	18.48	42.46	29.33	8.31	1.43	100.00
	1999-2000	20.65	43.19	30.93	3.35	1.88	100.00
	2000-01	15.29	41.01	26.42	12.31	4.98	100.00
EExotic &	1991-92	22.10	31.90	31.60	12.90	1.50	100.00
Cross-bred Cows	1992-93	5.80	24.00	33.60	29.00	7.60	100.00
	1993-94	3.80	21.40	31.40	31.70	11.70	100.00
	1994-95	5.70	22.80	30.10	27.60	13.80	100.00
	1995-96	18.28	35.92	27.80	13.72	4.28	100.00
	1996-97	22.75	34.31	23.67	11.62	7.55	100.00
	1997-98	28.94	37.51	21.45	8.60	3.50	100.00
	1998-99	21.98	39.18	28.05	8.77	2.02	100.00
	1999-2000	23.18	36.98	29.74	8.12	1.88	100.00
	2000-01	11.82	40.07	29.44	11.33	7.33	100.00

Source: Integrated Sample Survey, (various years)

Appendix Table 6.12
Trends in Number of Veterinary Institutions in Tamil Nadu

Year	*Number of Veterinary institutions*	*Number of Bovines Treated*	*Number of Animals Castrated*	*Bovines treated per veterinary institutions*	*Animals castrated per veterinary institutions*
1956-57	107	230188	70053	2151	655
1961-62	224	670720	184561	2994	824
1965-66	278	695820	90861	2503	327
1970-71	516	1255122	108245	2432	210
1975-76	606	2045718	113461	3376	187
1980-81	671	4871041	242640	7259	362
1985-86	772	6743744	437498	8735	567
1990-91	837	8639723	556316	10322	665
1995-96	883	9077194	598204	10280	677
1997-98	955	8597303	687209	9002	720

Source: Director, Department of Animal Husbandry, Chennai.

Appendix Table 6.13
Trends in Milch Bovines Per Veterinary Institution in Tamil Nadu

Year	*Total Veterinary Institutions*	*Total Milch Animal Population*	*Milch Bovines per Veterinary Institution*
1956	107	3710256	34675
1961	224	3865584	15257
1966	303	4082287	13472
1974	582	4232079	7272
1977	637	4529242	7110
1982	722	5208790	7214
1989	814	4765499	5854
1994	881	4641014	5268
1997	995	4753301	4777

Source: Director, Department of Animal Husbandry, Chennai and Livestock Census, Tamil Nadu, various years.

Appendix Table 6.14

Quantity (in litres) and Value (in Rs.) of (i) Consumption of Home Produced Milk and (ii) Purchase of Milk Per Person Per Month by Household Monthly Per-Capita Expenditure (HMPCE) Groups in Tamil Nadu, 1975-76

			Rural				*Urban*				*Share of Purchased Milk to the Total Milk*			
HMPCE Group	*% of households reporting consumption of milk*		*Home Produced*		*Purchased*		*Home Produced*		*Purchased*		*Rural*		*Urban*	
	Rural	*Urban*	*Qty*	*Value*	*Qty*	*Value*	*Qty*	*Value*	*Qty*	*Value*	*Qty*	*Value*	*Qty*	*Value*
Up to Rs. 9		8.33					0.18	0.35	0.02	0.06			10.00	14.63
Rs. 10 –19	6.94	17.31			0.05	0.07			0.15	0.24	100.00	100.00	100.00	100.00
Rs. 20-29	16.14	31.07	0.19	0.22	0.11	0.15	0.06	0.09	0.27	0.48	36.67	40.54	81.82	84.21
Rs. 30-39	21.22	42.45	0.27	0.35	0.18	0.24	0.10	0.16	0.56	0.95	40.00	40.68	84.85	85.59
Rs. 40-49	25.86	53.92	0.39	0.50	0.28	0.39	0.25	0.36	0.91	1.52	41.79	43.82	78.45	80.85
Rs. 50-59	40.45	63.63	0.80	1.02	0.55	0.78	0.29	0.47	1.36	2.35	40.74	43.33	82.42	83.33
Rs. 60-69	42.97	67.55	1.04	1.34	0.73	1.01	0.41	0.63	1.81	3.16	41.24	42.98	81.53	83.38
Rs. 70-79	47.45	72.64	1.42	1.91	0.84	1.19	0.50	0.80	2.45	4.30	37.17	38.39	83.05	84.31
Rs. 80-89	57.90	77.73	1.73	2.26	1.15	1.62	0.72	1.20	3.20	5.64	39.93	41.75	81.63	82.46
Rs. 90-99	47.89	74.16	2.44	3.30	1.13	1.65	0.63	0.96	3.65	6.26	31.65	33.33	85.28	84.71
Rs. 100 & +	65.70	74.24	3.34	4.56	1.66	2.39	0.65	1.13	6.36	12.00	33.20	34.39	90.73	91.39
Not Recorded	14.49	33.33	0.24	0.24	0.57	0.95			2.48	4.16	70.37	79.83	100.00	100.00
All Classes	31.46	60.69	0.64	0.83	0.41	0.57	0.33	0.53	1.92	3.43	39.05	40.71	85.33	86.62

Source: Government of India (1978a).

Appendix Table 6.15
Salient Features about the Activities of AAVIN, Tamil Nadu, 2001-02

Infrastructure	*Particulars*	*Unit*	*Figures*
Milk Products Factories	Number of Factories	in Nos.	5
	Processing Capacity	Lakh litres per day	9.12
	Drying Capacity	M.Ts per day	70
District Dairies	Dairies	in Nos.	20
	Processing Capacity	Lakh litres per day	18.27
Chilling Centres	Centres	in Nos.	38
	Chilling Capacity	Lakh litres per day	11.51
Milk Collection Centres	Societies	in Nos.	8921
Marketing Network	Automatic Vending Machine Units	in Nos.	217
	Fibre Reinforced Plastic Tanks	in Nos.	182
	Booths (in sachets)	in Nos.	509
	Parlours	in Nos.	34
District Cooperative Union	Regular Veterinary Units	in Nos.	100
	Emergency Units	in Nos.	37
	Societies with AI facilities	in Nos.	2517
Cattle Feed Plants	Number of Plants	in Nos.	3
	Capacity	M.Ts. per day	300

Source: AAVIN, Chennai.

Appendix Table 6.16
Trends in State and Per Capita Income in Tamil Nadu, 1970-71 to 2001-02

	Net State Domestic Product (in lakh Rs.)		*Per-Capita Income (in 0.00 Rs.)*	
Year	*Current*	*Constant (1970-71)*	*Current*	*Constant (1970-71)*
1970-71	237110	237110	581	581
1971-72	269617	249075	648	599
1972-73	283895	249978	669	589
1973-74	343231	260934	793	603
1974-75	363872	226574	826	514
1975-76	372740	267904	831	597
1976-77	430388	276324	944	606
1977-78	470987	303090	1017	654
1978-79	502302	314224	1069	669
1979-80	609524	318263	1280	668
1980-81	721816	301385	1498	625
1981-82	867670	334541	1776	685
1982-83	882089	316489	1777	638
1983-84	1022224	333608	2024	661
1984-85	1200775	376507	2341	734
1985-86	1368233	392051	2620	751
1986-87	1530500	388740	2885	733
1987-88	1819519	413021	3379	767
1988-89	1955980	453161	3581	830
1989-90	2296601	459489	4370	874
1990-91	2767374	518725	4983	934
1991-92	3258365	532650	5798	948
1992-93	3792154	560103	6680	987
1993-94	5164330	611300	8955	1066
1994-95	6127581	675652	10503	1167
1995-96	6971916	687881	11818	1177
1996-97	7912106	718836	13270	1218
1997-98	9268985	799698	15388	1335
1998-99	10579315	835675	17394	1382
1999-2K	11274064	882368	18367	1446
2000-01	12609957	948602	20367	1541

Source: Tamil Nadu Economic Appraisal, (various years).

Appendix Table 6.17

Trends in Whole Sale and Retail Prices of Milk, Ghee, Fish, Meat and Egg in Tamil Nadu

	Whole Sale Prices (0.00 Rs.)					*Retail Prices (0.00 Rs.)*						
Year	*Milk per 100 litres*	*Ghee per quintal*	*Fish-Pom per quintal*	*Fish-Cat per quintal*	*Eggs per 100*	*Milk per litre*	*Goat Meat per kg.*	*Pork per kg.*	*Beef per kg*	*Cat fish per kg.*	*Egg per dozen*	*Chicken per kg*
1965	111.50	973.48	303.75	179.33	19.71	1.12	4.78	3.69	1.69	2.20	2.43	3.02
1970	165.00	1372.65	290.00	140.00	25.33	1.28	6.50	6.00	2.50	1.25	3.48	3.04
1975	233.33	2143.84	550.00	225.00	38.92	1.80	11.92	9.75	4.17	3.31	4.72	8.50
1980	312.50	2487.50	1100.00	350.00	34.50	2.31	20.54	12.64	6.50	N.A	4.65	12.09
1985	475.00	4100.00	1541.67	1041.67	40.58	4.75	29.33	16.00	10.00	12.25	5.62	18.00
1990	600.00	7158.00	2400.00	1400.00	57.00	4.99	42.17	21.17	10.67	30.08	7.71	N.A
1995	1000.00	11496.00	4808.00	1787.00	102.00	8.60	N.A	38.10	N.A	26.00	14.25	40.00
2000	1125.00	13541.18	6808.00	2087.00	129.51	11.38	118.03	48.10	N.A	38.58	16.44	N.A
	Index Numbers (1965 =100)							*Index Numbers (1965 = 100)*				
1970	147.98	141.00	95.47	78.07	128.51	114.29	135.98	162.60	147.93	56.82	143.21	100.66
1975	209.26	220.22	181.07	125.47	197.46	160.71	249.37	264.23	246.75	150.45	194.24	281.46
1980	280.27	255.53	362.14	195.17	175.04	206.25	429.71	342.55	384.62	N.A	191.36	400.33
1985	426.01	421.17	507.55	580.87	205.89	424.11	613.60	433.60	591.72	556.82	231.28	596.03
1990	538.12	735.30	790.12	780.68	289.19	445.54	882.22	573.71	631.36	1367.27	317.28	N.A
1995	896.86	1180.92	1582.88	996.49	517.50	767.86	N.A	1032.52	N.A	1181.82	586.42	1324.50
2000	1008.97	1391.01	2241.32	1164.78	657.08	1016.07	2469.25	1303.52	N.A	1753.64	676.54	N.A

Source: Government of India (various years) Agricultural Prices in India, Ministry of Agriculture, various issues.

Appendix Table 6.18

Per Capita Monthly Consumption Expenditure by Broad Group of Items and Consumer Expenditure as Percentage to Total Consumer Expenditure Based on Different NSS Rounds in Tamil Nadu by Regions

	Rural						*Urban*					
	NSS Rounds and Period						*NSS Rounds and Period*					
Items of Expenditure	*27th 1972-73*	*32nd 1977-78*	*38th 1982-83*	*42nd 1986-87*	*50th 1993-94*	*55th 1999-2000*	*27th 1972-73*	*32nd 1977-78*	*38th 1982-83*	*42nd 1986-87*	*50th 1993-94*	*55th 1999-2000*
In Value Terms (0.00 Rs.)												
Cereals & its Substitutes	15.71	23.00	39.42	43.47	73.32	93.78	14.18	21.33	38.84	42.84	72.65	105.90
Pulses & Pulse Products	1.40	2.21	3.83	6.09	11.66	22.68	1.97	3.12	5.20	9.02	15.02	30.21
Milk & Milk Products	1.14	1.94	3.73	5.82	13.23	25.22	3.39	5.14	9.88	15.26	27.40	57.95
Edible Oils	1.31	1.84	3.73	6.12	11.48	16.81	1.89	2.90	5.63	9.70	15.74	22.20
Meat, Egg & Fish	1.43	2.29	4.20	5.80	12.64	24.52	2.02	3.11	5.87	9.32	18.45	34.49
Vegetables	1.30	2.47	4.26	7.62	16.79	32.58	1.85	3.15	6.49	11.24	20.95	46.67
Fruits & Nuts	0.52	1.04	1.92	3.34	6.04	11.71	1.02	1.17	3.43	6.29	9.41	20.67
Sugar	0.67	1.03	1.79	2.45	4.96	7.03	1.28	1.61	2.71	4.25	7.06	10.13
Salt	0.07	0.14	0.16	0.24	0.51	1.12	0.07	0.13	0.15	0.26	0.52	1.39
Spices	1.78	2.85	3.97	6.59	11.30	29.51	1.86	3.07	4.37	7.89	11.67	42.24
Beverages & Refreshments	1.81	3.15	5.98	11.31	22.54	36.89	5.08	7.04	13.21	20.27	40.27	70.33
Total Food	27.14	41.61	73.01	98.86	184.49	301.90	34.61	52.37	95.70	136.36	239.33	443.17
Total Non-Food	10.56	21.72	39.20	55.43	109.12	213.16	19.41	33.77	68.04	112.43	198.96	523.46
Total Expenditure	37.70	63.33	112.23	154.29	293.62	514.06	54.02	86.14	163.74	248.79	438.29	971.64

Contd...

Items of Expenditure	Rural						Urban					
	NSS Rounds and Period						NSS Rounds and Period					
	27th 1972-73	32nd 1977-78	38th 1982-83	42nd 1986-87	50th 1993-94	55th 1999-2000	27th 1972-73	32nd 1977-78	38th 1982-83	42nd 1986-87	50th 1993-94	55th 1999-2000
In Percentages												
Cereals & its Substitutes	41.67	36.32	35.12	28.17	24.97	18.24	26.25	24.76	23.72	17.22	16.58	10.90
Pulses & Pulse Products	3.71	3.49	3.41	3.95	3.97	4.41	3.65	3.62	3.18	3.63	3.43	3.11
Milk & Milk Products	3.02	3.06	3.32	3.77	4.51	4.91	6.28	5.97	6.03	6.13	6.25	5.96
Edible Oils	3.47	2.91	3.32	3.97	3.91	3.27	3.50	3.37	3.44	3.90	3.59	2.28
Meat, Egg & Fish	3.79	3.62	3.74	3.76	4.30	4.77	3.74	3.61	3.58	3.75	4.21	3.55
Vegetables	3.45	3.90	3.80	4.94	5.72	6.34	3.42	3.66	3.96	4.52	4.78	4.80
Fruits & Nuts	1.38	1.64	1.71	2.16	2.06	2.28	1.89	1.36	2.09	2.53	2.15	2.13
Sugar	1.78	1.63	1.59	1.59	1.69	1.37	2.37	1.87	1.66	1.71	1.61	1.04
Salt	0.19	0.22	0.14	0.16	0.17	0.22	0.13	0.15	0.09	0.10	0.12	0.14
Spices	4.72	4.50	3.54	4.27	3.85	5.74	3.44	3.56	2.67	3.17	2.66	4.35
Beverages & Refreshments	4.80	4.97	5.33	7.33	7.68	7.18	9.40	8.17	8.07	8.15	9.19	7.24
Total Food	71.99	65.70	65.05	64.07	62.83	58.73	64.07	60.80	58.45	54.81	54.61	45.61
Total Non-Food	28.01	34.30	34.93	35.93	37.16	41.47	35.93	39.20	41.55	45.19	45.39	53.87
Total Expenditure	100.00	100.00	100.00	100.00	100.00	100.00	100.00	100.00	100.00	100.00	100.00	100.00
% share of Milk and Milk Products to the Total Food Expenditure	4.20	4.66	511	5.88	7.17	8.35	9.79	9.81	10.32	11.19	11.45	13.08

Source: Joshi P.D., (1998)

7

CONCLUSION

We began with the objective of examining the factors determining the size, composition and productivity of bovine holdings in Tamil Nadu. As a prelude to the analysis, we reviewed the empirical studies on India's bovine economy spanning over the past few decades. In the light of the review, we formulated the general hypothesis that the size, composition and productivity of bovine stock in India has been shaped by socio-economic, institutional, ecological and technological factors and not by religious factors. We have verified this hypothesis at length by undertaking an in-depth study of Tamil Nadu.

The study of Tamil Nadu roughly covered the twentieth century. The analysis of the historical evolution of the bovine economy during the first half of the 20th century indicated a steady increase in the size of the bovine population from 1920 onwards, significantly in the case of male cattle, thanks to increase in the requirement of work animals in agriculture. In fact, there existed shortage of male cattle for work a problem that used to be met by using female stock also as draught animals. But from1935 onwards, a steady increase in the population of adult female bovines took place, reflecting itself in the slow decline in the sex ratio due mainly to the expansion of the urban demand for milk.

The trends in size, composition and sex-ratios of bovines in Tamil Nadu during the second half of the 20th century showed a differential pattern. The total bovine population increased up to the early 'sixties, remained unchanged up to the early 'eighties and declined slowly thereafter. The composition of bovines has been getting oriented towards the cattle stock, particularly, towards cows from the early 'eighties onwards. The reversal of sex ratios which began from the early 'sixties indicated that the importance of milch animals that gained momentum from the mid-1930s has increased in more recent decades. The density of work animals per hectare of gross cropped area had been increasing in the 1950s, remaining unchanged till the mid-1960s and declining thereafter. The dominant influence was agricultural mechanization especially tractorisation that led to reduction of the work animal stock. The reduction in the average size of landholding has been another factor that significantly influenced work animal density; but the influence of this factor seems to have been declining in recent years.

The role of cows as a producer of males for work has undergone change over time, in the context of the declining work animal requirements. To capture this dimension, the factors determining the density of breeding cows were examined. It was found that though the density of work animals continued to be the dominant factor determining the density of breeding cows, the influence of this factor has been declining over time, and that other (unexplained) factors gaining in importance in recent years. Both the price and the non-price factors, including technology have played significant roles in determining the density of breeding cows.

The trends observed in the work and the milch animal populations appear to have been taking place at varying rates across size classes of land holdings. The growing importance of milch animals, has been particularly striking in the marginal and small holdings. However, it was the reduction of the work animal stock that has been striking in the case of medium and large holdings. This contrast obviously was due to differential patterns of development and impact of agricultural mechanization across size groups of holdings. The replacement of work animals with milch animals in the lower size holdings has also been a reflection of the growing opportunities to take up milk production as a supplementary source of income and employment in rural areas.

Available estimates show significant increase in milk production in the state in recent decades. Growth in milk production is contributed by both increases in milch animal population and in the productivity of milch animals. Though the contribution of cow milk to the total milk production has been gaining in importance, both 'population effect' and 'yield effect' have contributed to the growth in milk production obtained from cows and she-buffaloes. However, the latter factor has been far more important than the former.

Growth in productivity has taken place due to improvements in breeding, feeding and other management practices of milch animals; the expansion of marketing and processing infrastructure for milk have facilitated the growth in productivity too. During the 'eighties, there was considerable expansion in the artificial insemination (AI) facilities as a result of which significant increase was registered in the milch animal population covered by the AI programme. This development contributed to the increase in the population of crossbred cows and upgraded buffaloes in the milch stock. Along with the increase in the proportion of improved animals, the feeding practices of milch stock have also been undergoing change: from grazed and stall-fed to stall-fed with fodder and concentrates. Available estimates also show an increase in the per head availability of feed. Although the relative price of milk and concentrate feeds has not been very favourable in recent years, farmers have not reduced the use of concentrates since marginal revenue was still higher than marginal cost.

Increase in commercialisation has been contributed to a large extent by the expansion of dairy cooperatives. The overall efficiency of the milch animal stock has been also on the increase not only because of the increase in the proportion of improved animals, but also reduction in the proportion of low productive and unproductive animals. The available estimates show that the aggregate demand for milk has been steadily on the increase. Milk has now moved from the category of a luxury to that of a necessary, as reflected in the sharp fall in expenditure elasticities. Milk prices have been increasing at a slower pace than of its close substitutes and complementary goods in the food basket. It is seen that, over time, the per capita consumption of milk has increased in both the rural and the urban areas.

The importance of bovines as an important source of draught power in agriculture has sharply declined; they are now considered mainly a source of milk production. Consistent with these changes, the reproductive role of female bovines has shifted to that of a producer of female calves to be raised as milch animals. There exist several constraints, which need to be resolved to sustain the growth and development of the bovine sector, especially dairying and milk production.

The decline in the draught animal population is accompanied by intensive input use of non-renewable sources of energy in various agricultural operations. The data thrown up by the 59th round of the National Sample Survey (GOI 2005a) show that out of the total farmer households in the state, 30 percent used non-renewable sources of energy on ploughing, 0.3 percent for irrigation, 13 percent for harvesting and 14 percent for threshing. The use of animal energy is confined only to a small proportion of farmers, especially in the small and marginal categories. While the intensive use of non-renewable energy has released feed resources in favour of milch animals, there have been often changes taking place in the agricultural economy that offset this advantage. The shift in the cropping pattern from food crops to commercial and tree crops and the near-stagnation in cropping intensity appear to be contributing to the slow growth of the overall availability of feeds and fodder for the bovine sector. The changes in the pattern of land utilisation, especially the decline in the proportion of area under permanent pastures and grazing land have reduced the access of the landless households to common grazing lands for raising their animals. In a situation of this kind, when milch animal holdings have been shifting to households with weak resource base, they have had to increasingly depend on the market for procurement of feed resources for milk production. Thus, milk production has become increasingly sensitive to the relative prices of milk and feed. Sustaining milk production in such a situation would require increase in the supply of feed and enhancing its nutritive value, as also adoption of breeding and other complementary technologies for reducing cost of production per unit of milk output.

Augmentation of the supply of feed and fodder will become increasingly feasible if the link between agriculture and dairying is strengthened by promoting mixed farming that produces more by-products per unit of crop output. The possibility of promoting cultivation of green fodder is limited due to bleak prospects for expanding irrigation. Various types of technologies are available for enhancing the nutritive value of dry fodder that could reduce the requirement for concentrate feed to milch animals. However, the diffusion of such technologies is taking place at a slow pace due to weak links in the extension system.

There exists considerable scope for improving breeding efficiency by enhancing the effectiveness of artificial insemination. Though effective techniques like embryo transfer are available, their large-scale application in the field conditions in India is yet to come. Therefore, artificial insemination is likely to continue to play a major role for some more years. Improvement of AI efficiency would require not only the expansion of its infrastructure, but also improvement of the quality of the technical personnel delivering AI services and also of the level of knowledge of farmers in its effective adoption. Since the draught power constraint has disappeared, the choice of animals for cross-breeding has become easier. However, the attempt to introduce high-yielding exotic breeds of animals will make dairying a costly proposition to farmers. This is so not only because animals would be more expensive, but also because they are more prone to diseases and would need more expensive feed than indigenous breeds. Such technological up-gradation should therefore be accompanied by an effective system of animal insurance to compensate the farmers for loss of animals or fall in incomes due to diseases and other calamities like drought.

In the present situation, the formal extension system in the animal husbandry sector of the state appears to be weak. The data provided by the 59th round of the NSS (GOI 2005b) show that the proportions of farmer households receiving information on modem technology for animal husbandry in the state are 22 percent on breeding, 18 percent on feeding, 65 percent on health care and 8 percent on management. In order to improve effectiveness of the extension system and to provide more cost-effective supports to the dairy farmers, privitisation of veterinary and other related services is advocated by several international agencies (Ahuja et al 2000, Morrenhof 2004). The issue is actively under the consideration also of the Central and State governments. However, in a situation characterised by households owning one or two animals with weak resource base, the extent to which privitisation of services would work in favour of the vulnerable segments of the animal owners is an issue that needs to be seriously considered. There exists scope for enhancing effectiveness of the public sector institutions in the animal husbandry sector if it can be made part of the local governance system and accountable to local communities.

In the years to come, demand for milk and milk products would tend to increase, not only because of income growth, but also changes in the consumption pattern. Therefore, demand constraints for milk are unlikely to emerge in the state. However, from the point of view of providing more income to farmers, the task of increasing the value per unit of milk produced through product diversification and effective marketing network will remain a major challenge. The cooperative sector has taken a leading role in the procuring and processing of milk in the state. However, with liberalisation, private investment in the dairy-processing sector is already taking place on a significant scale. Therefore, the cooperative sector has to work in a competitive environment.

At present, the elimination of unproductive animals in the state takes place largely through their export to the neighbouring state of Kerala for slaughter. While the meat is consumed in Kerala, the hides and skin are sent back to Tamil Nadu as raw materials for its leather industry. The possibility of development of the meat industry within the state itself is limited because of the relatively low demand for beef and the constraints of retaining unproductive animals. Given the severe constraints on feed resources, fattening of male calves for meat purposes is also a very difficult proposition. Therefore, development of the meat industry based on the bovine stock is unlikely to emerge as a viable proposition in Tamil Nadu. However, the state should initiate steps for effective organisation for marketing of live animals by bringing appropriate regulations and measures for transportation, disease control and more proper treatment of animals.

ANNEXURE

NOTE ON LIVESTOCK STATISTICS IN TAMIL NADU[1]

The basic statistics on livestock include total number of livestock population, composition in terms of breed, sex and age; distribution by size categories of landholding; and livestock utilization pattern. Information is also available on different livestock products and by-products and their costs of production, as well as on the quantities and prices of inputs and products. These data, provided by various agencies such as the Ministry of Agriculture, the National Sample Survey Organization (NSSO), Department of Economics and Statistics and the State Animal Husband-ry Departments, are available in various forms and relate to different reference periods.

Indian Livestock Census

The origins of the Livestock Census may be traced to the early eighties of the nineteenth century. The question of a livestock census in India was discussed first at the All-India Statistical Confer-ence of 1883, which recommended a prescribed form for regular cattle censuses in India, to be undertaken at fixed intervals of time. Based on that recommendation, livestock details were collected first in 1887-88, but the area covered was confined to the Madras pro-vince. Starting with that year, data on livestock were collected annu-ally up to 1915-16. The major draw-backs of these censuses were the following: (a) the information collec-ted was neither complete nor comprehensive; (b) neither were the data collected simultaneously nor were the methods of collection uniform throughout the country. These limitations led to inaccuracy and non-comparability of data.

During the First World War, Government of India realized the importance of livestock statistics and decided to standardize the methods of enumeration and make the data more useful. Accordingly, it decided in 1916 that a Livestock Census should be conducted throughout British India during the winter months of 1919-20 and that the Census should be repeated quinquennially thereafter. Thus, on the initiative of Government of India, the first Livestock Census on an all-India basis was conducted in 1920.

The first two Censuses suffered from two defects. First, the period of enumeration was too long, viz. from December to April. Second, since there used to be large-scale inter-provincial movements of cattle during these months, the results were probably inaccurate to some extent. To overcome these difficulties, on the basis of the recom-mendations made by the Royal Commission on Agriculture, 1928, enumeration was undertaken from the third Census onwards in a short period of one month, all over the country. The data were collec-ted with the assistance of village *chowkidars,* headmen and police personnel.

The type of data collected in the Livestock Censuses has undergone changes over time. During the pre-Census period, i.e. prior to 1919-20, livestock data had been grouped under five categories: working cattle, cows, working buffaloes, she-buffaloes, and young stock which included calves of both cows and buffaloes. In the first three Censuses (for the years 1919-20, 1924-25 and 1930), cattle and buffaloes were divided into four categories, viz. bulls, bullocks, cows and young stock. The group 'young stock' referred to animals not old enough for work or breeding. In the 1935 Census, a revised classification was introduced to obtain more information. Accordingly, the details of utilization of adult males (used for breeding purposes, used for work, and not in use for work and breeding) and adult females (used for breeding, used for work, and not in use) were collected separately. In addition, data on pigs and poultry were included.

The details of number of items and the coverage in each Livestock Census are given below:

Year	*Series*	*Coverage*	*Number of Items Covered*
1987-88		Madras Province	14
1919-20	First Livestock Census	All India Level	17
1925	Second	All India Level	17
1930	Third	All India Level	68 (Agricultural Implements included)
1935	Fourth	All India Level	68
1940	Fifth	All India Level	101 (Sex, age classification included)
1945	Sixth	All India Level	101
1951	Seventh	All India Level	103 (Common sets of items introduced)
1956	Eighth	All India Level	103
1961	Ninth	All India Level	121 (Fishing crafts included)
1966	Tenth	All India Level	121
1972	Eleventh	All India Level	241 (Agricultural implements and machinery included)
1977	Twelfth	All India Level	241
1982	Thirteenth	All India Level	258 (Varieties like breeds included)
1989	Fourteenth	All India Level	347 (Varieties and use pattern included)
1994	Fifteenth	All India Level	347
1997	Sixteenth	All India Level	462 (Rabbit and other small ruminants included)

Source: Report on 16th Livestock Census, 1997, Department of Economics and Statistics, Chennai.

In the 1940 Census, working animals were sub-classified into (i) castrated and (ii) un-castrated.. Similarly, breeding cows were sub-grouped into (i) in milk, (ii) dry and (iii) not calved even once. The young stock was sub-divided into animals that were less than one year old and those that were one to three years old. Another important feature of the 1940 Census was that data were collected separately for rural and urban areas in each district. The 1940 classifi-cation continued unaltered till 1960.

In the 1961 Census, information on 'yaks' and on *desi* and improved varieties of fowls were collected and tabulated separately. In the 1966 Census, data on sheep under one year, camels four years old, and male and female pigs were also collected. Female goats of one year and over of age were further classified into 'in milk', 'dry' and 'others'. In the 1972 Census, a further break-up of male and female pigs acc-ording to age groups was introduced. In the 1982 and 1987 Censuses, classification of the data was further modified. The breed dimension statistics of the bovine population also began to be collected. The breed groups were identified as exotic, native pure, cross-bred and indigenous in the case of cattle, and *murrah,* graded and indigenous in the case of buffaloes. Though such modifications and improve-ments in successive Livestock Censuses are necessary and have taken into account the changing data needs, these changes result in inherent problems of comparability of statistics over time. Moreover, the criteria used by enumerators in the identification of breeds were ambiguous. Therefore, the reliability of the data collected remains questionable and data interpretation calls for extreme caution.

From the above discussion, it is obvious that frequent changes in classification, adoption of different groupings, and lack of uniformity in the year and the duration of the Census are the major limitations of the Livestock Censuses. These limitations have made the comparison of Census figures over time and across regions difficult. It is also unfortunate that the Livestock Censuses scheduled for recent periods were not conducted in time. For instance, the 15th Livestock Census should have been conducted in 1992, but it was conducted during 1994 only in Tamil Nadu. One of the other major limitations of the Livestock Censuses has been the inordinate delay in the publi-cation of results. In certain years, the reports remained unprinted for years together.

Agricultural Census and Input Survey

The World Agricultural Census (WAC) is designed basically to collect detailed information on factors which influence agricultural production, provides significant data on the livestock sector. It owes its origin to the International Institute of Agriculture, Rome, which had proposed a World Census of Agriculture as early as in 1924. The first Census actually took place in 1930, with the participation of 63 countries. India took part in the WAC for the first time in 1950, the fieldwork for which was undertaken during July 1954-April1955 by the National Sample Survey Organization (NSSO). The Census provided all-India and state-wise figures for landholdings, livestock population, etc., classified according to size. In the 1960s, the Census was conducted by the NSSO during July 1960-June 1961 and September 1961-July 1962.

On realizing the wide use to which these data could be put, the coverage and the scope of the survey were widened in the 1970 Cen-sus. A complete enumeration spread over 50,000 villages and cover-ing 60 to 65 million holdings, was done. In order to obtain reliable data on inputs (including animals), it was decided to conduct Input Surveys using systematic sample survey methods, as part of the Agricultural Census, from 1976-77 onwards. The Input Survey provides detailed information on animal population and agricultural implements across size classes of land-holdings. Since the categories of livestock information collected are almost the same as those in the Livestock Census, the Input Surveys provide an independent set of data for comparison and analysis. However, this source too has its limitations, like non-availability of published information for all the years and delays in publishing the results.

The National Sample Survey Organization

The NSSO has conducted periodic surveys on various aspects of livestock. The type of data available on livestock from this source includes distribution of bovines of various categories across landholding classes and regions, production and consumption of milk, productivity of milch animals, consumption of feed, and age distribution and mortality rates of livestock. Data on the size and composition of livestock and its distribution across regions and landholding categories are also available in the NSSO surveys on landholdings. Data on consumption expenditure on livestock prod-ucts are available in the consumer expenditure surveys.

Information on the average monthly expenditure on milk and milk products, and egg and fish, across monthly per-capita expenditure classes for rural and urban areas of states is being esti-mated in every round of the Consumer Expenditure Survey of the NSSO, right from the first round (1950-51). After the 26th round of the survey, the NSSO decided to undertake the survey on consump-tion expenditure once every five years. Accordingly, the first quin-quennial Survey on Consumption Expenditure was conducted in the 27th round (1972-73). The second, third and fourth quinquennial surveys were conducted during the 32nd round (1977-78), 38th round (1983) and 43rd round (1987-88). To maintain the continuity of survey data on consumption expenditure, it was decided later to carry out the enquiry in every NSS round, based on a smaller sample, in addition to the full-sample quinquennial surveys, starting from the 42nd round (1986-87). The 50th round (1993-94) and the 55th round (1999-2000) provided details about consumption of certain important commodities including milk and milk products.

The 59th round (2000) of the NSS initiated a new series "Situation Assessment Surveys of Farmers" that provides various items of information about farmers' cultivation practices, use of modern technologies, the availability and quality of technologies and its services, and the access to them.

Some of the NSS rounds-the 16th and 17th rounds (1960 and -'62), the 26th round (1971-72), the 37th round (1982), and the 48th round (1992)-collected data on the number of cattle and buffaloes according to landholding categories with break-downs for age, sex and use. The 16th and the 17th rounds provided information about the average area of pasture and grazing land per household across size classes of landholding. The 30th round (1975-76) of the survey collected information on livestock numbers, livestock products and livestock enterprises, thus covering various aspects of animal hus-bandry activities. Data were collected on the number of livestock and poultry with break-downs for age, sex, use, breed, type of acqui-sition and disposal of animals, etc. As regards livestock products, information on the production of milk, eggs and wood was collected.

Data on consumption including consumption of milk by type of milk (cow and buffalo), milk products, meat (goat, sheep, pig, cattle and buffalo) and eggs were also collected. Information on the average quantity of concentrate feeds fed to the animals was also collected in the 30th round. The All-India Debt and Investment

Surveys, con-ducted by the Reserve Bank of India during the years 1951-52, 1961-62, 1971-72, 1981-82 and 1991-92, provide data on the asset value of livestock (including poultry) across regions and asset groups in the country. This source of data is also useful to get an in-sight into the spatial and temporal changes in investment in livestock.

Farm Management Studies and Cost of Cultivation Surveys

The Directorate of Economics and Statistics of Government of India (GOI) initiated a comprehensive programme of Farm Management Studies in 1954. These studies-provided details of the livestock economy, such as the size and composition of livestock, pattern of utilization of draught animals, productivity of milch animals, etc. They were conducted in certain districts of selected states and were limited in their scope and coverage. Based on the recommen-dations of the Standing Technical Committee on Indices of Input Cost, GOI implemented a Comprehensive Scheme for Studying the Cost of Cultivation of Principal Crops in India with effect from 1970-71. The Cost of Cultivation surveys collect a large volume of household-level information on livestock, particularly on bovines. Some of the specific items of information are: size, sex and age com-position of bovine holdings per household, employment pattern of draught animals, production of milk, milk products, dung etc., con-sumption and disposal of milk and milk products, feeding and man-agement of bovines, and income realized from animal rearing. To understand the farm-level changes in the livestock sector, this is the most valuable source of data available. However, the data collected are not processed and published and they remain unutilized.

Integrated Sample Survey

The Integrated Sample Survey Scheme was introduced to estimate annual production of major livestock products like milk, eggs, meat and wool, and to study livestock management practices annually in a regular and continuous manner at the state level. The sampling and estimation procedures for the survey were developed by the Indian Agricultural Statistics Research Institute (IASRI). This survey has been in progress in Tamil Nadu since 1977-78, under a central scheme coordinated by the Ministry of Agriculture, GOI.

This survey covers the entire state of Tamil Nadu. The year has been divided into three seasons as summer (March-June), rainy (July – October) and winter (November-February) so as to capture the seasonal fluctuations in the production of livestock products. A three stage stratified random sampling design had been adopted and the stages are: selection of village, selection of households in the selected villages and selection of animals in the selected households.

This survey provides data on the size and breed composition of bovines, feeding practices, average quantity of green and dry fodders and concentrates fed per day, production and utilization of dung, average milk yield per animal by season, milk production by species and by season, distribution of animals by order of lactation and daily milk yield, milk utilization pattern, layers and their composition, egg production per layer by variety, total egg prod-uction, particulars of animals slaughtered, and production of meat and wool.

Though the Integrated Sample Surveys provide a wide range of valuable statistics on the livestock sector, only a small part of the available information is compiled and published.

Cost of Production Survey

The IASRI has conducted methodological studies to estimate the cost of production of livestock products such as milk, wool, hide and skin, poultry and eggs. Based on the procedures developed on the basis of these studies, Cost of production studies were intro-duced at the state level in recent years. The IASRI has also developed methodologies for working out the economics of rearing calves and maintenance of adult cattle and buffaloes, and the economics of production of pigs and rearing of sheep and goats. But no systematic surveys have been initiated so far on the lines of these methodologies.

Nutrition Surveys

The National Nutrition Monitoring Bureau undertakes Nu-trition Surveys that provide information on intake of milk and milk products per day across various categories of the human population (by sex, age, educational status, etc.). The results of the Nutrition Surveys are published by the National Institute of Nutrition, Hydera-bad. However, the coverage of the surveys is limited to a few states and the data already collected are yet to be properly used by resear-chers and policy-makers.

Other Sources of Data

In addition to the above sources of data, the Registrar of Cooperatives provides information on the organized sector of milk marketing; the Directorate of Economics and Statistics on the price of animals, milk, milk products and feed inputs; and the Department of Animal Husbandry, Tamil Nadu on the infrastructure relating to livestock development, health aspects of livestock and the provision of other services to livestock.

In the foregoing discussion, we have dealt in detail with the availability of livestock statistics and their limit-ations. Nevertheless, the database on the livestock sector is substantial.

Notes

1. This note draws heavily from Nair KN and AC Dhas (2001).

BIBLIOGRAPHY

Acharya, T.K.T. and T.C. Pawar (1980), "The Economics of Milk Production by Different Types of Milch Animals", *Indian Journal of Agricultural Economics,* Vol. 24, No. 4.

Acharya,T.K.T., Jaganath Rao, R. Pawar and J.D. Bhadage (1973), "Economics of Milk Production in Tribal Area of Ahmednagar District (Maharashtra State", *Agricultural Situation in India,* 28, No. 2.

Agarwal, S.B. and K.N.S. Sharma (1986), "Dairy Management Practices of Bovines in Key Village and Non-Key Village Areas Around Karnal", *Indian Journal of Dairy Science,* Vol. 39, No 1.

Aggarwala, A.C. and R.M. Sharma (1961), *A Laboratory Manual of Milk Inspection,* Asia Publishing House, Bombay.

Ahuja, Vinod., P.S. George, Sunil Ray, Kenneth E.McConnell, M.P.G.Kurup, Vasanth Gandhi, Dina Umali-Deininger and Cees de Haan (2000), *Agricultural Services and the Poor: Case of Livestock Health and Breeding Services in India,* Indian Institute of Mnanagement, Ahmedabad, The World Bank and Swiss Agency for Development and Cooperation, Bern.

Alderman, Harold (1989), *Cooperative Dairy Development in Karnataka, India: An Assessment,* IFPRI Research Report 64.1, International Food Policy Research Institute, Washington D.C.

Alderman, Harold, George Mergos and Roger Slade (1987), *Cooperatives and the Commercialization of Milk Production in India, A Literature Review,* International Food Policy Research Institute, Working Paper, No. 2.

Amble,V.N. (1965), "Feed Requirements of Bovines and Problems of Meeting Them", *Indian Journal of Agricultural Economics,* Vol. 20, No. 1.

Amble, V.N., V.V.R. Murthy, K.V. Sathe and B.B.P.S. Goel (1965), "Feed Requirements of Bovines and Possibilities of Meeting Them", *Indian Journal of Agricultural Economics,* Vol. 20, No. 1.

Apte, D.P. (1982), *Evaluation of an Integrated Dairy Development Scheme (Warnanagar),* Gokhale Institute Monograph Series No. 21, Gokhale Institute of Politics and Economics, Pune.

Arora, S.P. (1978), *Feeding of Dairy Cattle and Buffaloes,* Indian Council of Agricultural Research, New Delhi.

Arya, S.L. and B.S. Rawat (1989), "Growth Trends in Bovine Population in Haryana-A District-wise Analysis" *Agricultural Situation in India,* Vol. 43, No. 10.

Aswathi, Maya Kant (2004), "Livestock Export Growth Potential", *Indian Journal of Agricultural Economics,* Vol. 59, No. 3.

Badal, P.S. and J.P. Dhaka (1998), "An Analysis of Feeding Pattern and Cost of Milk Production in GopalGani District of Bihar", *Indian Journal of Dairy Science,* Vol. 51, No. 2.

Baker, C.J. (1984), *An Indian Rural Economy:1880-1955, The Tamilnad Countryside,* Oxford University Press, New Delhi.

Bandyopadhyay, D. (1988), "Direct Intervention Programmes for Poverty Alleviation: An Appraisal", *Economic and Political Weekly,* Vo. 23, No. 26.

Banerjee, A. (1996), "Indian Agri-Exports: Developing Competitive Advantage in Dairy Products", *Indian Dairyman,* Vol. 48, No. 3.

Bardhan, Pranab. (1974), "On Life and Death Question", *Economic and Political Weekly,* Special Issue, Vol. 9, No. 32-34.

Barjee, Munjushree and S.R. Yadev (2003), "Production and Marketing of Milk in Central Uttar Pradesh, *Productivity,* Vol. 44, No. 3.

Basu, Alaka Malwade (1995), "Women's Roles and the Gender Gap in Health and Survival" in Gupta, M.D., L.C.Chen and T.N. Krishnan (ed) *Women's Health in India: Risk and Vulnerability,* Oxford University Press, Bombay.

Bhat,P.N.Mari (2002), "On the Trail of Missing Indian Females: Search for Clues", *Economic and Political Weekly,* Vol. 37, No. 51.

Bhote,R.A. and S.Jayaraman (1967): "Trends in Milk Production during 1956-61". *Agricultural Situation in India,* Vol. 22, No. 6.

Birthal, P.S. (1996), Nutrient Consumption Pattern in Rural Areas of Western Uttar Pradesh, *Agricultural Review,* Vol. 9, No. 2.

Birthal, P.S. and A. Ravishankar (1999), Sources of Growth in the Livestock Sector of Karnataka, Part II, in Birthal *et.al.*, (1999) *Sources of Growth in the Livestock Sector* Policy Paper 9, National Centre for Agricultural Economics and Policy Research (NCAP), New Delhi.

Birthal, P.S. and P. Parthasarathy Rao (2004), Intensification of Livestock Production in India: Patterns, Trends and Determinants, *Indian Journal of Agricultural Economics,* Vol.59, No.3.

Birthal,P.S., Anjani Kumar, A.Ravishankar and U.K.Pandey (1999), *Sources of Growth in the Livestock Sector,* Policy Paper 9, National Centre for Agricultural Economics and Policy Research (NCAP), New Delhi.

Bose, Dev Kumar (1960), "Expenditure Consumption Curves for Some Selected Commodities", in *Studies on Consumption Behaviour,* Indian Statistical Series 6, Asia Publishing House, Bombay and Statistical Publishing Society, Calcutta.

Bowonder, B., B. Das Gupta, Sanjeev Gupta and S.S.R. Prasad (1987), "Further Evidence on the Impact of Dairy Development Programme" *Economic and Political Weekly,* Vol. 22, No. 13.

Brown, W. Norman (1964), "The Sanctity of the Cow in Hinduism", *The Economic Weekly,* Vol. 16, No. 5-7.

Chand, Ramesh (1995), "Livestock in Himachal Pradesh: Factors Affecting Growth, Composition and Intensity", *Indian Journal of Agricultural Economics,* Vol. 50, No. 3.

Chopra, R.P. and A.L. Katyal (1980), "Input-Output Relationship in Milk Production and Employment Potential-A Livestock Enterprise in Haryana", *Indian Journal of Agricultural Economics,* Vol. 35, No. 4.

Chunkath, Sheela Rani and V.B. Atherya (1997), "Female Infanticide in Tamil Nadu: Some Evidence", *Economic and Political Weekly,* Vol. 32, No. 17.

Clouston, D. (1920), "The Fodder Problem in Relation to Cattle Breeding", *Agricultural Journal of India,* Vol. 20, No. 4.

Crotty, Raymond (1980), *Cattle, Economics and Development,* Common Wealth Agricultural Bureaux, England.

Dandekar,V.M. (1970), "Sacred Cattle and More Sacred Production Functions", *Economic and Political Weekly,* Vol. 5, No. 12.

Dandekar, V.M. (1964), "Problems of Numbers in Cattle Development" *The Economic Weekly,* Annual Number, Vol. 16, No. 5-7.

Dandekar,V.M. (1967), "Cattle Problem" in Shah, A.B. (ed) *Cow-Slaughter: Horns of a Dilemma,* Lalvani Publishing House, Bombay.

Dandekar,V.M. (1969), "India's Sacred Cattle and Cultural Economy", *Economic and Political Weekly,* Vol. 4, No. 39.

Dandekar, V.M. (1980), *The Cattle Economy of India,* Indian Secular Society, Pune.

Das Gupta, Monica (1998), *"Missing Girls" in China, South Korea and India; Causes and Policy Implications,* Harvard Center for Population and Development Studies, Cambridge MA Working Paper Series, No. 98-03.

Das Gupta, Monica and P.N. Mari Bhat (1997), "Fertility Decline and Increased Manifestations of Sex bias in India, *Population Studies,* Vol. 51, No. 3.

Desai, Ashok V. (1978), "India's Energy Consumption: Composition and Trend", *Energy Policy,* Vol. 6, No. 3.

Desai, B.M. (1972), *Analysis of Consumption Expenditure Pattern in India,* Occasional Paper No.54, National Sample Survey Organisation, Department of Statistics, Ministry of Planning.

Desai, M.B and S.K. Verma (1978), *An Evaluation of Dairying Assistance Programme,* Department of Agricultural Economics, University of Baroda.

Dhas A.C. (1984), *Economics of Milk Production with Special Emphasis on Optimum Feed Compounding by the use of Linear Programming Technique for Sulur Block of Coimbatore District,* (Unpublished) M.A. Project Report, PSG College of Arts and Science, Coimbatore.

Dhas, A.C. (1986), *Structure of Milk Production in Tamilnadu: An Analysis of Trends and Sources of Growth,* Unpublished M.Phil Thesis, Centre for Development Studies, Jawaharlal Nehru University, New Delhi.

Dhas, A.C. (1989), "Changes in Draught Animal Population and Its Effect on the Composition of the Bovine Stock in Tamilnadu", in *Livestock Economy of India,* edited by Indian Society of Agricultural Economics, Oxford & IBH Publishing Co.Pvt.Ltd, New Delhi.

Dhas, A.C. (1990), Structure of Milk Production in Tamil Nadu: An Analysis of Trends and Sources of Growth, in *Resources,*

Institutions and Strategies: Operation Flood and Dairying, edited by Doornbos and Nair, Indo-Dutch Studies on Development Alternatives-4, Sage Publications, New Delhi.

Dhas, A.C. (2001), "Trends and Sources of Growth of Milk Production in Tamil Nadu", *Southern Economist,* Vol. 40, No. 15 & 16.

Dhas, A.C. (2002), "Milk Production Technology and Its Impact: Evidence from Tamil Nadu", in *Livestock in Different Farming Systems in India,* edited by Birthal, Pratap,S., Anjani Kumar and Laxmi Tiwari, Agricultural Economics Research Review, Agricultural Economics Research Association, National Centre for Agricultural Economics and Policy Research, New Delhi.

Dhondyal, S.P. and P. Singh (1965), "Economics of Livestock Enterprise in Uttar Pradesh", *Indian Journal of Agricultural Economics,* Vol. 20, No. 1.

Dixit,V.B., D. Lall., R.K. Sethi and U. Arora (1998), "Assessment and Refinement of Traditional Feeding System in Murrah Buffaloes", *Indian Journal of Dairy Science,* Vol. 51, No. 3.

Dolberg, Frands (1982), Livestock Strategies in India, Institute of Political Science, University of Aarhus, Denmark.

Doornbos, Martin and K.N. Nair (1990), *Resources, Institutions and Strategies: Operation Flood and Dairying,* Indo-Dutch Studies on Development Alternatives-4, Sage Publications, New Delhi.

Doornbos, Martin, Frank van Dorsten, Manoshi Mitra and Piet Terhal (1990), *Dairy Aid and Development; India's Operation Flood,* Indo-Dutch Studies on Development Alternatives-3, Sage Publications, New Delhi.

Dreze, Jean (1990), "Poverty in India and the IRDP Delusion", *Economic and Political Weekly,* Vol. 25, No. 39.

Fahimuddin, M. (1963), *Animal Production in Bihar,* Asia Publishing House, Bombay.

Fernandez, C.J. (1939), "The Problem of Milk in India", *Indian Veterinary Journal,* Vol. 15, No. 4.

Franco, F. and P.G.Vijaya Sherry Chand (1991), *Operation Flood and the Voluntary Sector; A Study of Tribal Dairy Cooperatives in South Gujarat,* Indian Social Institute, New Delhi.

Gandhi,Vasanth P. and Gyanendra Mani (1995), "Are Livestock Products Rising in Importance?: A Study of the Growth and

Behaviour of their Consumption in India", *Indian Journal of Agricultural Economics,* Vol. 50, No. 3.

Gangadharan,T.P. (1980), "Feed Economy in Milk Production: A Probe Under New Dairy Farm Technology in Kerala", *Indian Journal of Agricultural Economics,* Vol. 35, No. 4.

Ganguly, Amalendu (1960), "Consumption Pattern in Different Occupation Groups", in *Studies on Consumption Behaviour,* Indian Statistical Series 6, Asia Publishing House, Bombay and Statistical Publishing Society, Calcutta.

Gangwar,A.C. and H.C.Bhatia (1980), "Economics of Milk Production: A Probe Under New Dairy Farm Technology in Kerala", *Indian Journal of Agricultural Economics.* Vol. 35, No. 4.

Gangwar, A.C., B.S. Panghal and Kuldeep Kumar (1989), An Economic Analysis of Milk Production and Consumption of Different Sizes of Farm in Haryana State, *Indian Journal of Dairy Science,* Vol. 42, No. 4.

Ganpule, S.P. and R.N. Desai (1983), "Comparative Efficiency of Milk Production of Indigenous and Cross-Bred Cows", *Indian Journal of Animal Science,* Vol. 53, No. 7.

Gebert, Rita (1989), "Poverty Alleviation and Village Politics in Tamil Nadu: Whose Interests First?", *Economic and Political Weekly,* Vol. 24, No. 4.

George, J. (1985), "Bovine Milk Production Estimate in India-An Exercise in Decomposition" *Agricultural Situation in India,* Vol. 40, No. 1.

George,J. (1988), "Sources of Growth in Bovine Milk Production in India", *Agricultural Situation in India,* Vol. 42, No. 10.

George, J. (1989), *Dairy Development Planning in India,* Unpublished Ph.D. Thesis, Department of Economics, University of Delhi.

George, P.S. (1996), Dairying and Livestock Economy of India–A Review", *Indian Journal of Agricultural Economics,* Vol. 51, No. 1 & 2.

George, P.S. and K.N. Nair (1990), *Livestock Economy of Kerala,* Centre for Development Studies, Tiruvananthapuram.

George, Shanti (1985), *Operation Flood: An Appraisal of Current Indian Dairy Policy,* Oxford University Press, New Delhi.

George, Shanti (1994), *A Matter of People: Cooperative Dairying in India and Zimbave,* Oxford University Press, New Delhi.

GOI (various years), *Results of Consumption Expenditure Surveys,* 17th round, 19th round, 27th round, 32 round, 38th round, 42 round, 50th round and 55th round, National Sample Survey Organisation, Department of Statistics, Ministry of Planning.

GOI. (1938), *Report on the Cost of Production of Crops in the Principal Sugarcane and Cotton Tracts in India,* Vol. IV, Madras, Imperial Council of Agricultural Research, New Delhi.

GOI. (1939), *Report on A Village Enquiry Regarding Cattle and Production of Milk in Seven Breeding Tracts in India,* Imperial Council of Agricultural Research, Delhi.

GOI. (1950), *Report on the Marketing of Milk in the Indian Union,* Agriculture Marketing in India, Ministry of Food and Agriculture, Delhi.

GOI. (1956), *Report on the Marketing of Cattle in India,* Directorate of Marketing and Inspection, Ministry of Food and Agriculture, New Delhi.

GOI. (1962), *Tables with Notes on Farming Conditions and Practices in Rural Areas: 1953-54,* The National Sample Survey, Eighth Round: July 1954-April 1955, No-60.

GOI. (1969), *Tables with Notes on Consumer Expenditure,* NSS 17th Round (July 1961 to June 1962), Report No.200, National Sample Survey Organisation, Department of Statistics, Government of India.

GOI. (1974), *Report of the Committee on Livestock Feeds and Fodders,* Ministry of Agriculture and Irrigation, New Delhi.

GOI. (1976), *Report of the National Commission on Agriculture, Part VII, Animal Husbandry; and Part III, Demand and Supply,* Ministry of Agriculture and Irrigation, Government of India, New Delhi.

GOI. (1978a), "Livestock Numbers & Products and Consumption of Livestock Products", NSS 30th Round, (July 1975-June 1976), *Sarvekshana,* Vol. 2, No. 2, National Sample Survey Organisation, Department of Statistics, Ministry of Planning.

GOI. (1978b), *Tables with Notes on Consumer Expenditure,* NSS 27th Round (October 1972 to September 1973), Report No.284, National Sample Survey Organisation, Department of Statistics, Government of India.

GOI. (1979), *A Note on Some Characteristics of Household Dairy Enterprises Based on the Data Collected in the Survey of Livestock Number, Product and Enterprises,* NSS 30th Round (July 1975 to June 1976), Report

No.268/1, National Sample Survey Organisation, Department of Statistics, Government of India.

GOI. (1982), "Survey Results on Land Holdings", National Sample Survey: 26th round, July 1971-September 1972, *Sarvekshana,* Vol. 5, No. 2 & 4, Department of Statistics, Ministry of Planning.

GOI. (1983), "A Note on Per Capita Per Diem Intake of Calories, Protein and Fat Based on the Data Collected in the Household Survey on Consumption Expenditure", NSS 27th Round (October 1972 to September 1973), *Sarvekshana,* Vol. 6, No. 3-4, Issue No. 18, Department of Statistics, Ministry of Planning and Programme Implementation, Government of India.

GOI. (1984), "A Note on Number of Bovines and Yield of Milk Classified by Various Correlates and Estimates of Number, Birth, Death and Calving Interval of Bovines", NSS 30th Round (July 1975-June 1976), *Sarvekshana,* Vol. 8, No. 1, Department of Statistics, Ministry of Planning and Programme Implementation, Government of India.

GOI. (1986a), *Per Capita Per Diem Intake of Nutrients,* NSS 32nd Round (July 1973 to June 1974), Report No.329, National Sample Survey Organisation, Department of Statistics, Government of India.

GOI. (1986b), "Some Results on the Second Quinquennial Survey on Consumption Expenditure" NSS 32nd round, *Sarvekshana,* Vol. 9, No. 3, Issue No. 26, National Sample Survey Organisation, Department of Statistics, Ministry of Planning, Government of India.

GOI. (1986c), "Survey Results on the Third Quinquennial Survey on Consumption Expenditure" NSS 38th round, *Sarvekshana,* Vol. 9, No. 4, Issue No. 27, National Sample Survey Organisation, Department of Statistics, Ministry of Planning, Government of India.

GOI. (1988), "A Note on Some Aspects of Operational Holdings" and "Results on Some Aspects of Operational Holdings", NSS 37th round (1982), *Sarvekshana,* Vol. 12, No. 1, Issue No. 36, National Sample Survey Organisation, Department of Statistics, Ministry of Planning, Government of India.

GOI. (1989a), "A Note and Survey Results on Monthly Per Capita Consumption of Cereals for Various Sections of Population" and " Note and Survey Results on Per Capita Per Diem Intake of Calories, Protein and Fat and Perception of the People on the

Adequacy", NSS 38th Round (1983), *Sarvekshana,* Vol. 13, No. 2, Issue No. 41, Department of Statistics, Ministry of Planning and Programme Implementation, Government of India.

GOI. (1989b), *Results on Consumer Expenditure,* NSS 42nd Round (1986-87), *Sarvekshana,* Vol. 12, No. 4, Issue No,39, National Sample Survey Organisation, Department of Statistics, Government of India.

GOI. (1990), "Estimates of Livestock and Agricultural Implements Classified by Household Operational Holding", National Sample Survey: 37th round, January- December 1982, *Sarvekshana,* Vol. 13, No. 3, Department of Statistics, Ministry of Planning.

GOI. (1993), "Proportion of Households Benefiting from Specified Poverty Amelioration Programmes by Socio-Economic Status ", National Sample Survey: 43rdround, July1987-June 1988, *Sarvekshana,* Vol. 17, No. 2, Issue No. 57, Department of Statistics, Ministry of Planning.

GOI. (1996), *Level and Pattern of Consumer Expenditure in India: 1993-94,* NSS 50th Round (July 1993-June 1994), Report No.402, National Sample Survey Organisation, Department of Statistics, Ministry of Planning & Programme Implementation, Government of India.

GOI. (1997a), "A Note on Nutritional Intake in India" and "Survey Results on Nutritional Intake in India" - NSS 50th Round (July 1993 to June 1994), *Sarvekshana,* Vol. 21, No. 2, Issue No. 73, October - December 1997, Department of Statistics, Ministry of Planning and Programme Implementation, Government of India.

GOI. (1997b), *Consumption of Some Important Commodities in India 1993-94,* NSS 50th Round, Report No. 404, National Sample Survey Organisation, Department of Statistics.

GOI. (1997c), "IRDP Assistance and Participation in Public Works: 1993-94", 5th Quinquennial Survey of Consumer Expenditure, National Sample Survey: 50th round, July 1993- June 1994, Report No. 423, National Sample Survey Organisation, Department of Statistics, Ministry of Planning.

GOI. (1997d), Land and Livestock Holdings Survey, *Operational Land Holdings in India,* 1991-92, Salient Features, NSS 48th Round (January-December 1992), NSSO, Report No.407, Department of Statistics, Government of India.

GOI. (1998a), "Livestock and Agricultural Implements in Operational Holdings" and "Results on Livestock and Agricultural Implements in Operational Holdings", NSS: 48th round, January- December 1992, *Sarvekshana,* Vol. 22, No. 1, Department of Statistics, Ministry of Planning & Programme Implementation, Government of India.

GOI. (1998b), *Ownership of Livestock, Cultivation of Selected Crops and consumption Levels,* 5th Quinquennial Survey of Consumer Expenditure, NSS 50th Round (July 1993 to June 1994) Report No. 424, National Sample Survey Organisation, Department of Statistics, Government of India.

GOI. (2001a), *Consumption of Some Important Commodities in India 1999-2000,* NSS 55th Round (July 1999-June 2000), Report No. 461, National Sample Survey Organisation, Department of Statistics, Ministry of Planning & Programme Implementation, Government of India.

GOI. (2001b), *Level and Pattern of Consumer Expenditure in India: 1999-2000,* NSS 55th Round (July 1999-June 2000), Report No. 457, National Sample Survey Organisation, Department of Statistics, Ministry of Planning & Programme Implementation, Government of India.

GOI. (2001c), *"IRDP Assistance and Participation in Public Works: 1999-2000",* National Sample Survey: 55th round, July 1999-June 2000, Report No. 467, National Sample Survey Organisation, Department of Statistics, Ministry of Planning.

GOI. (2001d), *"Reported Adequacy of Food Intake in India, 1999-2000",* National Sample Survey: 55th round, July 1999-June 2000, Report No.466, National Sample Survey Organisation, Department of Statistics, Ministry of Planning

GOI. (2002), *Report of the National Commission on Cattle,* Vol. 1, Department of Animal Husbandry and Dairying, Ministry of Agriculture, Government of India, 2002.

GOI. (2003a): National Accounts Statistics, Central Statistical Organisation, Government of India, New Delhi.

GOI. (2003b), *Report on Village Facilities,* NSS: 58th round, July-December 2002, Report No. 487, National Sample Survey Organisation. Department of Statistics, Ministry of Planning & Programme Implementation, Government of India.

GOI. (2005a), *Access to Modern Technology for Farming,* NSS: 59th round, January-December 2003, Report No.499, Situation Assessment

Survey of Farmers, National Sample Survey Organisation. Department of Statistics, Ministry of Planning & Programme Implementation, Government of India.

GOI. (2005b), *Some Aspects of Farming,* NSS: 59th round, January-December 2003, Report No. 496, Situation Assessment Survey of Farmers, National Sample Survey Organisation. Department of Statistics, Ministry of Planning & Programme Implementation, Government of India.

GOI. (2005c), *Tamil Nadu Development Report,* Planning Commission, Academic Foundation, New Delhi.

Gopal, R., U.G. Nadkarni and Bhagwan Dass (1986), "Age at Calving in Bovines of Punjab and Gujarat", *Indian Journal of Dairy Science,* Vol. 39, No. 2.

Gopalappa, D.V. (1996), "Crop Diversification and Income Levels in Karimnagar District of Andhra Pradesh", *Indian Journal of Agricultural Economics,* Vol. 51, No. 3.

Gopalaswamy,T.P. and V. Radhakrishnan (1979), *Techno-Economic Feasibility of Dairy Development in Dharmapuri District,* Centre for Agriculture and Rural Development, Indian Institute of Management, Bangalore.

GOTN. (1972), *Towards a White Revolution: Report of the Task Force on Animal Husbandry, 1972-84,* The Perspective Plan for Tamil Nadu, State Planning Commission, Plan Document No.4, Ezhilagam, Madras.

GOTN. (2003), *Tamil Nadu: Human Development Report,* Government of Tamil Nadu in association with Social Science Press, Delhi.

Government of Madras (1960), *Techno- Economic Survey of Madras,* Report of the NCAER, Department of Industries, Labour and Cooperation, Government of Madras, Madras.

Grewal, S.S. and A.S. Kahlon (1973), "Impact of Tractorisation on Draft Animals", *Agricultural Situation in India,* Vol. 27, No. 11.

Gulati, A., S. Bhinde and V. Raheja (1996), Indian Dairy Policy and Protection:1975-95, *National Council of Applied Economic Research,* New Delhi.

Gupta, P.R. (ed.) (1997), *Dairy India 1997,* Gupta Publishers, New Delhi.

Gurumurthi, S. (1999), "Miracle in Milk Procurement", *Economic and Political Weekly,* Vol.34 No.18, May 1.

Harris, Marvin (1966), "The Cultural Ecology of India's Sacred Cattle", *Current Anthropology,* Vol. 7, No. 1.

Harris, Marvin (1975), *Culture, People, Nature: An Introduction to General Anthropology,* ThomasY. Crowell, New York

Heston, Alan (1971), "An Approach to the Sacred Cow in India", *Current Anthropology,* Vol. 12, No. 2.

Hirway, Indira (1988), "Reshaping IRDP: Some Issues", *Economic and Political Weekly,* Vol. 23, No. 26.

Huria,Vinod K. and K.T. Achaya (1980), "Dairy Development in India: Some Critical Issues", *Economic and Political Weekly,* Vol. 15, No. 45 & 46.

ICAR Survey (undated), *Survey of Animal Draught Power in Various Agro-Climatic Zones of the Country: Socio-Economic Features and Current Husbandry Practices,* ICAR Adhoc Scheme, Department of Animal Husbandry Economics, Madras Veterinary College, Tamil Nadu Veterinary and Animal Sciences University, Madras.

Iyenger and Jain (1969), "Projections of Consumption in Rural/Urban India, 1970-71 and 1975-76", *Economic and Political Weekly,* Vol. 5, No. 48.

Iyer, A.K., Yegnanarayana (1919), "The Improvement of Indian Dairy Cattle", *Agricultural Journal of India,* Vol. 14, No. 4.

Jabbar, M.A. and D.A.G. Green (1983), *The Status and Potential of Livestock Within the Context of Agricultural Development Policy of Bangladesh,* Department of Agricultural Economics, The University College of Wales, Aberystwth.

Jacob, T., R.K. Srivatsava and V.N. Amble (1971), "A Study of Resource Productivity in Milk Production", *Indian Journal of Agricultural Economics,* Vol. 26, No. 1.

Jain D.K. and R.K. Patel (1987), "Inter-district Variations in Consumption Pattern of Milk and Milk Production in Haryana State", *Agricultural Situation in India,* Vol.42, No.4.

Jain, M.M. (1986), *Growth Pattern of Dairy Sub-Sector in Rajasthan,* Himalaya Publishing House, Bombay.

Jain,D.K. and J.C. Kalla (1981), "A Study of Shifts in Consumption of Essential Commodity Groups for Rural and Urban Population in Rajasthan", *Agricultural Situation in India,* Vol. 36, No. 3.

Jamaluddin,M. (1924), "Improvement of Cattle Breeding in India", *The Indian Veterinary Journal,* Vol. 1, No. 1.

Jarvis, Lovell S. (1982), "To Beef on Not to Beef? Portfolio Choices of Asian Smallholder Cattle Producers" in Fine,J.C. and R.G.Lattimore (ed), *Livestock in Asia: Issues and Policies,* International Development Research Centre, Ottawa, Canada.

Jatrana, Santhosh and S.K.Sangwan (1996), "Sex Differentials in the Child Care in Rural Mewat of Haryana", *Agricultural Review,* Vol. 9, No. 2.

Jeyaranjan,J. (2004), *Some Aspects of Change in Iluppakkorai Village,* Kerala Research Programme on Local Level Development, Centre for Development Studies, Trivandrum.

Jha, Brajesh (2004), "Implications of Trade Liberalisation for the Livestock Sector", *Indian Journal of Agricultural Economics,* Vol. 59, No. 3.

Jha, Brajesh and B. Debroy (2000), "Towards Globalising Indian Dairy Sector", *Asian Economic Review,* Vol. 42, No. 2.

Jonas, P. (1971), *An Analysis of Bovine Milk Consumption in Major Indian Metropolitan Areas,* DP/E-United States Agency for International Development (USAID), Mission to India, New Delhi.

Joshi, P.D. (1998), *Changing Pattern of Consumption Expenditure in India and Some Selected States,* Sarvekshana Analytical Report Number 2,National Sample Survey Organisation, Department of Statistics, Ministry of Planning Implementation, GOI. and NSS , Various issues.

Kalamani,A. (1984), *Comparative Efficiency of Milk Production of Cross-bred and Non-descript Cows and Murrah Graded Buffaloes in Sulur Block, Coimbatore District,* M.A. Thesis (unpublished), Department of Economics. PSG College of Arts and Science, Coimbatore, Tamil Nadu.

Kalyankar, S.P. (1980), "Economics of Milk Production in Different Breeds of Cows and Buffaloes", *Indian Journal of Agricultural Economics,* Vol. 35, No. 4.

Kaur, Maninder and G.S. Gill (1989), Milk Production, Consumption and Disposal Pattern in the Rural Areas of Ludhiana District (Punjab), *Indian Journal of Dairy Science,* Vol. 42, No. 4.

Kaura, R.L. (1944), "Deterioration of Cattle in Certain Parts of India and Its Probable Causes with Some Practical Suggestions to Overcome Them", *Indian Journal of Veterinary Science and Animal Husbandry,* Vol. 14, No. 2.

Kesavan, V.K. (1982), *An Economic Analysis of the Consumption of Milk and Milk Products in Kerala,* Unpublished Ph.D. thesis, Kurukshetra University, Kurukshetra, cited in Singh and Singh (1986).

Keshari, Sangeeta and B.S. Malik (1998), "Consumption of Milk and Milk Products by Dairy Farmers of Karnal District", *Indian Journal of Dairy Science,* Vol. 51, No. 3.

Klasen, Stephen and Winik (2003), "Globalisation and Women's Work: Expanding Freedom" *Feminist Economics,* Vol. 9 Nos. 2 & 3.

Krishnaswami, S.Y. (1947), *Rural Problems in Madras-Monograph,* Government Press, Madras.

Kumar, Vinod (2004), "Export Prospects of Livestock Products, Policy Intervention and World Trade Organisation", *Indian Journal of Agricultural Economics,* Vol. 59, No. 3.

Kumar, Virender., H.R. Sharma and R.K. Sharma (2004), "Livestock Economy of Himachal Pradesh: Growth Patterns, Ecological Implications and State Policy", *Agricultural Economics Research Review,* Vol. 17, No. 1.

Kumar, A. and U.K. Pandey (1999), "Growth Performance of Livestock Sector in India", Part-I, in Birthal *et.al., Sources of Growth in the Livestock Sector* Policy Paper 9, National Centre for Agricultural Economics and Policy Research (NCAP), New Delhi.

Kumar, P. and R.P. Singh (1980), "Dynamic Feed-Milk Relationship and Technological Change in Milk Production", *Indian Journal of Agricultural Economics,* Vol. 30, No. 3.

Kumar, R., V.N. Autkar and Y.P. Mahalle (1995), "Family Consumption Pattern in Rural Sector: A Case Study of Vidarbha Region", *The Bihar Journal of Agricultural Marketing,* Vol. 3, No. 2.

Kurup, M.P.G. (2003), *Livestock in Orissa–The Socio-Economic Perspective,* Manohar Publishers and Distributors, New Delhi.

Kurup. M.P.G. (1997), "Cattle Numbers and Draught Animals" in *Dairy India 1997,* edited by Gupta, P.R., Gupta Publishers, New Delhi.

Lakshmann R., Vishva Raj, K.S. Ramesh, Nandita Ray, S. Subrahmanyam and S. Waelty (1994), *Bovine and Dairy Development in Andhra Pradesh,* Indo-German Project, Andhra Pradesh, Hyderabad.

Lal, Deepak (1988), *The Hindu Equilibrium,* Vol. 1, *Cultural Stability and Economic Stagnation, India, c1500 BC - AD 1980,* Clarendon Press, New York.

Lata, Swarn and Kuber Ram (1986), Rural-Urban Inequalities in Expenditure on Milk and Milk Products, *Indian Journal of Dairy Science,* Vol. 39, No. 2.

Lavania, G.S., B.D. Shukla and R.S. Dixit (1975), "An Economic Analysis of Milk Production in Kashi Vidyapeeth Block, Varanashi District", *Indian Journal of Agricultural Economics,* Vol. 30, No. 1.

Leake, H.M. (1923), "The Cattle Problem of the United Provinces", *Agricultural Journal of India,* Vol.23, No.4.

Low, C.E. (1912), "The Supply of Agricultural Cattle in India", *Agricultural Journal of India,* Vol. 7, No. 4.

Lucas, R.D. (1944), "The Cooperative Movement-Its Future Development", *The Indian Cooperative Review,* Vol. 10, No. 1.

Madras Institute of Development Studies (1988), *Tamilnadu Economy-Performance and Issues,* Oxford & IBH Publishing, New Delhi.

Mascarenhas, R.C. (1988), *A Strategy for Rural Development: Dairy Cooperative in India,* Sage Publications, New Delhi.

Mathur, G.K., C.L. Malik and S.P. Singh (1982), "Milk Production Estimates in India for the Years 1977-78, 1978-79 and 1979-80", *Agricultural Situation in India,* Vol. 36, No. 11.

Matson, J. (1922), "The Cattle Question in India", *Agricultural Journal of India,* Vol. 17, No. 4.

Mellor, John W. and Bruno De Ponteves (1964), "Effect of Growth in Demand for Milk on the Demand for Concentrate Feeds in India, 1951-66", *Indian Journal of Agricultural Economics,* Vol. 19, No. 3 & 4.

Mergos, George and Roger Slade (1987), *Dairy Development and Milk Cooperatives: The Effects of a Dairy Project in India,* World Bank Discussion Paper No-15, World Bank, Washington D.C.

Miller, Barbara (1981), *The Endangered Sex: Neglect of Female Children in Rural North India,* Bhaca, NY, Cornell University Press.

Minhas, B.S. and A. Vaidyanathan (1965), "Growth of Crop Output in India, 1951-54 to 1958-61: An Analysis by Component Elements", *Journal of Indian Society of Agricultural Statistics,* Vol. 17, No. 2.

Mishra, S.N. (1978), ***Livestock Planning in India,*** Vikas Publishing House, New Delhi.

Mishra, S.N. and Rishi K. Sharma (1990), *Livestock Development in India: An Appraisal, Institute of Economic Growth,* Vikas Publishing House Pvt. Ltd., New Delhi.

Mohan, C. Madan (1989), *Dairy Management in India; A Study in Andhra Pradesh,* Mittal Publication, Delhi.

Morrenhof, Jan., Vinod Ahuja and Ashok Tripathy (ed.) (2004), *Livestock Services and the Poor, Swiss Agency for Development and Cooperation,* Swizerland and Food and Agriculture Organisation of the United Nations, Rome.

Murali, R.S. and A.C. Dhas (1992), "Systems Analysis of Dairy Development in Kerala, *People and Development,* No. 5, June-July.

Murthi, Mamta, A. Guio and J. Dreze (1995), "Mortality, Fertility and Gender Bias in India; A District Level Analysis", *Population and Development Review,* Vol. 21, No. 4.

Muruganathan, P. (1996), *Extent of Mechanization in Paddy Farms in Select Districts of Tamil Nadu-An Assessment,* MBM Thesis (unpublished), Tamil Nadu Agricultural University, Coimbatore.

NABARD (1987), *Dairy Development Schemes in Karnal and Rohtak Districts of Karnataka: An Ex-post Evaluation Study,* Evaluation Study Series No. Chandigard-2, National Bank for Agriculture and Rural Development, Regional Office, Chandigarh.

Naganathan, M. (ed) (2002), *Tamil Nadu Economy: Trends and Prospects,* University of Madras, Chennai.

Naidu, Muthukrishna (1948), "The Madras Cooperative Milk Supply Union", *Indian Cooperative Review,* Vol. 14, No. 1&2.

Nair, K.N. and A. Vaidyanathan (1979), *Inter-state Differences in Milk Consumption in India- A Preliminary Analysis,* Working Paper No. 62, Centre for Development Studies, Trivandrum.

Nair, K.N. (1977), "Size and Utilization of Draught Animals in Kerala", *Indian Journal of Agricultural Economics,* Vol. 32, No. 4.

Nair, K.N. (1979), "To Butcher or Not to Butcher: Cattle Holdings and Milk and Meat Production in Kerala", *Economic and Political Weekly,* Vol. 14, No, 17.

Nair, K.N. (1980), Operation Flood: Some Constraints and Implications", *Economic and Political Weekly,* Vol. 15, No. 8.

Nair, K.N. (1981a), *Bovine Holdings in Kerala: An Analysis of Factors Governing Demand and Supply,* Unpublished Ph.D. Thesis, Centre for Development Studies, Kerala University, Trivandrum.

Nair, K.N. (1981b), Animals and Tractors in Agrarian Economies: An Assessment of Some Issues Concerning Cultivation Techniques in Agriculture" in *Maximum Production from Minimum Land,* edited by M.G.Jackson, Bangaladesh Agricultural University, Mymen Singh, Bangladesh.

Nair, K.N. (1982), "Technological Change in Milk Production: A Review of Some Critical Issues with Reference to South Asia', *Economic and Political Weekly,* Vol. 17, No. 13.

Nair, K.N. (1985), "White Revolution in India: Facts and Issues", *Economic and Political Weekly,* Vol. 20, Nos. 25 &26.

Nair, K.N. (1987), Animal Protein Consumption and the Sacred Cow Complex in India, in Marvin Harris and Eric Rose (ed.) *Food and Evolution,* Temple University Press.

Nair, K.N. and A.C. Dhas (1989), "Cattle Breeding Technology and Draught Power Availability in Indian Agriculture: An Unresolved Contradiction", in *Livestock Economy of India,* Indian Society of Agricultural Economics, Oxford & IBH Publishing Co.Pvt.Ltd, New Delhi.

Nair, K.N. and A.C. Dhas (1990), "Cattle Breeding Technology and Draught Power Availability: An Unresolved Contradiction" in *Resources, Institutions and Strategies: Operation Flood and Dairying,* edited by Doornbos, Martin and K.N.Nair, Indo-Dutch Studies on Development Alternatives-4, Sage Publications, New Delhi.

Nair, K.N. and A.C. Dhas (2001), Livestock Statistics in India, in *India's Socio Economic Data Base: Surveys of Selected Areas,* edited by Chandrasekhar C.P. and Jandhyala B.G. Tilak, Tulika, New Delhi.

Nair, K.N. and M.C. Jackson (1981), "Alternatives to Operation Flood II Strategy", *Economic and Political Weekly,*Vol. 16, No. 52.

Nair, K.N. (1979), "Milk Production in Kerala - Trends and Prospects", *Economic and Political Weekly,* Vol. 24, Nos. 12 &13.

Natarajan, B. (1940), "Gangaikondan (Tirunelveli District)", in *Some South Indian Villages: A Resurvey,* edited by Thomas, P.J. and K.C. Ramakrishnan, University of Madras, Madras.

Natarajan, B. (1950), An Enquiry Into the Economics of Milk Production and Distribution in the City of Madras, *Indian Journal of Agricultural Economics,* Vol. 5, No. 2.

National Council of Applied Economic Research (1967), *All India Consumer Expenditure Survey II: Pattern of Income and Expenditure,* National Council of Applied Economic Research, New Delhi.

National Council of Applied Economic Research (1972), *All India Household Survey of Income, Saving & Consumer Expenditure (With Special Reference to Middle Class Households),* National Council of Applied Economic Research, New Delhi.

National Dairy Development Board (1978), *Operation Flood II, A Proposal* by the National Dairy Development Board, (revised Edition), NDDB, Anand.

National Dairy Development Board (1980), *Breeding and Feeding for Milk Production in Operation Flood II,* NDDB, Anand.

National Dairy Development Board (2003), *Annual Report 2002-2003* and previous issues, Anand.

Nirman, K.P.S., S. Singh and K.C. Raut (1982), "Estimation of Crop Residues Using Grain to Strawn Ratios", *Agricultural Situation in India,* Vol. 37. No. 2.

Odend'hal, Stewart (1972), "Energetics of Indian Cattle in Their Environment," *Journal of Human Ecology,* Vol. 1, No. 1.

Odend'hal, Stewart (1988a), "Human and Cattle Population Changes in Deltaic West Bengal, India Between 1977-1987," *Journal of Human Ecology,* Vol. 16, No. 1.

Odend'hal, Stewart (1988b), "Human and Cattle Population Changes in Upland West Bengal, India Between 1977-1978 and 1987," *Journal of Human Ecology,* Vol. 16, No 2.

Oliver, Arthur (1943), "Animal Husbandry in India", *The Indian Veterinary Journal,* Vol. 19, No. 4.

Pandey, R.C. and D.S. Yadav (1982), "Environmental Management and Fodder Availability in Haryana", *Agricultural Situation in India,* Vol. 37, No. 8.

Pandey, R.N., A.C. Gangwar and S.K. Goyal (2002), "Economics of Cattle and Buffaloes in Haryana", in *Livestock in Different Farming Systems in India,* edited by Birthal, Pratap, S., Anjani Kumar and Laxmi Tiwari, Agricultural Economics Research Review, Agricultural Economics Research Association, National Centre for Agricultural Economics and Policy Research, New Delhi.

Pandy, J.N. and H.R. Mishra (1985), "Productive and Reproductive Performance of Indigenous and Crossbred Cows Under Village Conditions", *Indian Dairyman,* Vol. 37, No. 3.

Panse,V.G., Amble,V.N and K.C. Raut (1963), *Cost of Milk Production in Madras State,* ICAR Report Series No. 10., Indian Council of Agricultural Research, New Delhi.

Parisot, Rajarajeswari (1990), "Cattle Development, Nutritional Requirements and Environmental Implications" in *Resources, Institutions and Strategies: Operation Flood and Dairying,* edited by Doornbos, Martin and K.N.Nair, Indo-Dutch Studies on Development Alternatives-4, Sage Publications, New Delhi.

Pattabhiraman, D. (1958), *Statistical Information of Department of Animal Husbandry,* Government of Madras, Madras.

Patel, Jahaverbhai (1958), *The Village Oil Industry,* Khadi Village Industries Commission, Bombay.

Patel, R.K., C.B. Singh and J.P. Dhaka (1984), "Economic Analysis of Different Species of Dairy Animals", *Indian Dairyman,* Vol. 36, No. 3.

Patel, R.K., R.V. Singh, A.S. Saini and R.C. Nagpal (1982), "Energy Input and Cost of Milk Production" *Agricultural Situation in India,* Vol. 36, No. 11.

Patel, R.K., (1993), "Present Status and Promise of Dairying in India", *Indian Journal of Agricultural Economics,* Vol. 48, No. 1.

Patel, R.K., P. Kumar and J.K. Khera (1974), "A Study of Consumption Pattern of Milk and Milk Products", Proceedings of the *XIX International Dairy Congress,* India, New Delhi.

Pitcholiya, R.R. (1975), "Bovine Economy of Panchmahals District-A Study", *Indian Journal of Agricultural Economics,* Vol. 30, No. 1.

Prabaharan, R. (1991), *Survey of Animal Draught Power in Various Agro-Climatic Zones of the Country: Socio-Economic Features and Current Husbandry Practices,* I.C.A.R. Sponsored Adhoc Scheme, Final Report, Department of Animal Husbandry Economics, Madras Veterinary College, Tamilnadu Veterinary and Animal Sciences University, Madras.

Prabaharan, R. and C. Ramasamy (1984), "Influence of Certain Selected Factors on Marketed Surplus of Milk", *Cheiron,* Vol. 13, No. 2.

Prabaharan, R. and S.N. Sivaselvam (1986), "A Study on Marketed Surplus and Supply Functions for Milk in Chengalpattu District of Tamil Nadu", *Indian Journal of Dairy Science,* Vol. 39, No. 1.

Prakash, Anand and S.D. Bokil (1983), "Estimation of Production of Cultivated Fodder" *Agricultural Situation in India,* Vol. 37, 11.

Prasad, Y. (1978), "Livestock Development Programme in India" in M.G,Cooper (ed), *Livestock Development Programme for the Asian Small Farmers,* Australian Vetrinary Association, Australia.

Pukan, Umananda and D.Gohain (1975), "Dairy Farming in the Brahmaputra Valley of Assam: A Case Study", *Indian Journal of Agricultural Economics,* Vol. 30, No. 3.

Puri, T.R. and Bhupal Singh (1964), "Statistical Studies on the Economics of Milk Production", *Indian Journal of Dairy Science,* Vol. 17, P. 29-35.

Raj, Dev and J.N.Gupta (1994), "An Economic Analysis of Milk Production in Cheru District of Rajasthan", *Indian Journal of Dairy Science,* Vol. 47, No. 4.

Raj, K.N. (1969), "Investment in Livestock in an Agrarian Economy: An Analysis of Some Issues Concerning Sacred Cows and Surplus Cattle", *Indian Economic Review,* Vol. 4, No. 1.

Raj, K.N. (1971), "India's Sacred Cattle: Theories and Empirical Findings", *Economic and Political Weekly,* Vol. 4, No. 13.

Raj, K.N. (1972), "Mechanisation of Agriculture in India and Sri Lanka (Ceylon)", *International Labour Review,* Vol. 106, No. 4.

Rajalakshmi, N. (2001), *Tamil Nadu Economy,* Business Publications, Mumbai.

Rajan, S.I., U.S. Mishra and K. Navaneetham (1991), "Decline in Sex Ratio: An Alternative Explanation", *Economic and Political Weekly,* Vol. 26, No. 51.

Rajapurohit, A.R. (1975), "Bovine Feed Availability and Requirements in Karnataka with Reference to Dairy Development Programme", *Indian Journal of Agricultural Economics,*Vol. 30, No. 1.

Rajendran, K. and R. Prabaharan (1989), *A Study on Resource Use Efficiency Among Buffaloes, Cross-bred and Desi Cows in Dharmapuri District,* Department of Animal Husbandry Economics, Madras Veterinary College, Madras.

Rajendran, K. and R. Prabaharan (1993), "A Study on Production, Consumption and Disposal of Milk in Dharmapuri District of Tamil Nadu", *Indian Journal of Dairy Science,* Vol. 46, No. 10.

Raju, A. Sarada (1941), *Economic Conditions in the Madras Presidency 1800-1850,* University of Madras, Madras.

Ram, Kuber and Kulwant Singh (1974), "Production and Disposal of Milk on Farms in Milk Shed Areas of Karnal", *Agricultural Situation in India,* Vol. 28, No. 11.

Ramakrishnan K.C. (1930), "Environment and Economic Activities in the Madras Presidency", *The Journal of the Madras Geographical Association,* Vol. 3, No. 4.

Ramakrishnan K.C. (1939), "Milk Supply in the City of Madras", *The Journal of the Madras Geographical Association,* Vol. 14, No. 4.

Ramakrishnan K.C. (1944), "Milk Supply and Cooperation", *The Indian Cooperative Review,* Vol. 10, No. 1.

Ramasamy, C., V. Pugazhendi and R. Prabaharan (1981), "Economics of Milk Production with Cross-bred Cows" *Cherion,* Vol. 10, No. 3.

Ramesh, Babu P. (1995), "Trends, Patterns and Effects of Diffusion and Adoption of Crossbreeding Technology: An Assessment in the Context of Kerala", *Indian Journal of Agricultural Economics,* Vol. 50, No. 3.

Randhawa, M.S. (1958), *Agriculture and Animal Husbandry in India,* Indian Council for Agricultural Research, New Delhi.

Ranganath, K. (1977), "Livestock Resources and Their Utilisation in Karnataka" *Journal of the Mysore University,* Section-A, Vol. 38, No. 3.

Rao, Ananda (1919), "Dairy Industry Around Coimbatore" *Agricultural Journal of India,* Vol. 14, No. 2.

Rao, B. Sambasiva (1985), "Factors Affecting Milk Production: A Study", *Indian Journal of Agricultural Economics,* Vol. 40, No. 2.

Rao, C.H. Hanumantha and R. Rangaswamy (1988), "Efficiency of Investments in IRDP: A Study of Uttar Pradesh", *Economic and Political Weekly,* Vol. 23, No. 26.

Rao, C.H. Hunumanatha (1969), India's Sacred Cattle: Some Empirical Results, *Economic and Political Weekly,* Vol. 4, No. 52.

Rao, Neeraj, Prasanth Kumar, Govind Pal and Chandra Sen (2004), "Economics of Milk Production in District Kanpur (Dehat), Uttar Pradesh", *Indian Journal of Agricultural Economics,* Vol. 59, No. 3.

Raut, K.C. and V.N. Amble (1969), "Breed Variation in Cost of Milk Production", *Agricultural Situation in India,* 23, No. 11.

Reddy, T.R.K., J.V.Venkataram and S. Suryaprakash (1980), "An Economic Analysis of Dairy Enterprise in Bangalore District, Karnataka", *Indian Journal of Agricultural Economics,* Vol. 35, No. 4.

Reddy, Y.V.R. and S.C. Mathur (1980), "A Comparative Study on the Cost of Milk Production of Cross-bred Cows and Buffaloes", *Indian Journal of Animal Science,* Vol. 50, No. 5.

Reddy, Y.V.R. and S.C. Mathur (1981), "Economics of Milk Production with Special Emphasis on Proper Allocation of Concentrate Feed to Dairy Animals," *Indian Journal of Dairy Science,* Vol. 33, No. 4.

Rekib, A., D.P. Handa and S.K. Rajpali (1987), "Analysis of Factors Affecting Cost of Milk Production in Buffaloes", *Agricultural Situation in India,* Vol. 42, No. 7.

Research Team (CED) (1982), *Operation Flood: Development or Dependence?,* CITE Publication, Bombay.

Retnam, V.C.V., Vineetha Menon and K.N. Nair (2004), "Continuity and Change in Tamil Sambavar Village", *Journal of Indian School of Political Economy,* Vo. 16, Nos. 2&3.

Retnam,V.D. (1943), "The Madras City Milk Supply", *The Indian Veterinary Journal* ,Vol. 16, No. 4.

Roy, J. and R.G. Laha (1960), "Preliminary Estimates of Relative Increase in Consumer Demand in Rural and Urban India", in *Studies on Consumption Behaviour,* Indian Statistical Series 6, Asia Publishing House, Bombay and Statistical Publishing Society, Calcutta.

Rudra, A. and B. Roy (1960), "Some Results in Consumption Studies", in *Studies on Consumption Behaviour,* Indian Statistical Series 6, Asia Publishing House, Bombay and Statistical Publishing Society, Calcutta.

Saini, A.S., D.S. Thakur and D.C. Thakur (1991), "Resource Use Efficiency on Dairy Farms in Himachal Pradesh", *Agricultural Situation in India,* Vol. 46, No. 2.

Sangeeta Keshari and B.S. Malik (1998), Consumption of Milk and Milk Products by Dairy Farmers of Karnal District, *Indian Journal of Dairy Science,* Vol. 51, No. 3.

Sangu, K.P.S. (1995), "Comparative Economics of Milk Production for Buffalo, Desi Cow and Crossbred Cow in Village and Town Conditions", *Indian Journal of Dairy Science,* Vol. 48, No. 4.

Sardana, Parveen K., V.P. Manocha and Manocha (1995), "Spatio-Temporal Changes in Consumption of Livestock Product in India", *Indian Journal of Agricultural Economics,* Vol. 50, No. 3.

Sastry, N.S.R., D.P.R. Reddy and R.R. Hermon (1993), *Planning for Development of Animal Husbandry Sector: A Study in Pondicherry,* National Institute of Rural Development, Hyderabad and Borklinks Corporation, Hyderabad.

Saxena, Rakesh (1995), *Status and Utilization of Draught Animal Power in Gujarat,* Working Paper No. 93, Institute of Rural Management, Anand.

Saxena, Rakesh (2000), *Comparative Advantage and Competitiveness of the Indian Milk Sector,* Working Paper No. 142, Institute of Rural Management, Anand.

Seabright, Paul (1989), "Failure of Livestock Investments Under IRDP: Evidence from Two Villages in Tamilnadu", *Economic and Political Weekly,* Vol. 24, No. 39.

Seabright, Paul (1991), "Identifying Investment Opportunities for the Poor: Evidence From the Livestock Market in South India" *The Journal of Development Studies,* Vol. 28, No. 1.

Seabright, Paul (1992), "Quality of Livestock Assets Under Selective Credit Schemes: Evidence From South Indian Data" *Journal of Development Economics,* Vol. 37, No. 2.

Shah, Deepak (1997), "Bovine Stock in Maharashtra: Changing Structure of Draught Power", Productivity, Vol. 37, No. 4.

Shah, Deepak and K.N.S. Sharma (1994), "Economics of Milk Production in Bulandshar District of Uttar Pradesh", *Indian Journal of Dairy Science,* Vol. 47, No. 11.

Shah, A.B. (ed.) (1967), *Cow–Slaughter: Horns of a Dilemma,* Lalvani Publishing House, Bombay.

Sharma, A.K. and K. Ram (1991), "Seasonal Variation in Consumption Pattern of Weaker Section Households With Special Reference to

Milk and Milk Products in Saharanpur District", *Indian Journal of Dairy Science,* Vol. 44, No. 8.

Sharma, A.K. and Kuber Ram (1991), Seasonal Variations in Consumption Pattern of Weaker Section Households with Reference to Milk and Milk Products in Saharanpur District, *Indian Journal of Dairy Science,* Vol. 44, No. 8.

Sharma, K.N.S., D.K. Jain and R.K. Patel (1987), Milk Production Projections for Different States and Union Territories", *Agricultural Situation in India,* Vol. 42, No. 9.

Sharma, K.N.S., R.K. Patel and Surendra Singh (1975), "Projections of Bovine Population, Requirement and Economic Demand for Milk", *Indian Journal of Agricultural Economics,* Vol. 30, No. 1.

Sharma, R.K. (1981), *Draught Power Planning in Indian Agriculture,* Ph.D. Thesis, (Unpublished), Department of Economics, University of Delhi.

Sharma, R.K. (1987), *Animal Energy in Agriculture: A Case Study of Uttar Pradesh,* Agricultural Economics Research Center, University of Delhi, New Delhi.

Sharma, R.K. (1989), "Green Revolution and Draught Power (A Case Study of a Village in West Uttar Pradesh)", in *Livestock Economy of India,* Indian Society of Agricultural Economics, Oxford & IBH Publishing Co. Pvt. Ltd., New Delhi.

Sharma, R.K. (2001), *Livestock Economy of Haryana; Recent Trends and Prospects,* Agricultural Economic Research Centre, University of Delhi, New Delhi.

Sharma, V.P. (2000), "Assessing the Effects of the WTO Agreement on Indian Dairy Industry: What Can We Learn From Past Five Years", *Indian Dairyman,* Vol. 52, No. 11.

Sharma, V.P. (2001), "Exim Policy Changes and Their Implications for Indian Dairy Sector", *Indian Dairyman,* Vol. 53, No. 4.

Sharma, V.P. (2002), "Policy Initiatives for Countering Imbalances in Dairy Sector in the Post-WTO era", *Indian Dairyman,* Vol. 55, No. 3.

Sharma, V.P. (2004), "Livestock Economy of India: Current Status, Emerging Issues and Ling-Term Prospects", *Indian Journal of Agricultural Economics,* Vol. 59, No. 3.

Sharma,V.P. and Ashok Gulati (2003), *Trade Liberalisation, Market Reforms and Competitiveness of the Indian Dairy Sector,* MTID

Discussion Paper No. 61, Markets, Trade and Institutions Division, International Food Policy Research Institute, Washington, D.C., U.S.A.

Sharma, V.P. and G.D. Vashist (1992), "Trends in Milk Production in Himachal Pradesh" *Agricultural Situation in India,* Vol. 46, No. 11.

Sharma, V.P. and Pritee Sharma (2002), *Trade Liberalisation and Indian Dairy Industry,* Oxford& IBH Publishing Co Pvt. Ltd., New Delhi.

Sharma, V.P. and Pritee Sharma (2002a), "Implications of Agricultural Trade Liberalisation for Indian Dairy Industry", in *Livestock in Different Farming Systems in India,* edited by Birthal, Pratap, S., Anjani Kumar and Laxmi Tiwari, Agricultural Economics Research Review, Agricultural Economics Research Association, National Centre for Agricultural Economics and Policy Research, New Delhi.

Sharma, V.P. and R.V. Singh (1993), Resource Productivity and Allocation Efficiency in Milk Production in Himachal Pradesh, *Indian Journal of Agricultural Economics,* Vol. 48, No. 3.

Sharma, V.P. and R.V. Singh (1994a), "An Economic Analysis of Milk Production, Consumption and Disposal Pattern in Rural Areas of Himachal Pradesh", *Indian Journal of Dairy Science,* Vol. 47, No. 3.

Sharma, V.P. and R.V. Singh (1994b), "An Economic Analysis of Milk Production by Different Breeds of Milch Animals in Humid-Temperature Zone of Himachal Pradesh", *Indian Journal of Dairy Science,* Vol. 47, No. 9.

Sharma, V.P. and R.V. Singh (1994c), "Economics of Milk Production in Himachal Pradesh", *Agricultural Situation in India,* Vol. 48, No. 10.

Shiyani, R.L. (1996), "An Economic Enquiry into the Impact of Dairy Cooperatives on Milk Production", *Indian Journal of Agricultural Economics,* Vol. 51, No. 3.

Shiyani, R.L. and U.K. Dev (1998), "Technological Efficiency of Cooperatives and Individual Milk Producers", *The Asian Economic Review,* Vol. 40, No. 2.

Singh Katar and V. Mukunda Das (1984), *Impact of Operation Flood–I at the Village Level,* IRMA, Anand.

Singh, Bhupal (1981), Inequalities in Consumption Pattern of Milk and Milk Products in Muzaffarnagar(Uttar Pradesh), *Journal of the Indian Society of the Agricultural Statistics,* Vol. 34, No. 3.

Singh, D., B.B.P.S. Goel, V.V.R. Murty, D.V.S. Rao and B. Singh (undated), *Sample Survey for Estimation of Milk Production and Study of Bovine Practices* (Report of the survey conducted in Tamil Nadu State during 1965-66), Institute of Agricultural Research Statistics, New Delhi.

Singh, Dalbir (1989), "Common Property Resources and Livestock Farming in Chila Village of Himachal Pradesh", in *Livestock Economy of India,* Indian Society of Agricultural Economics, Oxford & IBH Publishing Co. Pvt. Ltd, New Delhi.

Singh, Parmatma and Dayanantha Jha (1975), "Economic Optimum in Milk Production", *Indian Journal of Agricultural Economics,* Vol. 30, No. 3.

Singh, Satya Prakash and Raghbir Singh (1986), "Consumption of Milk Products and Income", *Margin,* Vol. 19, No. 1.

Singh, Surendar (1979), "Operation Flood II: Some Constraints and Implications', *Economic and Political Weekly,* Vol. 14, Nos. 42&43.

Singh, Surendra and K.N. Sharma (1979), "Trends in Breedable Bovine Population and in Milk Production", *Agricultural Situation in India,* Vol. 34, No. 8.

Singh, Virender and K.N. Rai (1998), "Economics of Milk Production and Marketing of Buffalo Milk in Haryana", *Indian Journal of Agricultural Economics,* Vo. 53, No. 1.

Singh, B. (1979), "Economics of Milk Production and Bovine Livestock Compositions in a Growing Economy", *Indian Journal of Agricultural Economics,* Vol. 34, No. 2.

Singh, B.B. (1975), "Economics of Production of Milk", *Indian Journal of Agricultural Economics,* Vol. 30, No. 3.

Singh, I.J. and A.C. Gangwar (1989), "Bovine Economy of Haryana: An Economic Analysis", in Livestock Economy of India, *Indian Society of Agricultural Economics,* Oxford & IBH Publishing Co. Pvt. Ltd., New Delhi.

Singh, J. and C.B. Singh (1981), " Economic Performance of Different Species of mIlch Animals", *Agricultural Situation in India,* Vol. 36, No. 9.

Singh, R.K.P., K.P. Rajan and Alok Jha (1996), "Declining Milk Availability and Nutrition Security in Bihar", *Agricultural Review,* Vol. 9, No. 2.

Singh, R.K.P., K.P. Ranjan and Alok Jha (1996), "Declining Milk Availability and Nutrition Security in Bihar", *Agricultural Economics Research Review,* Vol. 9, No. 2.

Singh, R.P., M.K. Chaudhry and Himmat Singh (1975), "Growth Trends in Bovine Population in Himachal Pradesh", *Indian Journal of Agricultural Economics,* Vol. 30, No. 3.

Singh, Rajendra, C. Tiwari and Parmatma Singh (1990), "An Analytical View of Bovine Population in Uttar Pradesh" *Agricultural Situation in India,* Vol. 45, No. 5.

Singh, S.P., P. Singh, R. Prakash and C.B. Tewari (1986), "An Economic Analysis of Inter-State Disparities in Milk Production and Institutional Facilities in India", *Agricultural Situation in India,* Vol. 40, No. 10.

Sinha, P. and A.K. Giri (1989), "Consumption of Livestock Products-Analysis and Comparison of Data of NSS 32nd and 38th Rounds", in *Livestock Economy of India,* Indian Society of Agricultural Economics, Oxford & IBH Publishing Co. Pvt. Ltd., New Delhi.

Sirohi, Smita (2002), "World Global Trade Liberalisation Provide a LevelPlaying Field for Indain Dairy Industry: Lessons for Future WTO Negotiations", in *Impact of WTO on Indian Agriculture,* IX Conference Proceedings, Agricultural Economics Research Review, Agricultural Economics Research Association, National Centre for Agricultural Economics and Policy Research, New Delhi.

Sivakumar, S.S. (1978 a), "Aspects of Agrarian Economy in Tamilnadu: A Study of Two Villages-II. Constraints on Production and Marketing", *Economic and Political Weekly,* Vol. 23, No. 13.

Sivakumar, S.S. (1978 b), "Aspects of Agrarian Economy in Tamilnadu: A Study of Two Villages-III. Structure of Assets and Indebtedness", *Economic and Political Weekly,* Vol. 23, No. 14.

Smith, W. (1919), "The Importance of the Development of the Dairy Industry in India", *Agricultural Journal of India,* Vol. 14, No. 4.

Srivatsava H.L. and G.N. Singh (1975), "Economics of Milk Production in Rural Areas of Kanpur District (A Case Study)", *Indian Journal of Agricultural Economics,* Vol. 30, No. 1.

Subrahmanyam, S. and R. Nageswara Rao (1995), "Bovine Sector in Agriculturally Prosperous and Backward Regions: A Comparative Study", *Indian Journal of Agricultural Economics,* Vol. 50 (3).

Subrahmanyam, S., N. Jagadeshwara Rao, C. Ratnam and R. Nageswara Rao (1999), *Dairy Development in Andhra Pradesh: An Analysis of Regional Variations,* Booklinks Corporation, Hyderabad.

Subrahmanyam, S., V. Rama Raju and R. Nageswara Rao (1996), "Inter-linkages between Agriculture and Dairy Development", *Agricultural Situation in India,* Vol. 53, No. 1.

Sudha, S. and S. Irudaya Rajan (1999), "Female Demographic Disadvantage in India1981-1991: Sex Selective Abortions and Female Infanticide", *Development and Change,* Vol. 30, No. 3.

Sundaresan, C.S. (2001), "Multilateral Trade and Dairy Commodity Markets in LDCs: Recent Evidence from Delhi", *Economic and Political Weekly,* Vol. 35, No. 34.

Suryanarayana, M. (1980), *Growth and Income Distribution in India,* M.Phil. Thesis (Unpublished), Centre for Development Studies, Trivandrum.

Tamil Nadu Veterinary and Animal Science University (1991), *Survey of Animal Draught Power in Various Agro-Climatic Zones of the Country: Socio-Economic Features and Current Husbandry Practices,* ICAR ADHOC Scheme, Final Report, Department of Animal Husbandry Economics, Madras Veterinary College, Madras.

Telang, M.A . and B.W. Chavan (1965), "Role of Bovine Population in Maharashtra's Economy with Special Reference to Milk Production", *Indian Journal of Agricultural Economics,* Vol. 20, No. 1.

The Agriculturists (1914a), "Cattle Supply to the Southern Districts", *The Agriculturists,* Vol. 6, No. 2.

The Agriculturists (1914b), "The Use of Cows for Ploughing", *The Agriculturists,* Vol. 6, No. 2.

Thirunavukarasu, M., R. Prabaharan, and C.Ramasamy (1992), "Operation Flood-A Dent on the Consumption of the Rural Poor", *Indian Journal of Dairy Science,* Vol. 45, No. 1.

Thomas, P.J. and K.C. Ramakrishnan (1940), *Some South Indian Villages: A Resurvey,* University of Madras, Madras.

Thompson, F.M.L. (ed) (1983), *Horses in European Economic History: A Preliminary Canter,* The British Agricultural History Society, Great Britain.

TIVJ (1938), "Milk Supply in Madras: Marketing Survey Results", *The Indian Veterinary Journal,* Vol. 15, No. 1.

Tripathi, Hema and O.N. Kunzru (1994), "Milk Production, Consumption and Disposal Behaviour of Rural Dairy Animal Owners", *Indian Journal of Dairy Science,* Vol. 47, No. 3.

Tripathi, R.S. (1995), "Cow Milk Production in H.P. Hills: An Economic Approach", *Indian Journal of Dairy Science,* Vol. 48, No. 2.

Tripathi, R.S., J.S. Garg and G.N. Singh (1986), "An Economic Analysis of Dairy Enterprise in Bundelkhand Region of Uttar Pradesh", *Indian Journal of Dairy Science,* Vol. 39, No. 1.

Vaidyanathan, A. (1978), "Aspects of Indias's Bovine Economy: Some Preliminary Results", *Indian Journal of Agricultural Economics,* Vol. 33, No.1.

Vaidyanathan, A. (1982), Milk Production in Tamil Nadu and Kerala: Contrasts and Implications", *Bulletin,* Madras Development Seminar Series, Vol. 11, No. 4.

Vaidyanathan, A. (1983), *Vegetarianism and Animal Protein Consumption in India,* Wenner-Gren Foundation for Anthropological Research.

Vaidyanathan, A. (1988), *Bovine Economy in India,* CDS Monograph Series, Centre for Development Studies, Trivandrum and Oxford & IBH Publishing Co. Pvt. Ltd., New Delhi.

Vaidyanathan, A. (1989), "Research on the Livestock Economy: An Overview" in *Livestock Economy of India,* Indian Society of Agricultural Economics, Oxford & IBH Publishing Co. Pvt. Ltd, New Delhi.

Vaidyanathan, A. and K.N. Nair (1979), *A Comment on Questions in the Sacred Cow Controversy,* CDS Working Paper No.95, Centre for Development Studies, Trivandrum.

Vaidyanathan, A. and K.N. Nair (1980), "On the Sacred Cow Controversy", *Current Anthropology,* Vol. 21, No. 3.

Vaidyanathan, A., K.N. Nair and Marvin Harris (1982), "Bovine Sex and Species Ratios in India" *Current Anthropology,* Vol. 23, No. 4.

Vashist, G.D. and Pradeep Katiha (1988), "A Comparative Economic Analysis of Milk Production for Different Milch Animals in Himachal Pradesh", *Agricultural Situation in India,* Vol. 43, No. 2

Vashist, G.D. and V.P. Sharma (1991), "Production Functions for Milk Production in Kangra District of Himachal Pradesh", *Agricultural Situation in India,* Vol. 45, No. 12.

Veeraraghavan, A.K. (1940), "Eruvellipet (South Arcot District)", in *Some South Indian Villages: A Resurvey,* edited by Thomas, P.J. and K.C. Ramakrishnan, University of Madras, Madras.

Venkatasubramanian, V.S., A.K.Singh and S.V.N. Rao (2003), *Dairy Development in India: An Appraisal of Challenges and Achievements,* Concept Publishing Company, New Delhi.

Wadley, S. and B. Derr (1987), "Child Survival and Economic Status in a North Indian Village", Proceedings of the workshop on *Differential in Mortality and Health Care in South Asia,* BAMANEH/ SSRC, Dhaka.

Wani, S.A. and S.C. Mathur (1992), "Relative Efficiency of Milk Marketing Channels in Rural Kashmir", *Agricultural Situation in India,* Vol. 46, No. 10.

Whyte, R.O. and M.L. Mathur (1965), "An Analysis of the Feed and Fodder Resources for the Livestock Population in India", *Indian Dairyman,* Vol. 17, No. 1.

Whyte, R.O. (1967), *Milk Production in Developing Countries,* Faber and Faber Ltd., London.

Whyte, R.O. and M.L. Mathur (1968), *The Planning of Milk Production in India,* Orient Logmans, New Delhi.

Yadav, M.C. and R.K. Singh (1982), "Relative Economic Efficiency of Cross-bred Cows and Murrah Buffaloes", *Livestock Adviser,* Vol. 7, No. 10.

Yeshwanth (1990), "Livestock Economy in Kerala", *Journal of Rural Development,* Vol. 9, No. 4.

Government Publications and Reports (Regular and Undated).

Agricultural Prices in India (various issues), Directorate of Economics and Statistics, Department of Agriculture and Cooperation, Ministry of Agriculture, Government of India.

All-India Report on Input-Survey, 1976-77, Vol.1, Agricultural Census Division, Department of Agriculture and Cooperation, Ministry of Agriculture and Rural Development, New Delhi.

Annual Reports, (various years), AAVIN, Tamil Nadu Cooperative Milk Producer's Federation, Ltd., Chennai.

Annual Statistical Abstract of Tamil Nadu, various years, Directorate of Economics and Statistics, Government of Tamil Nadu.

Basic Animal Husbandry Statistics, 2002 and previous volumes, Department of Animal Husbandry and Dairying, Ministry of Agriculture, Government of India.

Census in Tamil Nadu, (various years), Chennai, Government of Tamil Nadu.

Economic Survey *2004-05 and previous years, Ministry of Finance, Economic Division, GOI, New Delhi.*

Indian Agricultural Statistics Various Issues, Directorate of Economics and Statistics, Department of Agriculture and Cooperation, Ministry of Agriculture, Government of India.

Indian Livestock Census (various years), Directorate of Economics and Statistics, Department of Agriculture and Cooperation, Ministry of Agriculture, Government of India.

Policy Note, Milk Supply Schemes (various years), Dairy Development Department, Government of Tamil Nadu.

Report on Livestock Census, Tamil Nadu-1997 and previous years, Directorate of Economics and Statistics, Chennai.

Report on the Integrated Sample Surveys (ISS), various years, Department of Animal Husbandry and Dairying, Directorate of Economics and Statistics, Government of Tamil Nadu.

Input Survey (various years), Tamil Nadu Agricultural Census, Commissioner of Statistics, Madras.

Season and Crop Report of Madras Presidency (various years), Department of Statistics, Government of Madras, Madras.

Season and Crop Report of Tamil Nadu (various years), Department of Statistics, Government of Tamil Nadu, Chennai.

Statistical Abstracts of Madras Presidency (various years), Department of Statistics, Government of Madras, Madras.

Statistical Atlas of Madras Presidency (various years), Department of Statistics, Government of Madras, Madras.

Statistical Handbook of Tamil Nadu (various years), Directorate of Economics and Statistics, Government of Tamil Nadu, Chennai.

Studies in the Economics of Farm Management in Coimbatore District (Tamil Nadu): Combined Report for 1953-54 to 1956-57, Directorate of Economics and Statistics, Ministry of Agriculture and Irrigation, Government of India.

Studies in the Economics of Farm Management in Coimbatore District (Tamil Nadu): Combined Report for 1970-71 to 1972-73, Directorate of Economics and Statistics, Ministry of Agriculture and Irrigation, Government of India.

Survey of Animal Draught Power in Various Agro-Climatic Zones of the Country: Socio-Economic Features and Current Husbandry Practices, (undated), ICAR Adhoc Scheme, Department of Animal Husbandry Economics, Madras Veterinary College, Tamil Nadu Veterinary and Animal Sciences University, Madras.

Tamil Nadu-An Economic Appraisal (various years), Department of Evaluation and Applied Research (DEAR), Kuralagam, Government of Tamil Nadu, Chennai.

Tenth Five Year Plan (2002-2007), Volume II, Sectoral Policies and Programmes, Planning Commission, GOI, New Delhi.

Tenth Five Year Plan (2002-2007), Planning Commission, Government of India.

INDEX

M

N